How Anyone Can Negotiate With The IRS— And WIN!

*A DARING EXPOSE' OF THE VULNERABILITY
OF THE SYSTEM AND THE PEOPLE WHO RUN IT.*

by Daniel J. Pilla

WINNING Publications
St. Paul, Minnesota

WINNING Publications
506 Kenny Road, Suite 120
St. Paul, Minnesota 55101

First Edition, November, 1988

Printed in the United States of America

Library of Congress Catalog Card Number: 88-051374

ISBN: 0-9617124-5-7

Notice from the Author and Publisher

This book is designed to provide the author's findings and opinions based on research, analysis and experience with the subject matter covered. This information is not provided for purposes of rendering legal, accounting or other professional advice. It is intended purely for educational purposes.

The author and publisher disclaim any responsibility for any liability or loss incurred as a consequence of the use and application, either directly or indirectly, of any information presented herein.

Because the United States currently functions under an evolutionary legal system, the reader bears the burden of assuring that the principles of law stated in this work are current and binding at the time of any intended use or application. Caution: The law in this country is subject to change arbitrarily and without prior notice.

Dedication

To Anthony and MacKenzie

Writings by Daniel J. Pilla

How Anyone Can Negotiate With The IRS—And WIN!

Pilla Talks Taxes, A Monthly Newsletter

The Naked Truth

Understanding Taxes and Court Procedure

"*Who would believe the ironic truth that the cooperative taxpayer fares much worse than the individual who relies upon his constitutional rights!*"

— US Federal Judge Cummings
writing in **United States v. Dickerson**,
413 F.2d (7th Cir. 1969)

Table of Contents

CHAPTER SIX - 3 IRS Tools of Collection— And How to Neutralize Them

CHAPTER SEVEN - 2 Ways to Eliminate Taxes You Cannot Pay

INTRODUCTION

*"To Tax and to Please, no more than to
Love and be Wise, is not given to men."*
— **Edmund Burke**
Speech on American Taxation, 1774

Since 1913, America has been burdened with a progressive income tax which was born out of the passage of the 16th Amendment.[1] With it came the Internal Revenue Service, an organization which started out in relative obscurity with little power but which has, through both the passage of time and legislation, grown to be the most powerful—and feared—of our myriad of federal agencies and bureaus.

Until 1943, income taxation in the United States was a simple, painless process. The rates were low, the taxable income thresholds were high and the paperwork necessary to comply was brief and to the point. The Victory Tax Act changed that, apparently forever. With the Victory Tax Act, the "temporary" wage withholding provision was placed in the law. So that the United States could immediately raise sufficient funds to prosecute World War II, every wage earner was required to pay his taxes in regular installments through wage withholding. As with most "temporary" taxing measures, the withholding requirement became permanent not long after its adoption by Congress.

By 1954, the Internal Revenue Code became monstrous in size and impossibly complex. As long as I can remember, selected congressmen, senators and presidential candidates have promised to "simplify" the tax laws. As the latest effort (the Tax Reform Act of 1986) has shown, simplification is not to be. Why? I believe the answer lay deep in the bowels of the Minneapolis Public Library's Government Documents section. It is there where I finally laid my hands on the text of testimony given by Senator Henry Bellmon before the Senate Finance Committee in 1969, while Congress was

---

[1] Many believe that the 16th Amendment was not a product of a legitimate undertaking. Evidence collected in the past few years has indicated that records reflecting ratification of the amendment by the several states were falsified in Washington, D.C. To date however, no federal court has ruled favorably regarding the argument.

considering another effort at "simplification"—the Tax Reform Act of 1969.

Part of Senator Bellmon's remarks appear on the cover of this book. Without question, that is a powerful statement, but perhaps more telling are the Senator's observtions on why the income tax laws are so complex. Listen:

> "I believe that the main purpose of our tax system should be to raise revenue. During the period since the 1930s, the idea of using our revenue-raising laws to accomplish certain social aims has complicated and caused great confusion in the administration of these laws.
>
> "With the passage of vast quantity of social legislation in other fields, with the increased socially oriented activities of the United States Supreme Court, and with the creation of many additional federal programs to deal with social problems, it occurs to me that any tax reform legislation passed by the present Congress might well take note of the fact that the need for using our tax system for social purposes may no longer require the same high priority.
>
> *"If this concept can be adopted, the law can be vastly simplified.* It can be much more easily understood and followed by individual taxpayers, and it can be much more effectively enforced by those who are charged with its administration." Testimony before Senate Finance Committee, October 2, 1969, Record of H.R. 13270, Vol. 5, pages 4675-76. (Emphasis added.)

Senator Bellmon had the courage to say what few others have said either before or after that October morning in Washington. The underlying purpose of the tax laws, claimed Bellmon, has been perverted. What began as a vehicle for raising revenue to fund the *legitimate* functions of the federal government has evolved into a process whereby the social end of redistribution of the wealth could be accomplished. The United States is a land with many facets, faces and needs. As a result, any legislation which undertakes to evenly distribute the wealth of such a nation will naturally be enormously complex, cumbersome and difficult to comply with as well as administer.

It seems that the Powers That Be *do not* appreciate it when public figures call a spade a spade with respect to taxes. It seems that those Powers will tolerate all of the garden variety rhetoric about simplification which the average politician can spew forth in a given campaign, but when somebody hits the nail on the head as did Bellmon, his words find themselves hidden from public view. That is right. I said, "hidden."

My efforts to discover Bellmon's words, of which I had seen glimpses prior to my research, led me to the Minnesota State Law Library, the Supreme Court Law Library, and two major public libraries designated as depositories of government documents. Bellmon's name has been deleted from all of the indexes compiled for the Congressional record for 1969. Even though Bellmon played a significant role in the committee hearings on H.R. 13270 (the Tax Reform Act of 1969), nowhere is his name found in any of the indexes! Why?

It seems he had the answer to the single most compelling question which has plagued American government for three decades. How do we simplify the tax laws? His answer, however, was not what the Powers wanted to hear. Continuing with Bellmon's testimony:

> "In a recent conversation with an official of the Internal Revenue Service, I was amazed when he told me that, 'If the taxpayers of this country ever discover that the Internal Revenue Service operates on 90% bluff, the entire system would collapse.' He further went on to tell me that when he first joined the Service in the 1940s, his reference manuals occupied thirteen inches of shelf space. At the present time, he must rely upon books of instructions and interpretations that make up a total of thirty-three feet of shelf space in his office. Plainly, simplifying of our tax laws should have a high priority. Much of the statement I have prepared for the Record is aimed in this direction.
>
> "There seems to be a danger, that in its effort to administer the present complex and confusing law, the Internal Revenue Service is resorting to tactics which frequently seem to border on coercion. Many innocent taxpayers who are accused by the Internal Revenue Service of irregularities, find it less costly to pay the additional taxes and penalty than to go to court and prove their innocence * * *" (Ibid.)

Currently, twenty years after Bellmon's testimony was given, no tax lawyer worth his salt has a library consisting of less than 50 feet of shelf space. The bizarre part is that much of the material is now on *microfilm!*

Confusing and complex tax laws have not only been the cause of much IRS abuse of the innocent, these factors have been responsible for zapping much production from the private sector over the years. Capital that would otherwise have been invested to create jobs and eliminate high prices has been pumped into the business of *tax avoidance*. Charles Adams, in his epic *Fight, Flight, Fraud, The Story of Taxation*[2] writes:

> "Tax avoidance, like evasion, is an inherent aspect of income taxation. Opportunities for tax avoidance have given birth to a new industry. The brightest lawyers and accountants often move into the business of tax planning, along with a few promoters. Most high-bracket taxpayers soon learn that a tax dollar saved is much larger than an ordinary dollar earned. A few hours of skillful planning can often save tens of thousands of dollars for the rich. In what other pursuit can a lawyer make so much for his clients with such a small expenditure of time?"

The rich have creative lawyers and accountants to hide their incomes from the tax man. The poor have no income to worry about. Those left are the defenseless middle class upon whose shoulders the heaviest burden of taxation has always fallen. On top of that is heaped the callousness and outright coercion and intimidation of the IRS.

But Senator Bellmon's report that the IRS operates on "90% bluff" comes as a breath of fresh air at a time when oppressive tax rules and IRS bullying has caused middle class Americans to cower in life's corner like terrified schoolchildren. Now that we know that the IRS collects much of their additional tax claims through bluff, we can undertake to call those bluffs and to counter the IRS' hand.

Until now, the tactics used by the IRS have been largely a mystery known only to those within the system. The unfortunate citizens who have fallen victim to the ploys report only the bleakest of messages, "You just have to pay, *or else.*" Unable to recognize the baseless threats for what they are, Americans by the millions have turned out their pockets believing they had no other choice.

How Anyone Can Negotiate With The IRS—And Win is an instruction book to those faced with the unenviable task of fencing with the tax man. Based upon experience in hundreds of cases, you

---

[2] Euro-Dutch Publishers, Buffalo, NY 1982, page 270

will learn just how you can effectively counter the threats, intimidations and bluffs routinely served to unsuspecting taxpayers.

The era of taxpayer ignorance has come to an end.

— Daniel J. Pilla
St. Paul, Minnesota

Chapter One

15 BLUFFS AND INTIMIDATIONS— AND HOW TO COUNTER

Introduction

In testimony before the Senate Finance Committee in 1969,[1] Senator Henry Bellmon of Oklahoma told his colleagues:

> "In a recent conversation with an official of the IRS, I was amazed when he told me, 'If the taxpayers of this country ever discover that the Internal Revenue Service operates on 90% bluff, the entire system will collapse'."

My own experience with the IRS has shown, through a preponderance of the evidence, that the IRS lives and breathes on bluffs and intimidation. Like a poker player, the art of intimidation and the use of the bluff is an integral part of IRS training and practice, though its employees and its manuals never admit it. History speaks plainly however, and it is clear that without the bluff, the IRS, in many cases, just simply *would not* collect money.

Sometimes the bluffs are subtle. In one case, an IRS agent explained that he would hate to see the citizen "run up all kinds of legal fees fighting a case that he couldn't win." By not taking the bait, this particular taxpayer did fight, and did win—and *without* running up "all kinds of legal fees."

Other times the bluffs are not so subtle, unless you think a train wreck is subtle. An example of this is where a doctor was harassed to within an inch of his life on the question of his personal and corporate income taxes. After the IRS made literally hundreds of thousands of dollars in mistakes and *lost* the doctor's receipts, the case went into collection. The IRS demanded that $55,000 in back taxes be paid "now." After listening to the doctor's explanation that he did not have the money to pay "now," and pleas for time to allow him to raise the funds, the revenue officer told him, "Our experience with doctors who say they don't have the money is, if we just squeeze them hard enough, the money they don't have just seems to come from someplace."

---

[1] October 2, 1969. Report of Hearings on H.R. 13270, Part 5, page 4676.

A few days later, the doctor phoned the same revenue officer and again pleaded for help in resolving the problem of his delinquence. Shouting into the receiver, the officer arrogantly demanded, "Why are you calling me?! You say you want to resolve the problem, SIR!, but if you want to resolve the problem, SIR!, then the way you resolve the problem, SIR!, is, you *pay the money!!*"

Whether subtle or blatant, a bluff is recognizable for what it is; an attempt to induce the citizen to take some action that he is less than excited about taking. Sometimes, the bluff is an outright lie, as in the case where a revenue agent informs a citizen that he has no right to appeal an adverse audit decision. Other instances involve bluffs that, while technically correct, are so far removed from the facts as to render them meaningless, as is often the case when an Appeals Officer threatens to impose the $5,000 penalty for fighting a "frivolous Tax Court appeal."

In either instance, the success of the bluff or intimidation is dependent upon two things. First, the hope that the individual will not recognize it as a bluff. Secondly, that his own lack of confidence in the case will move him off his position and into an emotional condition that will cause him to accept the "bad news" the IRS has to offer.

In a poker game, even the inexperienced card player cannot be bluffed if he holds all the aces. Aces win, it is that simple. To insulate yourself from IRS bluffs and intimidations, you must be able to recognize the aces. If you hold them, you cannot be bluffed. If you do not know what they look like, you will easily be convinced that the IRS agent holds all of them. When that happens, you are done. Pack up the briefcase and go home. Get ready to write a check.

Beginning with this chapter, I will turn the cards "face up." I am going to distinguish the aces from the deuces, so that in your next poker game with the IRS, *if* you end up paying any money, it will be because you owe it, not because you were bluffed out of the game.

PART I — The Audit
A. The Bluff: "You must appear at the audit when told."

One of the most common complaints I hear from people is that the IRS is insensitive and inconsiderate when it comes to setting the time for an audit. IRS letters state that the examination *must* be conducted on "Thursday, at 9:00 a.m." or an arrogant phone message demands that if you are not in the office by "the 20th, enforcement action will be taken." Citizens are left—quite deliberately—with the impression that they have no say in determining the date or time in which their tax audit will take place. More times than not, they are bullied into believing that they must jump through whatever hoop happens to have been hoisted by the tax examiner.

"To every thing there is a season, and time to every purpose under the heaven...," so says King Solomon in the Biblical Book of *Ecclesiastes*, Chapter 3, vs. 1. This scriptural passage is the genesis of the popular phrase, "There is a proper time and place for everything." The tax audit is no exception.

The ace which the IRS does not want the citizen to recognize is that you do indeed have a say in determining the time of your audit. Let us examine the authority for this proposition. Section 7605 of the Internal Revenue Code is entitled *Time and Place of Examination*. This section is far from exhaustive on the matter of who controls the time in which an audit may be set, but it is the *sum total* of all the Code's guidance on the matter.

Section 7605(a) states in part that:

> "The time and place of examination pursuant to the provisions (of the Code) shall be such time and place as may be fixed by the Secretary *and as are reasonable under the circumstances*." (Emphasis mine.)

The Code and regulations do not attempt to define what is "reasonable under the circumstances," and there does not appear to be an abundance of court authority to lead us. The conclusion I have reached over many years of applying this provision is that the grey language of §7605(a) is one of the few instances where the unclear provisions of the tax law actually work to the *advantage* of the citizen.

The phrase "reasonable under the circumstances," must be read to include circumstances which relate to the convenience of the citizen. An individual has the right, in my judgment, to have a voice in where the audit is to be conducted, and in setting the time and the date of the audit. On a regular basis I have made it my business to insist that pre-scheduled audits be re-set to accommodate either calendar concerns, or to facilitate further preparation and record-gathering by the subject citizen.

In the typical audit scenario, the IRS will not give you the option to assist in determining a date which is "reasonable under the circumstances." As I have pointed out above, generally a letter or phone call will "direct" you to appear at a pre-set time and place. If it appears that you have a conflict with that date or are unable to be prepared by that time, too bad! You will just have to make do. Such is the attitude of the IRS all too often.

If circumstances dictate that you claim your right under §7605(a) to have a voice in determining what is "reasonable," you must be assertive with regard to that right. Failure to assert it in a positive manner will mean that the IRS alone will dictate where and when you will meet, without regard to your needs. A barrage of audits in the western Wisconsin area illustrate how this can act to the distinct *advantage* of the unwitting citizen.

That case involved a tax preparer who underwent investigation by the IRS Criminal Investigation Division. Claims and counterclaims caused the IRS to look at the tax returns which this accountant had prepared over a number of years.

In order to determine whether the accountant was deliberately falsifying the deductions claimed by his clients, all of his clients were called in for an audit. The IRS has been less than congenial in their demands for examination of the various clients' returns. Some clients have been accused, some have been bullied, some have been misled regarding their appeal rights, and some have been cornered into paying more taxes than they probably owed. But *all* have been *told*—with no alternative offered—that they must appear at the time demanded by the auditor, period.

One couple was asked to appear at 12:30 in the afternoon on a particular day. The citizen informed the agent that he did not get off work until 3:00 p.m. She responded by saying, "We don't do things that way around here. You will be here at 12:30." Not knowing any better, the man and his wife were *both* forced to take a day off work to accommodate the "unreasonable" demands of the belligerent agent.

Contrast that with another example. This one involved a citizen of St. Paul who knew, if not in form then in substance, of his right under §7605(a). The IRS notified the man of the pending audit of his 1985 income tax return. The auditor set up a meeting, sent out a document request, and awaited the appointed date. Two factors, of which the agent was unaware, prevented the audit from coming off as the agent might have hoped.

The first was that the individual was an independent salesman on the road almost four full weeks per month. He worked in a season-sensitive business and had to travel from early March through October's end in order to reap the harvest his industry has to offer. Any time off during that period had a serious impact on his ability to make sales, and hence, earn commissions. The second important element was that he had moved subsequent to filing his 1985 tax return, and most of his records were lost. Those that were available were in a state of disarray, at best.

Much time would be needed to either locate the lost records, or reconstruct them if they could not be located. We also had to organize and make sense of those which were on hand. This had to be achieved during the industry's few off-peak months if the citizen were to earn any kind of respectable living. The agent was notified, *not asked*, that circumstances dictated that the scheduled meeting be postponed. An explanation of the facts was given to demonstrate that the request for additional time was "reasonable under the circumstances." The date originally set was ignored and the citizen went about his business.

This same sequence of events was then repeated several times: Letter from the IRS setting a date; response stating that the date was impossible to comply with for reasons given; date dropped by agent. The pattern continued for *over one year!* Finally, only *after* the records were located, *and* the peak season had come and gone, did the citizen attend the audit. During the audit, the agent made the remark that she had been handed, but did not want to delve into, the man's 1986 tax return. "I just want to get '85 finished and off my desk," she said. "You're just too hard to get a hold of."

Had the citizen sheepishly appeared at the audit on the date first set, two undesirable consequences would have been certain. First, his records were not in order so it is a *given* that many, if not all deductions would have been disallowed. Secondly, since the auditor did not seem to understand that appeal rights exist, (the last bluff discussed under Part I of this chapter) she may well have convinced the citizen to sign a waiver and *accept* the disallowances, surrendering all appeal rights. The outcome would have been the payment of thousands in taxes, interest and penalties which were not owed.

Do not be forced into attending an audit for which you are not prepared. Furthermore, I do not believe that the IRS has any statutory authority to force you to attend an audit at a time which would prove costly or otherwise inconvenient to you. I believe, as the above history indicates, that §7605(a) speaks substantially—although quietly—to the wary person on this issue.

B. The Bluff: "You must submit to a 'line audit'."

In recent years, particularly since putting into place the Strategic Plan,[2] the IRS has increased the number of Taxpayer Compliance Measurement Program (TCMP) audits dramatically. The TCMP audit is nothing more or less than a fishing expedition undertaken by the IRS to develop its Discriminate Function (DIF) scores. DIF is the computer program that uses regional and national averages to do line-by-line comparisons of tax form entries. Any entry which appears to be above the national or regional average causes that return to be electronically selected for audit.

The DIF audit focuses on the particular item which the computer determined was "out of sync." The TCMP audit, however, concentrates its attention on the entire tax return—each and every line—each and every claim. TCMP audits are completely arbitrary as to the manner in which returns are selected, and they are completely arbitrary as to the entries which are scrutinized by the auditor. They are, in the truest sense of the phrase, a "fishing expedition."

Still, it is a most uncomfortable posture to be thrust into, as we well know that the IRS, in conducting an audit, does so for the purpose of getting *more money*. In fact, IRS figures show that it collects on the average, over $5,500 per audit![3]

TCMP audits can easily be, and often are, abusive. This for the simple reason that since no particular item or claim seems to be in question, the examining agent is free to and often does, create problems as the audit develops. Without the forewarning that one usually receives in the typical DIF audit, the citizen must be prepared to react to *on the spot* demands and questions of the examiner, something that most people find difficult to do.

The TCMP bluff can be neutralized with just a little forethought and an understanding that the right to appeal any audit decision *does* exist. In fact, where, as in a TCMP audit, the examining agent has *caused* problems, the Appeals Office can effectively be used to *solve* those problems. Let me put this into perspective.

Under ordinary circumstances, a person will go into the audit, produce all of his records to the examiner, and—if the IRS has its way—will end up with a number of his deductions disallowed. Of course, this results in a tax bill. When the matter is taken to the

---

[2] IRS Document 6941, exposed in *The Naked Truth*, by Daniel J. Pilla. Winning Publications, 1986.
[3] IRS Highlights, Annual Report, 1987, page 31.

Appeals level by the citizen, the review is limited to whether the examiner correctly disallowed the deductions under all of the facts of the case.

With this in mind, we can work this knowledge to our advantage. Suppose you did not produce records at the audit. What would be your reasons for not doing so? What would be the IRS' reaction to your stance? And what would be the consequences? The following hypothetical dialogue will answer these questions:

AUDITOR: Good morning, Mr. Smith. My name is Jim Henderson. Thank you for coming this morning. Let's get right down to business. Did you bring all of your books and records for 1986? I would like to go through them.

MR. SMITH: Well, Jim, before we go in to any of that, tell me, what part of my return is in question?

AUDITOR: The entire return. This is a TCMP audit where we look at each item.

MR. SMITH: Why?

AUDITOR: To see if the return is correct, and to help the IRS keep accurate statistics for future audits.

MR. SMITH: Is there an item on the return which caused this audit?

AUDITOR: Well no, not exactly. We want to look at each item.

MR. SMITH: Are you saying that there is no one particular entry which caused my return to be selected?

AUDITOR: No. Your return was selected at random just to review it. That will help us to make adjustments to our data base and to more accurately select returns for future audits.

MR. SMITH: Why should I go to all the trouble of going through this hassle if there is nothing wrong with my return?

AUDITOR: You have to. When your return is called into question, you have to verify that the items shown are correct.

MR. SMITH: You just said there is nothing on my return that has been called into question. You said this audit is arbitrary to help you build your data base! I don't have to put up with that!

AUDITOR: Look, if you don't want to produce your records, I will just have to disallow all your deductions. Then you will have a bill to pay, with interest and penalties!

MR. SMITH: Are you saying I don't have any right to have your decision reviewed? Are you the one and only person I will ever deal with here?

AUDITOR: Of course not. But if you don't produce records, the Appeals Office will uphold my decision every time.

MR. SMITH: I am perfectly happy to verify anything which you feel is out of line. But I am not going to waste all my time going through this hassle just so you can beef up your computer system. Just tell me which item you think is out of line and we will talk about that item.

AUDITOR: I just explained that I must look at each item. We can take them one at a time if you like, but I must have proof for each item. And if you don't want to cooperate, I will just disallow your deductions and you can go from there.

MR. SMITH: I think you are the one who is not cooperating. I just told you that I am willing to verify my return if there is something wrong with it. But you keep saying there is nothing wrong with it. Then, in the next breath, you tell me I have to produce every scrap of paper I own to prove it. That doesn't make sense. So, unless you just tell me what is wrong, I guess I will take it to Appeals.

Later on, at the Appeals level:

APPEALS OFFICER: Mr. Smith, we are here to review the determination made by Examination that you owe additional taxes. It appears from the file that Examination disallowed your deductions because you refused to cooperate. Apparently, you refused to turn over your records. What is your contention here?

MR. SMITH: First of all, I didn't refuse to cooperate. I told the agent again and again I would produce any records he asked for if he would just tell me what was wrong with my return. He wouldn't—so I didn't.

OFFICER: Well, my job here is to review this bill you have gotten, and to decide whether it is correct. It appears to me that it's just a matter of verifying what you've claimed. If you are willing to cooperate, it will be just a simple matter. If not, there is nothing I can do. In the absence of records, we just can't allow any deductions. Are you willing to do that?

MR. SMITH: Yes. I was willing to do it at the audit, but the examiner would not cooperate with me. Let's just take the items one at a time. We can begin with . . .

What has been accomplished? The case has been transferred to the Appeals Division—which is responsible to *solve* problems— and away from the Examination Division—which is responsible for *creating* problems. You may ask, "How have I helped myself? I still had to produce my records! Why didn't I just give them to the auditor and be done with it?"

The answer is simple. The auditor's job is to find ways to collect *more money*. With records in hand, he could have found any number of reasons to say they were insufficient to satisfy this or that deduction. By contrast, the Appeals Officer was only to determine whether the auditor's actions were justified. At that point, it was simply a matter of verifying the deductions by producing the records. Since the auditor made a blanket disallowance, the resulting tax bill could have been overcome just by record production at the Appeals level.

Had records been produced at the audit level, the citizen would have been faced with an uphill battle in Appeals. The job of overcoming disallowance is much more formidable once the auditor has been given the ability to formulate reasons for their disallowance. Without any such reasons, it becomes just a matter of verifying that the records exist, and are sufficient to support the claims. The environment changes radically, and the advantage swings to the citizen's favor.

C. The Bluff: "Your proof for this deduction is not sufficient."

The most common bluff used in the tax audit is for the examiner to attack the sufficiency of one's form or method of proof. I have heard people say they were told by IRS agents that canceled checks were insufficient forms of proof. I have heard where receipts have been ignored. And, I have heard where year-end statements were said to be ineffective. Of course, most agents in the audit environment will *never* accept taxpayer testimony as valid, despite the rules which are examined in detail in Chapter Two.

The "Your Proof is No Good" bluff works under one condition, and one condition only. That is where the citizen believes that he has no recourse to contest the auditor's decision. As a matter of fact, most audit bluffs fall apart when used on a citizen who knows he has the right to appeal the examiner's decision. By taking the appeal, you obtain a fresh hearing before a fresh face in a fresh environment.

Provided your proof meets one or more of the criteria set out in Chapter Two, there is no need to fall victim to this bluff.

D. The Bluff: "You must fill out Form 4822."

IRS Form 4822 is entitled *Statement of Annual Estimated Personal and Family Living Expenses.* I was made aware of this form in an audit which took place some time ago. During the examination, the auditor took out the form, asked us to take it home and fill it out. The purpose, she said, was to allow her to determine whether the income shown on the income tax return was correct.

Income as reported on the return is one of the two basic items, the correctness of which the taxpayer bears the burden of proving in an audit. I examined the form. It asked that amounts of expenditures be reported in several categories of items, including personal expenses, household expenses, auto, and taxes. It also asked for reports of assets such as stocks, bonds, and boats, etc. One was to include the total amounts paid for each of these items, both in cash and by check, during the year in question.

The audit in which I was involved when this form first popped up covered the year 1985. The examination was taking place in January of 1988, over two years later.

"You've claimed only $18,000 income on your return," the examiner said. "That doesn't seem like much money. I want to verify that this amount was all you earned."

In addition to asking us to complete the form, she asked some questions, two of which I recall quite well. The first was "How much cash did you have on hand January 1, 1985?," and the next was "How much cash did you have on December 31, 1985?"

The citizen was expected to *remember* how much money he had in his possession on two specific dates in time over two years ago. In conjunction with Form 4822, this "exact" information was supposed to verify that his income was as stated on the tax return.

In reality, the form does nothing to shed any light on the correctness of the income tax return. In the first place, by its nature it is an "estimate" of the various expenses about which it inquires. Secondly, and more importantly, it is *impossible* to complete the form accurately. For example, I want *you* to tell *me* how much money you spent in 1985 on "Barber, beauty shop, and cosmetics." How about "Gifts and allowances?" Can you shed any light on "Furniture, appliances, and jewelry?"

The form has the effect of spinning the taxpayer into a direction which is unnecessary. Why go through all of the time, effort and hassle to complete a form which cannot possibly be correct, when, in order to prove your income, your Forms W-2, 1099, personal ledgers and bank statements will *accurately* show all of the income you had in the year? Since the IRS is in the business of verifying the *correctness* of a tax return, one would think that they should concern themselves with only the most *accurate* source of supporting documentation. Form 4822 is anything but accurate.

In my judgment, the effect of the 4822 most assuredly is to cause confusion, and to create the appearance of unreported income. Since it would be nearly impossible to accurately complete the form, one cannot be assured that the apparent "income" necessary to pay the bills shown on the Form 4822 will match the "income" shown on the tax return, and supported by other, more accurate data. Moreover, people tend to complete such forms using *current* expenditures as a guide. This of course would have the effect of *raising* one's income.

In this particular audit, we opted to prove income using other, more accurate data. I explained to the agent that since it would be impossible to accurately prepare the form, we elected not to do so. I pointed out, however, that I recognized that it was our burden to prove that the return was correct, and have chosen to do so using much more reliable methods.

We presented a statement from the man's employer showing the amounts of his monthly paychecks, and a statement from the employer's accountant to the effect that his review of the employer's books revealed no other payments to the citizen. "This," I insisted, "was reliable proof of income, and that is how we will fly."

Certainly our reasons for refusing to complete the form were reasonable. In the interests of accuracy and completeness, we opted for the more reliable method. How could she argue?

E. The Bluff: "I can't allow additional deductions."

One of the most common defense mechanisms used by citizens to combat an audit is this: All deductions to which one may be entitled *are not* claimed on the return. In the event of an audit, the additional receipts are presented as a means of offsetting any disallowances which may result.

While the wisdom of this approach is debatable, the IRS has developed a response of its own to this defense. Many times, additional receipts are not scorned by the IRS during an audit, but just as often, they are. In one case, a citizen was told that before any additional deductions would be considered, an amended return would have to be filed. This of course, put the citizen at a distinct disadvantage.

Procedurally, what was he to do? The amended return would no doubt cost some money as it would have to be prepared by a person knowledgeable in the field. More importantly, he was under audit *now*. Any amended return would first have to be filed with the service center for processing, and then, *maybe*, it would be accepted. In the meantime, the audit of the present return was progressing, with much dispatch. "I'll wait to see what happens," he responded. "After all, if I come out of this with a clean slate, there is no reason to spend money just to get back a few extra dollars."

Unfortunately, he did not come out "with a clean slate." He ended up with a small tax bill, which, after paying, he rationalized the same way. "It's just a few dollars. No big deal."

Contrary to my friend's logic, it was a "big deal." The reason is that he held an ace in his hand which he did not recognize, and which the IRS agent bluffed him out of using. The statement that additional deductions can only be claimed on an amended return is just flat wrong—period. In fact, revenue regulations *expressly* provide that any additional deductions which a citizen may have overlooked can rightfully be claimed at an audit.[4] The pertinent regulation reads, in part as follows:

> "* * *During the interview examination (the audit), the taxpayer *has the right* to point out to the examining officer any amounts included in the return which are not taxable, or *any deductions* which the taxpayer *failed to claim on the return.* * * *" (Emphasis added.)

This regulation gives the citizen two specific rights which the IRS sometimes likes to overlook. The first is the right to change the "income" shown on the return by demonstrating that certain amounts claimed as income were in fact, *not income* for whatever reason. This has the effect of *lowering* the taxable income shown on the return.

Secondly, the citizen has the right to assert entitlement to any *additional* "deductions" which were not claimed on the return. We all understand the effect of this.

Since asserting additional deductions is specifically provided for in the regulations, the regs themselves make quite an effective counter to the bluff.

---

[4] Rev. Reg. 601.105(b)(2)(ii).

F. The Bluff: "No witnesses are allowed in the conference."

It is not unusual for citizens to desire the presence of witnesses at an audit conference for one of two reasons. Either the witness is needed to present relevant evidence on the subject of a claimed deduction, or the witness is desired for the purpose of observing the audit proceeding for some future eventuality.

Most common is the need to present evidence on the subject of a claimed deduction. One example that comes to mind is the case of a man, Paul, who had taken a travel expense deduction for a trip he made to California. He brought with him a friend whom, he claimed, was along on the trip for business purposes. The two traveled to California, so goes the story, in order to research a possible investment which the second man was considering in Paul's business. Paul, who had already established the business as a viable income producing venture, took the deductions on his tax return.

During the course of the audit, the propriety of these deductions was called into question. In order to establish the business purpose of the trip, I intended to bring to a follow up conference, Paul's travel companion. Further, I intended to present his testimony regarding the purpose, length, and nature of the trip.

At the second meeting, we walked in the door with our witness present. We met with immediate opposition from the revenue agent. "These conferences are confidential," she said. "I cannot permit unauthorized persons to be present when Paul's confidential tax matters are being discussed." I explained that the man's presence was for the limited purpose of offering evidence and testimony on the matter of the travel expenses, and that once that portion of the meeting was concluded, the witness could be excused, hence not privy to any of the other matters to be discussed.

"I'm sorry," was the response. "The law is quite clear and I just can't allow it." The law referred to is section 6103 of the Code. That provision is the so-called confidentiality stipulation of the tax law. Under the law, the IRS is forbidden to release any confidential "tax returns or return information" to any "unauthorized person."

The intent of this law may well be noble. That is, to prevent persons in government from misusing what, potentially, could be quite damaging to a person in one way or another. Yet, the IRS deliberately uses the confidentiality provisions of the law to *handicap* the citizen.

Without the testimony of the eyewitness, we could have been at a decided disadvantage. The agent knew this and that is exactly why she flexed the §6103 muscle. However, I had anticipated the objection, and to counter her powerplay, prepared in advance IRS Form 2848D. Form 2848D is entitled *Authorization and Declaration.* The purpose of the form is to permit the citizen to give his consent, in writing, to the IRS in order that they may release confidential information relating to his tax affairs.

With Form 2848D in hand, the agent had no legitimate reason to preclude the presence of the witness and his important testimony in the matter.

One of the common "objections" I have heard from IRS agents when presented with a 2848D is that the "authorized" person, despite the written consent, nevertheless cannot be present, since, it is claimed, such a person is not an attorney, accountant, or enrolled agent. Revenue agents quite often, either deliberately or otherwise, mistake Form 2848D, *Authorization and Declaration,* for Form 2848, *Power of Attorney.* Since I have not yet met an IRS agent who was in fact functionally illiterate, I have trouble believing the mistake is inadvertent.

Still, one must take care to point out that the purpose of the 2848D is to authorize release of confidential information, and not for the purpose of appointing a representative who will speak on behalf of the taxpayer as is the case with the 2848. Attorney or not, a 2848D authorizes release of confidential tax information, and removes from the IRS the legal power to exclude a witness from the conference.

G. The Bluff: "You have to sign this waiver."

At the conclusion of the audit, it is not uncommon to be presented, either in person or through the mail, with a bill. Accompanying the bill is a form 870, Waiver. The Form 870, once signed, permits the IRS to assess the tax demanded and to move forward to collection, regardless of whether or not the citizen agrees with the amount claimed to be owed.[5]

Signing the form is of course, not mandatory. What's more, the IRS is powerless to force a signature. If you do sign, however, your only appeals recourse at that point is to pay the tax in full and then to file a claim for refund. To talk with the IRS, though, you would believe that unless you sign the form, "bad things will happen."

Some time ago, a man I will call Bud came into my office looking

---

[5] See Chapter Four for further details on this Form.

for help in connection with an audit. He had already gone through several conferences with the IRS case agent, his lawyer and accountant. The IRS had called into question the sale of some real estate which had occurred during 1984, but which had not been reported on the '84 tax return. A mistake had been made, but the principals could not decide whether Bud overlooked the sale or whether his accountant had simply neglected to schedule it into the return. Regardless, the agent analyzed the sale, made some adjustments to other entries on the return, and computed a new tax liability.

The bill presented for *immediate* payment was in the neighborhood of $14,000 before interest. The agent told Bud that he must "pay the bill." The audit was over and it was time to settle the case. The agent demanded, rather rashly, that Bud sign a Form 870, Waiver.

But Bud did not agree with the figures presented, and had no intention of paying the tax demanded if he could help it. The agent gave Bud no alternative. "Sign it," he said. "If you don't I'm going to write it up just the way it is!" Exactly what was meant by "I'm going to write it up" was never explained. The implications were left solely to Bud's imagination. And, as you might appreciate, one's imagination has a way of getting away in situations like this.

Bud turned to his lawyer and accountant for help. The accountant's advice was profound: "We've done all we can do. Looks like you're gonna have to pay." The lawyer's observation was even more compelling: "You haven't paid much taxes in the past four years anyway—might as well just give 'em the money." Great advice, huh? The best part is that he paid for the advice!

Now let us understand something important before we go any further. The IRS' computation was wrong—dead wrong. The agent had computed some important aspects of the sale improperly, and had completely overlooked several thousand dollars in expenses associated with it. In addition, a penalty was imposed which was totally out of line under the circumstances of the case. Why these facts had escaped the watchful eyes of the lawyer and accountant is anybody's guess. I pointed the errors out to Bud, and sent him back into the lion's den with the new ammo.

Bud returned just two days later. He had not gotten anywhere with the talks, and frustratedly reported that the agent had repeated his demand, even more adamantly now, that Bud sign the waiver or he would "close the case." The bold, unmistakable impression left by the ultimatum was that if Bud did not voluntarily sign the waiver, the IRS would just collect the tax anyway.

I explained to Bud his rights to appeal a decision of any auditor, a fact ignored by the agent. "Hey Bud," I said, "If you don't agree, let him 'write it up.' All it means is we have the chance to take the case into Appeals and then to the Tax Court. You have a right to trial before you have to pay 'em a dime. If they won't bend, that's fine. We'll go over his head."

"No kidding," replied Bud, in wide-eyed disbelief, "they never said I could do that."

"Of course not," I observed, "you might take them up on it."

Bud asked me to call the agent to explain his factual position on the matter, so I did. I pointed out the documents we had which demonstrated Bud's expenses and the details of the errors made in the IRS' computations. The agent agreed to look at our material more carefully. He set a date for a few days later at which he would release his findings and state his intentions with regard to the case.

Bud attended the meeting but was discouraged by the report. The agent was unimpressed with our evidence. Again he demanded that Bud sign the 870 or he would "write it up." Now that Bud knew what "write it up" meant, he challenged the agent. "Fine, write it up," he said. "I will just appeal."

Rather astonished, the agent replied, "Appeal? You will appeal?"

"That's right," touted Bud, more confident now. "I disagree with your figures and I have made a counter-offer which is correct. And if you don't accept it, I'm going to appeal!"

Apparently pushed into a corner, the agent said, "Fine. Appeal it. I'll issue the notice."

Bud left the office. Not more than three hours later Bud was contacted at home by the IRS agent. It seemed he had reconsidered. It seemed that the case was not worth hassling over any longer. It seemed that his computations had indeed overlooked several items of importance, and it looked as if he would be willing to settle the case as Bud had proposed.

"Great!" said Bud, "I'll write it up!"

The recomputation saved Bud over $8,000. It took a few phone calls. It took a few trips down to the IRS office. It took some understanding of his tax return. But most importantly, it took the intestinal fortitude to say "NO" and stick to it. With just a little information, Bud was not bluffed into paying thousands in taxes and penalties he did not owe.

The right of appeal within the IRS is very important. Unfortunately, the IRS does not always explain these rights very clearly, if at all. Ironically, however, they have produced a publication which does. You just have to know what to ask for. The document is IRS Publication 5. It explains your rights of appeal within the system, and the steps you must take to carry it off.

PART II—The Appeal
A. The Bluff: "If you pre-pay the tax, you can avoid interest."

At the conclusion of an income tax examination, it is established procedure for the IRS to ask for voluntary payment of any additional tax, interest and penalties which may have been found to be due.[6] The pitch which is generally made is that "if you pre-pay the tax, you will stop the interest from running and save yourself a lot of money. You can maintain your objections, but at least the interest stops accumulating."

Like a broken clock, this statement is *correct*, but it is also *incorrect*. Pre-paying a tax liability *does* indeed stop the running of interest, and that is a major consideration to be cognizant of when fighting the IRS. Interest on an unpaid tax bill can be crushing. First of all, the interest *does not* begin to run from the time the tax is adjusted to be due, it begins to run from the time the tax *should have been paid* in the first place.

For example, suppose your 1984 income tax return is selected for audit in June of 1986. At the conclusion of the audit, you take the case through appeals and into the Tax Court. A Tax Court decision is handed down on February 2nd, 1989. The Court held that there was a deficiency in your 1984 income tax payment of $2,516, and assessed a 5% penalty for negligence. The total bill is $2,614.80.

Interest on the $2,614.80 deficiency is computed, at established rates, beginning on April 15, 1985—the date the tax *should have been paid*, through the date the tax is fully paid, which would be sometime after February 2nd, 1989. Hence, even if one were to pay the tax immediately upon losing in the Tax Court, over three years of interest would be tacked on to the bill.

The prevailing rates of interest being what they are could easily *double* a tax bill. In fact, in the above example, I would consider

---

[6] Revenue Procedure 63-5, 1963-1 CB 484.

the time lapsed between filing the return and the Tax Court judgment to be somewhat *short*. It is not unusual for tax litigation which goes the distance, to take five years, or more.

In February of 1980, the rate charged by the IRS on unpaid tax liabilities jumped from six to 12 percent. As of February 1, 1982, the rate was *20 percent*. Because the interest rate charged by the IRS is computed at the rate of three points[7] above the average prevailing interest rate as announced by the Federal Reserve Board, the rate has seen much fluctuation over the years. The rate is subject to change every six months. In addition, beginning on January 1, 1983, interest is compounded *daily*.

The portion of the bluff which can be outright misleading to an ignorant citizen, is that once paid, a person can "continue to object" to the tax bill. Again, this is a true statement, but taken out of context, which it almost always is, creates a completely false impression. Under ordinary circumstances, the IRS cannot collect a dime without an assessment, and it cannot obtain an assessment without issuing a notice of deficiency to the taxpayer. Having received a notice of deficiency, the taxpayer has the right to petition the United States Tax Court *before* paying the tax, provided the petition is filed in a timely manner.[8]

A deficiency notice will be mailed *only* where there is an *underpayment* of income taxes determined to be due in a particular year. Code section 6211(a) states that a deficiency is *reduced* by the amount of tax collected by the IRS. Consequently, if after examination, it is determined that a $2,000 deficiency exists, and $2,000 is *paid* to the IRS pursuant to the bluff, a notice of deficiency *will not be mailed*. Consequently the citizen *will not* have an opportunity to petition the Tax Court for a redetermination of the bill.

After having paid the tax, the *only* remaining method by which to continue the battle is to file an administrative claim for refund. The difficulty is that this legal nuance is generally not explained when the request for pre-payment is made. Believing he will be notified by the IRS, the citizen will write the check, go home and await the next letter. The next letter, however, never comes. The reason is that the burden is now on the citizen to file a claim for refund, something which he either does not know, or does not know how to do. The result is that the IRS gets more money, but without

---

[7] Code §6621.
[8] Code §6213(a). One receiving a notice of deficiency has 90 days in which to petition the Tax Court. As a result, the notice of deficiency is commonly referred to as a "90-day letter."

a court fight.

Before a decision to pre-pay taxes is made, one must carefully and objectively weigh the chances of success in litigation.[9] This is done through the consideration of all of the appropriate factors, particularly the facts of the case and the governing law. Next, if a decision to pre-pay is made, it must be done in such a way as to preserve all possible avenues of pursuit, should one's desire to continue the fight prevail at a later time.

By designating in writing a pre-payment as a "deposit in the nature of a cash bond," rather than as "payment of the tax," not only will the interest on the deficiency cease to accrue, but one will nevertheless be mailed a notice of deficiency, thus preserving the right of a Tax Court appeal.[10]

B. The Bluff: "All bets are off!"

Throughout the course of your appeal, you would have met numerous times with the Appeals Officer assigned to the case. You would have had several meetings at which you presented your case in the form of documents, perhaps some affidavits of witnesses, and maybe even some oral testimony from a perspective witness. You would have gone to great lengths to research the law and to present to the Appeals Officer a picture of the points of law which you feel are dispositive to your view of the case.

The Appeals Officer having done likewise, you would then have undertaken to narrow the issues pending in the case in the hope that if a trial becomes necessary, you will move into such a trial with as *few* issues as possible yet on the table.

Narrowing the disputed issues is the sum total of the underlying purpose of any pre-trial negotiation. This is desirable from the citizen's standpoint for a number of reasons, most notably is that by carving out of the case as many disputed points as possible, one reduces, in corresponding measure, the inherent risk of litigation.

The process of a give and take negotiation with Appeals as described in the first paragraph of this section will eventually lead to one party or the other making an offer of settlement. Allow me to paint a factual scenario for purposes of illustration, and to elucidate on the manner in which this bluff is used. Suppose an audit of your tax return left you with an examination report

---

[9] For more information, see Bluffs and E of this Part.
[10] This procedure is more fully explained in Chapter Five, part 4.

demanding additional taxes. The tax was based upon the following:

1. $1,500 in travel expenses disallowed,
2. $2,500 in home office expenses disallowed,
3. $1,000 in charitable contributions disallowed, and
4. 25 percent in penalties added to the bill.

As a result of negotiation and presentation of evidence, the Appeals Officer makes to you this offer: "I will allow you all the contributions, I will give you $1,000 in travel expenses based on the proof you have offered, and I will allow one half of the office-in-home expenses."

As you see, since no specific mention of penalties was made in the offer, as far as the Appeals Officer is concerned, the penalties will remain in the case as part of the deal.

Your response: "I don't like it. I want the penalties out of there. I believe that the facts of my case justify removing the penalties."

The revenue officer is firm on his position: "I don't think you have shown the good faith required in order for me to wash the penalties out of the case."

Unwilling to budge on the penalty issue, you are now faced with a decision. Either you take the deal offered to you, or you litigate the issue of the penalties. Comfortable with the figures offered on the remaining issues, you state: "I am willing to settle this case on the basis of the deductions you offered, but I want the penalties out. If you are not willing to bend on that, I will litigate the penalties."

The Appeals Officer responds with the bluff: "If you want to litigate, all bets are off. I will withdraw my offer to settle the deduction issues, and you will have to litigate everything. The offer I made is to *settle the case*. If you don't want to settle the case, I withdraw my offer."

With this statement, your blood runs cold. By accepting the offer, at least you have a bird in the hand. If it is withdrawn and you are forced to try each issue in court, you stand to lose that bird in the hand. What to do?

I follow a two step process. The first is rather simple. Elicit an admission that this offer of settlement is based upon the proof that you provided during the course of the discussions. You could ask, "You would agree, wouldn't you, that the reason you are allowing $1,000 in travel expenses is because I have proven $1,000 in travel expenses?" When he says, "yes," proceed to the next issue.

"And you will also agree, wouldn't you, that you are permitting me to take one half of the home office expenses claimed, because I have proven that I spent that much?" Having elicited another affirmative response, proceed to the second step.

Step two is to make reference to Rule I, applicable to practice before the Office of Appeals. The rules governing practice before the Office of Appeals are found in Revenue Regulation §601.106(f). Rule I reads as follows:

> "An exaction by the U.S. Government, which is not based upon law, statutory or otherwise, is a taking of property without due process of law, in violation of the Fifth Amendment to the U.S. Constitution. Accordingly, an Appeals representative of his or her conclusions of fact or application of law, shall hew to the law and the recognized standards of legal construction. It shall be his or her duty to determine the *correct amount of the tax*, with strict impartiality between the taxpayer and the Government, and without favoritism or discrimination as between taxpayers." (Emphasis added.)

Rule I is, in my judgment, pretty strong language and a stiff admonition to the Appeals Officer to decide the case on the basis of the facts and the law, and *not* to make an offer or withdraw an offer solely on the basis of discouraging litigation on a legitimate issue. Moreover Rule II provides that Appeals Officers are to give serious consideration to any taxpayer proposal which:

> ". . . fairly reflects the relative merits of the opposing views in light of the hazards which would exist if the case were litigated. However, no settlement will be made based upon nuisance value of the case to either party. If the taxpayer makes an unacceptable proposal of settlement under circumstances indicating a good-faith attempt to reach an agreed disposition of the case on a basis fair both to the Government and the taxpayer, the Appeals official generally should give an evaluation of the case in such a manner as to enable the taxpayer to ascertain the kind of settlement that would be recommended for acceptance. * * *"

I approach the subject with three carefully worded questions.
1. "You of course recognize your obligation to resolve this case on the basis of the law and facts as have been shown to exist in the case, do you not?" Do you think he will say no? Of course not. Next question.

2. "And the offer you have made to settle the question of the deductions was based entirely on the law as you understand it and the facts as they have been presented, wasn't it?" What do you think his answer will be? Next question.

3. "So if you withdraw your offer and force me to litigate issues which you have already agreed have been proven, your case is no longer based on the law and facts is it?" What can he possibly say? And when he agrees with you, he is finished!

Successful use of this technique will allow you to carve out of the case those issues which are troublesome or which you cannot prove in court, yet will allow you to remain strong on those in which the law and facts are behind you. At the same time, you have substantially reduced the "hazards of litigation."

The "All Bets Are Off" bluff is generally used by Appeals in what are called "docketed cases." A docketed case is one in which a petition in the Tax Court has been filed, and the case is remanded to Appeals for settlement negotiations. In the typical case, one generally has two settlement opportunities when dealing with Appeals. The first comes after an examination report, or 30-day letter, has issued. The next comes after the notice of deficiency, or 90-day letter, has issued. In the case of the latter, the appeal is executed by filing a petition in the Tax Court, after which the Appeals Office is given exclusive settlement jurisdiction for a time.

Merely recognizing the "All Bets Are Off" bluff does not guarantee one's success in overcoming it. One must be sure that the law and facts support his position before this bluff can be called with any assurance of success.

C. The Bluff: "Just file an offer."

If I have heard it once, I have heard 30 times. It is a last resort plea used by Appeals Officers, and sometimes District Counsel attorneys, to induce a settlement on a case involving big numbers. Of course, one of the major indices used to determine whether an offer of settlement is acceptable to the citizen is the *bottom line.* "How much will I owe if I accept this offer?" In fact, if you *have not* asked this question upon being presented with an offer, or in making one for that matter, you are *cheating* yourself. Tax disputes are about money. Make no mistake about it.

It is not uncommon for settlement negotiations to stall because the proposal on the table would leave the citizen with just too large a tax bill with which to cope. This is particularly true where one considers not only the tax, but the implications of interest as well.

The bluff refers to the "offer in compromise" provided for by Code section 7122.[11] That provision of law allows the IRS to *reduce* the amount of any assessment if such a reduction is justified under the circumstances. There are just two reasons for which the law allows a tax to be compromised. The first is if it can be shown that there exists doubt as to one's actual *liability* for the tax. The second is if it can be shown that there exists doubt as to the *collectability* of the tax.

The subject of the offer in compromise is addressed in detail in Chapter Five, but for purposes of exposing the bluff, we will cover the basics here also.

First, jurisdiction to consider and pass upon offers in compromise rests with the Collection Division and Special Procedures. The Appeals Office has very little to do with the receipt of or processing of offers, particularly where the offer is based upon the ability of the IRS to collect the assessment. So while Appeals personnel may sometimes be rather flippant with regard to one's right to file an offer, they can afford to be. They have nothing to do with processing them.

More importantly, one must understand that having an offer in compromise accepted is rare and the consideration process is sometimes lengthy. One is not guaranteed any relief from collection while an offer is pending. The chances of having an offer accepted are even further reduced, maybe by half, if one's case has already gone through Appeals or Tax Court. The reason is simple. One of the only two recognized reasons for accepting an offer has been effectively *eliminated* by the Appeals and Tax Court process.

After a person has gone through the appeals process and has received a decision either from Appeals or from the Tax Court, the Collection Division and Special Procedures, those who do process offers, are of the opinion that *no doubt* exists as to one's actual liability for the tax. The issue has been litigated and the Appeals Division or the Tax Court has expressly found that a liability *does indeed* exist. IRS Manual Chapter 5700, part 57(10)7.43, speaks to the issue of investigating offers based on doubt as to liability. The manual provides:

> "A decision of a court of competent jurisdiction based upon
> the merits or upon stipulation, when it is final, constitutes a

---

[11] See Chapter Five, part 3.

valid judgment and therefore the liability is *conclusively determined.* * * *"

From the same paragraph, we learn that the Special Procedures section will, if the liability was "determined by the Appeals branch office," send the case to said Appeals Office for *verification* of the liability. When this happens, do you think that the Appeals Office will then change its mind, indicating you *do not* owe the tax they previously held you do owe?

In light of these manual provisions, I have concluded that any offer in compromise based upon doubt as to liability will be rejected where the case has been adjudicated by Appeals or the Tax Court. The only remaining alternative is to convince Collection and Special Procedures that doubt exists as to the collectability of the tax, and that is a matter which is more fully developed in Chapter Five.

The bottom line is that any hope, based upon a suggestion by the Appeals Officer, to the effect that an offer in compromise will provide relief from a large tax bill is marginal at best. Do not fall into the trap of accepting an otherwise unacceptable Appeals proposal simply because the offer in compromise carrot has been dangled under your nose.

D. The Bluff: "We will add the $5,000 penalty if you litigate."

A common threat used by both Appeals Officers and District Counsel attorneys is that if one is bound and determined to take an issue to trial in the Tax Court, the IRS will apply for an assessment of the $5,000 penalty provided for under Code §6673.

The maximum amount of the penalty was increased by TEFRA[12] from $500 to $5,000 for Tax Court cases filed after 1982. The idea behind the bluff is that if one loses a case in Tax Court, not only will he be required to pay the tax, but will be responsible for an additional $5,000 penalty to boot. This of course, is very dissuading indeed to the would-be litigant. Imposition of the penalty is not, however, automatic.

Under the law, the Tax Court has three reasons it can impose the penalty in any amount, but not in excess of $5,000. Those reasons are (1) if your legal position in the proceeding is "frivolous or groundless," (2) if the proceeding was instituted "primarily for delay," or (3) if you unreasonably failed to pursue "available

---

[12] Tax Equity and Fiscal Responsibility Act of 1982.

administrative remedies."

The Court on its own, or on motion of District Counsel, has the authority to impose the §6673 penalty when one or more of the above conditions exist. The third condition is new with the Tax Reform Act of 1986. The presence of this new language in the penalty makes it imperative that one do all he can to properly exhaust administrative remedies before petitioning the Tax Court.

In this regard, the 1986 Tax Act added *another* new section which relates directly to this issue. The section is §6212(d), and it gives the IRS the authority to "rescind" a notice of deficiency which was mailed in error, thereby eliminating the need to file a petition in the Tax Court. Filing in the Tax Court was *always* necessary before the new section was added.

In light of the added penalty language, it is advisable that one take full advantage of §6212(d). However, both the statute and regulations are silent on just what procedure one is to follow in contesting an "erroneous" deficiency notice after it has issued. I suggest contacting—in writing and well before the 90-day grace period expires—the office which issued the notice and begin at that level to make your claims. If this is unsuccessful, you will have no choice but to petition the Tax Court before the time period lapses.

With regard to the other areas of concern identified by the penalty statute, adversity can be avoided by following this general rule of thumb: If your claim has not been specifically rejected by the Tax Court repeatedly in previous cases, *and* your claim, if found in your favor, will lead to a *reduction*—in whole or in part—of the tax deficiency, the risk of incurring the $5,000 penalty is *de minimus*. As long as you are proceeding in good faith and for the purpose of *resolving* the dispute, *not* delaying the inevitable, one should have no problem overcoming this bluff.

E. The Bluff: "There is a 90% chance we will win the case."

After all other inducements to settle have failed, the Appeals Officer or District Counsel attorney will inform you of your chances of prevailing on the merits of the case. Glibly, he will claim that the government's chances of prevailing in the case are high, perhaps as high as 90%. "There really isn't much sense in going forward," he will report. "I can tell you what the court is going to say about this. There is a 90% chance that this is going to go our way. I don't see what you have to gain by pursuing this."

Let me say right now that anybody who has had any experience with trial work will tell you that the only thing certain about litigation is that the outcome is *uncertain.* The one aspect of litigation that is universally recognized by trial lawyers nationwide is that the risks of litigation are high. For that reason, our judicial system has been almost completely transformed into a forum for arbitration and settlement. Maybe that is good, maybe it is not. The point is, very seldom can any lawyer, or anybody else, accurately predict the outcome of a trial. IRS lawyers, while they often pretend to be capable of doing so, are no exception.

It is true that certain cases contain attributes which make them more or less likely to meet with success. An example comes to mind involving certain of the so-called "tax protester" cases. In past years, numerous individuals have brought cases into the Tax Court and other federal courts challenging the Constitutionality of the tax laws on any one or more of several grounds. Almost without exception, the courts have rejected the claims as meritless.

If someone were to ask me whether he had a chance of prevailing on the merits of a case in which he claimed to be exempt from the requirements of paying taxes because a belief that income taxes were unConstitutional, I would respond that the chances were almost non-existent by virtue of the track record of similar claims. But not every type of tax case has a record paved with the defeats of predecessor cases. And without some case history to go on, any attempt to place odds on the chances of success or failure on the merits of a given case is, at best, a shot in the dark.

I was once involved with a District Counsel attorney in negotiating a settlement in a Tax Court case. The issue involved the deduction of $12,000 for fees paid to a return preparer and business manager in a particular year. The IRS made an offer of settlement which proposed to allow just $4,000 of the $12,000 deducted. The offer proposed to disallow the remaining $8,000 on the ground that it was not proven that the entire amount was expended for the purposes of "earning income" in the year the deduction was taken.

Our position was that as a business manager, the person to whom the money was paid was performing services in an ongoing capacity which services were essential to maintaining the profitability of the company involved. In addition, a portion of the services were attributed to tax return preparation and bookkeeping services which surely were deductible expenses.

Early in the negotiations, the IRS held firm on its offer. Despite my protestations, the attorney and Appeals Officer were both convinced the IRS would be successful if we litigated the question. In fact, a letter written by the attorney suggested that the IRS stood a 95% chance of prevailing on this issue."

I phoned the attorney to discuss the matter further. "Mike," I asked, "on what do you base your statement that there is a 95% chance the IRS will be successful on this point?" He answered quickly, "You haven't shown that all of the consultant's work was directed at earning income for your clients."

Pointing to the evidence we submitted, I countered, "All of the consultant's time sheets detail with particularity the work the man did. In addition, you heard the testimony of my client as to what work the consultant did. Surely this evidence does satisfy the requirement."

Mike's only retort was, "Well, I don't think it does."

There was no question that the attorney was firm in his position, but I also knew that there was nothing tangible in the way of legal authority to back him up. So rather than *attack* his position, my tactic was to make *him* argue his position, in as strong of terms as he could. Knowing that his stance was weak at best, I believed that the most effective way to convince him of that was to allow him to convince *himself*.

I asked, "Mike, I want you to talk me out of litigating this case. What do you have in the way of case authority to dissuade me from taking this any further?" He responded flatly, "I don't have any."

Not surprised, I asked, "Well then what specific facts are you going to rely on to support the notion that we are not entitled to the whole deduction?" Smelling my approach, he got defensive. "Hey, he snapped, "you have the burden of proof in this case. I don't have to prove anything."

"That's true," I replied calmly, "and my proof consists of the testimony of my client and that of the consultant himself. You heard what each had to say. You are not saying these people are liars, are you?"

More reserved now, he said, "Of course not."

Pushing a little more, I asked, "In fact, Mike, you would have to agree that they are both quite believable people, wouldn't you?"

The attorney was no dummy and knew exactly what I was doing. He just could not prevent it. He said, "If you are asking me whether I think the court will find them to be believable, yes, it probably would."

My last question spelled the end of the fight. "Well then," I said, "what is there in your case that justifies your hardline position on this issue?" In light of all the previous admissions, he was forced to come to grips with the weaknesses which existed in his case and surrendered on the issue of the fees.

The bluff works when the citizen has no idea what the prevailing state of the law is on the issue in question. When you have a grip on reality in this respect, the bluff means nothing.

PART III—Collection
A.The Bluff: "You owe penalties."

With the advent of the Automated Collection System and its entry into the tax collection theater, more and more collection notices are being handled by advanced computer systems. Whereas in years past, collection notices and efforts were handled by humans, now they are being accomplished by machine. This makes it difficult to recognize bluffs and even more difficult to counter them.

The premier collection bluff is a computer-generated letter which states that for one reason or another, penalties have been added to your tax bill. The letter is very matter-of-fact in nature, and unlike other letters proposing additions to a tax bill, it offers no alternative to the assessment other than immediate payment. Because the problem is handled by Automated Collection, phone calls for help and guidance go unheeded, and lead only to greater frustration.

Some time ago, a man came into my office with a bill from the IRS for over $6,000 in late filing and negligence penalties. Ed had filed his 1986 tax return almost a year late, and though he paid the tax in full, the IRS now demanded payment of a potpourri of penalties which was equivalent to about 30% of the already quite high tax.

"What can I do," he asked. "They want over $6,000. That's a lot of money!" What was worse, the letter stated that if "immediate payment" was not received, the IRS would take "enforcement action."

The answer seemed simple. "Penalties are not automatic," I said. The statutes under which penalties are assessed, particularly the late filing and negligence penalties, have what is called a "good faith" provision built into them. Simply put, if the citizen makes the showing that his failure to file timely was due to "reasonable cause" and not due to "willful neglect," the penalties must be abated.[13]

We structured a letter to the Service Center which generated the bill. The letter included ammunition obtained from Revenue Regulation §301.6651-1 (c) (1). That regulation provides, in part:

> ". . . a taxpayer who wishes to avoid the addition to the tax for failure to file a tax return or pay tax must make *an affirmative showing* of all facts alleged as a *reasonable cause* for his failure to file such return or pay such tax on time in the form of a written statement containing a declaration that it is made under penalties of perjury. Such statement should be filed with the district director or the director of the service center with whom the return is required to be filed.. . If the taxpayer exercised *ordinary business care* and prudence and was nevertheless unable to file the return within the prescribed time, then the delay *is due to a reasonable cause.** * *"
> (Emphasis added.)

The regulation *does not* define what is "ordinary business care." It seems that a definition of that phrase is adapted from the way one may employ it in everyday usage. In a very general way, I believe it can be said that those steps which a "reasonable person" would take under identical facts and circumstances are the test for what is considered "ordinary business care." In all events, one must make an "affirmative showing" of the facts to support the conclusion that "ordinary business care" was exercised in the case.

Ed's tax return had been filed almost one year late. It was due to be sent in on April 15, 1987, but Ed filed a request for an automatic extension of time. This pushed his filing deadline back to August 15, 1987. By filing the extension, he was thus exempt from the failure to file penalty *up to* August 15, 1987. However, the return was not filed until March of 1988. By that time of course, the grace period created by the extension was long gone.

Still, Ed had an explanation, a good one. Lifted directly from his letter, the following statement unravels the facts behind the filing of his extension and the *missed* deadline:

> "The purpose for filing the extension was that records necessary for the accurate and truthful preparation of the

---

[13] Code §§6651 and 6653(a).

return in question were not in my hands by April 15, 1987. A request for automatic extension was filed.

"The needed records included documents showing the receipt of income and payment of deductible expenses in connection with a limited partnership of which I have been a limited partner for a number of years. The transmittal of the necessary tax information from the general partner to the limited partners is perennialy late. Ordinary business care and prudence dictate that before my return can be accurately prepared to correctly reflect my income and expenses, I must have this information in hand.

"Next, in December of 1986, my address had changed by reason of a move. After the move, I was unable to locate all of the other personal records which were necessary to correctly prepare the tax return. These records were lost through no fault of my own. After having gone through every box and searching in every conceivable location, I located the records and immediately bı ought them to my tax return preparer. This was in January of 1988, several months after the extension had run out. I did not believe that I had any right to file another request for extension, but was unable to file a correct income tax return by August 15, 1987, due to the missing records. Once those records were located, I took immediate and prompt steps to have the return prepared, and to pay the tax shown due thereon, in a prudent business manner.

"I believe and so state that I did not act in a 'willfully negligent' manner as that phrase is used in IRS Code §6651(a). My reason for not filing or paying on time was due, as shown above, to 'reasonable cause.' I delayed filing the return so to be sure that such return, once filed, would be true and accurate in all respects. It was impossible to file such a return without the information mentioned above. My actions of filing late were a direct result of the knowledge of the legal requirement to file a truthful return, and not an inaccurate one. For this reason, I have acted in a reasonable manner, and not due to willful neglect."

Ed concluded his letter by demanding that the assessed penalties for failure to file "be abated." By letter dated July 27, 1988, two months after Ed made his demand for abatement, the IRS responded. The Chief of the Taxpayer Assistance Section for the Atlanta Service Center stated, in writing that:

"The penalties have been abated for reasonable cause that you requested in your letter."

A review of Ed's letter shows, in more detail, how his protest was effective where others often fail.

First of all, the letter was *very specific* as to what happened and why. Ed was not vague about what information he was missing, and why he did not have it in his possession.

Secondly, Ed was *just as specific* in describing the steps he took to secure the needed material.

Thirdly, he identified the *specific facts* which he claims constitute "reasonable cause" and "ordinary business care." This is a most important item because the regulation expressly provides that such elements must be present before penalties will be abated.

Fourthly, he explained *with detail* how his acts were calculated to comply with the law, and were not an effort to avoid his legal obligations.

Lastly, he *demanded* the abatement. He did not *ask* for the abatement. In making the demand, he drew the pointed conclusion that his actions were not "willfully negligent," which allowed the IRS to comply with his wishes.

Most importantly, Ed did not *ask questions*. The steps he took were quick and decisive. Had he asked questions, surely his time limits under §6213(b) would have expired. The next section of this chapter contains further details on this time limit.

Exhibit 1-1 (consisting of two pages) is a reproduction of IRS Manual pages 5500-124 and 125. These pages include the "Reasonable Cause Criteria" used by the IRS itself to determine whether penalties should be abated. Also, you will find a list of the *questions* which the IRS looks to in determining whether reasonable cause exists in a particular case. This manual reference will be most helpful in structuring a letter such as that written by Ed, and thereby avoiding being victimized by the "You Owe Penalties" bluff.

Not all cases are the same. For that reason, each responsive letter of this kind must be tailored to the peculiar facts and circumstances of a given situation. What is certain, however, is that the revenue regulations we have examined *describe* the conditions under which the IRS will abate penalties. Anyone challenging an assessment of penalties would be wise to take note of their provisions before writing his letter.

EXHIBIT 1-1 (page one)

5500 Automated Collection Function Procedures

page 5500-124
(12-4-86)

Exhibit 5500-19

Reasonable Cause Criteria   ◊

(Reference: IRM 5552.3)

(1) The following are general guidelines which may be applied, when clearly established, to a situation where penalties are to be abated because of reasonable cause:

(a) Death or serious illness of the taxpayer or a death or serious illness in his/her immediate family. In the case of a corporation, estate, trust, etc., the death or serious illness must have been of an individual having sole authority to file the return (not the individual preparing the return) or make the deposit or payment or a member of such individual's immediate family.

(b) Unavoidable absence of the taxpayer. In the case of a corporation, estate, trust, etc., the absence must have been of an individual having sole authority to file the return (not the individual preparing the return) or make the deposit or payment.

(c) Destruction by fire, other casualty or civil disturbance of the taxpayer's residence, place of business or business records.

(d) The taxpayer is unable to obtain records necessary to determine the amount of tax due, for reasons beyond the taxpayer's control.

(e) A taxpayer mailed his/her return or payment in time to reach the IRS office within the prescribed time period with the normal handling of the mail. Through no fault of the taxpayer, the return was not delivered within the prescribed time period. Note: If the taxpayer erroneously addresses his/her federal return to the state taxing agency, it is not considered reasonable cause.

(f) The taxpayer did not file his/her return, or pay his/her tax, after receiving erroneous information from an employee of the Internal Revenue Service; or the taxpayer timely requested necessary tax forms and instructions, and the Service did not provide them timely.

(g) Taxpayer contacts a tax advisor who is competent on the specific tax matter, furnishes necessary and relevant information, and is then incorrectly advised that the filing of a return is not required, and the taxpayer exercises normal care and prudence based on his/her own information and knowledge in determining whether to secure further advice; then the taxpayer may have reasonable cause.

(2) The following questions must be addressed to determine if the taxpayer has established reasonable cause.

(a) Do the taxpayer's reasons address the penalty that was assessed?

(b) Does the length of time between the event cited as a reason and the filing or payment date negate the event's effect?

(c) Does the continued operation of a business after the event that caused the taxpayer's noncompliance negate the event's effect?

(d) Should the event that caused the taxpayer's noncompliance or increased liability have reasonably been anticipated?

(e) Was the penalty the result of carelessness or did the taxpayer appear to have made an honest mistake?

Has the taxpayer provided sufficient detail (dates, relationships) to determine whether he/she exercised ordinary business care and prudence?

(g) Is a nonliable individual being blamed for the taxpayer's noncompliance? What is the nature of the relationship between the taxpayer and this individual? Is the individual an employee of the taxpayer or an independent third party such as an accountant or lawyer?

EXHIBIT 1-1 (page two)

5500 Automated Collection Function Procedures

Exhibit 5500–19 Cont.

Reasonable Cause Criteria   ◊

(Reference: IRM 5552.3)

(h) Has the taxpayer documented all pertinent facts, i.e., death certificate, doctor's statement, insurance statement for proof of fire, etc.?

(i) Does the taxpayer have a history of being assessed the same penalty?

(j) Does the amount of the penalty justify closer scrutiny of the case?

(k) Could the taxpayer have requested an extension or filed an amended return?

(3) For tax years beginning in 1983 and prior, the estimated tax penalty cannot be waived for reasonable cause. For tax years beginning in 1984 and beyond, the penalty may be abated in the following circumstances:

(a) the underpayment is due to casualty, disaster or other unusual circumstances and the imposition of the penalty would be "inequitable and against good conscience";

(b) the taxpayer has retired at age 62 or older or has become disabled in the year the payment was due or the preceding year and the underpayment is due to reasonable cause; or

(c) an overpayment designated for application to estimated tax is offset for child support or a non-tax Federal obligation and the taxpayer is not notified of the offset prior to the due date of the estimated tax.

The Bluff: "You owe more taxes."

In my book *The Naked Truth*,[14] I spoke of the phenomenon brought about by the IRS Strategic Plan.[15] As a means of increasing "computer-generated contacts," and maximizing efficiency in tax collection, the IRS began a program of systematically notifying unsuspecting taxpayers that they had made a mistake in computing their tax liabilities, and that as a result, additional taxes were due.

The notice, what the IRS calls a "mathematical recomputation," but what I call an "arbitrary notice," would, with no explanation, set out the amount of tax alleged to be due together with a computation for interest and penalties. Just like the computer letter previously mentioned, it would state that if immediate payment was not received, "enforcement action" would be taken. It would also threaten the accrual of interest and further penalties. The form invited the recipient to, if any questions arose, phone the Automated Collection Site which issued the letter.

My experience with the "arbitrary notice" is that the claims of the IRS are dead wrong. That is to say, while the notice purports to hold that a mistake was made on the return and that additional dollars are due, careful review of the tax return revealed no mistake at all. Such was the case in the overwhelming number of circumstances of which I have knowledge.

The Internal Revenue Service's Annual Report, *Internal Revenue Service Highlights—1987*, shows, in Table 7A, (see Exhibit 1-2) that the Service Center "correction program" was responsible for making 463,000 taxpayer contacts and *collecting* $22 million in additional tax and penalties! Just how many of those 463,000 people paid taxes which were not legally due is completely unknown. The Annual Report for 1987 *does not* include a column entitled "Number of idiots who took the bait." But we do know that the IRS collected $22 million. I have my own opinion as to how much of that money was legally due.

We also know just how the IRS was successful, in probably the large majority of those cases, in collecting the $22 million. The plot would unfold in this matter: After receiving an arbitrary notice, the innocent victim would phone the toll free number shown at the top of the form. On the other end of the line he would talk to a representative within Automated Collection.

---

[14] WINNING Pulications, 1986.
[15] IRS Document 6941.

EXHIBIT 1-2

STATISTICAL TABLES

Table 7.—Continued

Recommended additional tax and penalties (Million)				Average tax and penalty per return			No-change Percent[4]		
Revenue agents	Tax auditors	Service centers	Total	Revenue agents	Tax auditors	Service centers	Revenue agents	Tax auditors	
3,885	1,286	740	5,911	12,235	2,107	4,084	12	14	Individuals, total
119	60	174	354	10,843	1,335	3,501	11	12	1040A, TPI under $10,000
48	25	8	82	5,567	1,033	892	16	21	Non 1040A, TPI under $10,000
59	80	16	155	2,368	919	662	16	14	TPI $10,000 under $25,000 simple
69	75	16	161	2,362	1,015	649	15	13	TPI $10,000 under $25,000 complex
236	301	49	586	3,107	1,280	1,490	14	13	TPI $25,000 under $50,000
1,932	556	402	2,890	20,254	5,817	12,030	10	18	TPI $50,000 and over
66	25	1	93	5,834	1,746	1,529	13	13	Schedule C-TGR under $25,000
163	62	19	243	7,277	3,380	9,147	9	11	Schedule C-TGR $25,000 under $100,000
954	89	42	1,085	29,399	8,015	15,835	12	16	Schedule C-TGR $100,000 and over
3	1	0	5	4,463	789	1,195	24	26	Schedule F-TGR under $25,000
9	3	0	12	4,436	1,158	569	19	19	Schedule F-TGR $25,000 under $100,000
226	8	13	247	70,391	4,766	18,236	14	20	Schedule F-TGR $100.00 and over
78			78	15,425			13		Fiduciary
							18		Partnerships
10,576			10,576	236,613			14		Corporations, total
208			208	108,439			13		Assets not reported
31			31	7,219			21		Under $50,000
40			40	11,428			20		$50,000 under $100,000
73			73	15,067			21		$100,000 under $250,000
48			0	17,339			20		$250,000 under $500,000
64			64	23,138			18		$500,000 under $1 mil
264			264	40,092			14		$1 mil under $5 mil
168			168	63,913			12		$5 mil under $10 mil
477			477	79,907			9		$10 mil under $50 mil
315			315	113,069			7		$50 mil under $100 mil
570			570	195,731			5		$100 mil under $250 mil
8,172			8,172	2,372,098			4		$250 mil and over
147			147	438,982			43		Form 1120F
6			6	657			35		Small business corporations
							29		Form 1120 DISC
963			963	63,697			8		Estate, total
159			159	18,121			9		Gross estate under $1 mil
278			278	50,172			8		Gross estate $1 mil under $5 mil
526			526	643,718			7		Gross estate $5 mil and over
227			227	135,913			14		Gift
15,735	1,286	740	17,761	37,982	2,107		13	14	Income, estate and gift, total
159			159	4,074			10		Excise
350	1		350	7,730	528		20	3	Employment
1,090		6	1,096	701,123		2,156	20	3	Windfall Profit
				18,383			0		Miscellaneous
			477			947			Service center corrections

[4] Service center no-change rate by class is not available. Service center examinations resulted in 14 percent no-change.

Table 7A.—Information returns and other corrections programs (1987)	Service center contacts	Additional tax and penalties recommended (million)
Underreporter program	2,242,000	$ 1,201*
Other correction programs	463,000	22

*351 million dollars of this total are included on table 7 in service center correction results.

"I got this notice today," he would say. "It says I made a mistake on my return and I owe $650. I don't understand. It doesn't say what the mistake was. I asked my accountant and he is sure the return was prepared correctly."

The friendly voice would say, "I'll bring up the file. What is your social security number, please?" Having given the number, the caller would hear the sound of computer keys being skillfully punched. After a time, the voice would say, "Yes, here it is. Your return was corrected due to an error. You owe $650."

"I know that," the caller would chirp. "But why?! My accountant says the return was done correctly." Responding abruptly, the voice would say, "I don't have that information in my computer. The file shows an assessment. When may we expect payment?"

Frustrated, the caller would bark, "What do you mean? I don't even know if I owe this and you can't tell me why. Why should I pay it?"

Firm now, the voice would threaten, "Sir, if you don't make prompt payment, enforcement action could be taken on this account. That can include the filing of tax liens and placing a levy against your wages or salary, as well as your bank account."

Anybody with sense enough to write with his inquiries just got a form letter in response. It read:

> "We are giving special attention to your inquiry about the tax account identified above. We will write you again within 45 days to let you know the action we are taking."

After the passage of some time, the next communication received from the IRS would be the levy or lien mentioned by the Voice. By that time, it was just a matter of biting the bullet and paying the tax.

The bluff is successful if one does not respond to the letter properly, as the poor souls in the above narrative surely did not do. Code section 6213(b) allows the IRS to correct "mathematical errors" made on tax returns, but subsection (b) (2) (A) expressly states:

> "... a taxpayer may file with the Secretary within 60 days after notice is sent...a request for an abatement of any assessment specified in such notice, and upon receipt of such request, the Secretary *shall abate the assessment.* * * *" (Emphasis added.)

Provided the citizen responds in a timely and appropriate manner, the IRS has *no choice*. It must abate the tax. Moreover, if it is convinced that the assessment was correct and the tax is in fact due, it must mail a notice of deficiency in accordance with §6213(a). The notice of deficiency gives the citizen a right to be heard in the Tax Court *before* he can be forced to pay a dime.

Any response which is (1) not in writing, (2) does not demand immediate abatement of the tax under §6213(b) (2) (A), and (3) is not made within 60 days, will render the tax fully collectable by "levy or proceeding in court for the collection of such assessment."

PART IV—The Unspoken Bluff
A. The Bluff: "You will go to jail!"

One of the most heinous elements of the IRS' Strategic Plan is that portion which calls for the IRS to "create and maintain a sense of presence" in all of America, in order that the IRS can "encourage and achieve the highest degree of voluntary compliance" possible. The term "presence" can mean a lot of things, but in this context, there can be little doubt that the IRS has taken it upon itself to become as an American Gestapo.

Of all the atrocities attributed to the German Gestapo, perhaps the most nefarious is the domestic surveillance in which it engaged against its own citizenry. It is one thing to spy on your enemies. It is quite another to spy on your own people, creating conditions such that those citizens are terrified of their own government. Under the auspices of collecting revenue, the IRS has done much the same thing.

You can ask an opinion of anyone you see on the street, and the answer would be the same: If you cheat on your income taxes, *you will* go to jail. The know-it-alls who so boldly give the legal advice on these matters have no knowledge of what it takes for the IRS to obtain a conviction in a criminal case, nor have they ever personally seen a criminal tax trial. They probably do not even know anybody who has met with the "fate worse than death." What they do know, however, is that the government is everywhere, and if you do not do what it says, *"you will* go to jail."

To ensure that this prevailing attitude continues, the IRS does its best to prosecute a "token" number of misfortunates each year. It is, of course, "coincidence" that the majority of these prosecutions takes place in the spring of each year, just as the tax return filing deadline approaches. Newspaper headlines cry out the horrible "truth:" "Minneapolis Man Charged With Tax Fraud—Faces 15 Years." Fifteen years?! Good God! Why didn't the idiot just pay the stupid tax?

As hardcore "believers" in the statements decreed in newspaper headlines, the good Americans who are bombarded with the propaganda not only have the poor stooge convicted even before a trial is held, but are themselves convinced that when you mess with the IRS, the fate certain to befall you is to have your name featured in the evening news. The one thing that has been most appalling to me has been to learn that an incredibly large majority of the population believes that one runs a risk of jail just by speaking out against the IRS, Not only are people certain that "all tax cheaters go to jail," they are equally certain that in speaking out against the IRS, one's chances of "going to jail" rival those of the garden variety tax cheater.

What has the IRS become if it commands that kind of respect? More importantly, what has it done to earn that kind of respect?

I believe it is high time we end the *myth*. That's right, I said, *"myth."* The reality is that not "all tax cheaters go to jail." And as much as the IRS would like to believe it has ubiquitous powers of perception and prosecution, it does not. That does not mean, however, that it is not striving to achieve such power. Indeed it is. The entire premise of the Strategic Plan underscores this proposition.

However, the criminal investigation and prosecution statistics are, I believe, telling. The table in Exhibit 1-3 is reproduced from the 1986 Internal Revenue Service Annual Report[16] at page 18.

Results of Criminal Investigation Activity—1986   *EXHIBIT 1-3*

	Fraudulent Tax Shelters		Illegal Tax Protesters		Narcotics Related		Bank Secrecy Act (Title 31)		All Other		Total	
	1986	1985	1986	1985	1986	1985	1986	1985	1986	1985	1986	1985
Investigations Initiated	312	326	338	447	1264	1188	354	338	3593	3766	5861	6065
Investigations Completed	335	334	464	608	1343	1277	369	250	3576	3442	6087	5911
Prosecution Recommendations	231	213	299	351	956	840	275	174	1763	1656	3524	3234
Indictments/ Informations	124	92	338	345	817	673	204	144	1471	1198	2954	2452
Convictions	107	55	296	302	666	515	108	91	1283	1062	2460	2025
Sentencings	80	50	319	304	662	514	111	97	1246	1126	2418	2091
Percent Receiving Prison Sentences	59%	66%	60%	61%	73%	80%	60%	57%	56%	58%	61%	64%

---

[16] Similar statistics were not available for 1987 at the time of this writing.

Reading in the far right column, we see that in 1986, 6087 criminal investigations were completed by CID.[17] Of these, only 3524 were *recommended* for prosecution. That is about 58%.

Of the 3524 recommended for prosecution, just 2954 were *actually* prosecuted. And of those prosecuted, 2460 were convicted or pled guilty. The conviction-to-prosecution ratio is good, about 83%, but the conviction-to-investigation ratio is not, only about 40%.

The most amazing statistic is the last one shown in the column. It indicates that even when *convicted* of a tax crime, the offender still has a 40% chance that he *will not* go to jail! Those facing the most realistic chances of doing time are those convicted for "Narcotics Related" offenses. Even that ratio, 73% in 1986, is *down* from 1985, when it was 80%.

In 1986, 101.75 million individual tax returns were filed with the IRS. Of those, just 2460 persons were convicted of a tax-related offense. That computes to a *24 thousandths* of a percent chance that you will be convicted of a tax crime this year! Honestly, who is kidding whom?

Not shown in Figure 1-3 is the cost of conducting all these investigations (not to mention prosecutions) and the personnel available to do the work. In 1986, 2800 Special Agents spent $221.3 million chasing what amounted to 2460 tax cheaters. 1987 saw a *decline* in CID's work force, leaving just 2715 supersleuths to snoop around the countryside. The 85 *fewer* Special Agents spent $44 million *more* to achieve approximately the same results as those realized in 1986.

As one can easily see from the above figures, the IRS, even with its 21st Century computers and its everybody-on-the-block-is-a-spy attitude, is not capable of prosecuting every person who fails to properly dot an "i" or cross a "t." I do not say this because I now wish to encourage people to charge out and begin cheating on income tax returns. On the contrary, whether or not one is "caught," deliberate tax cheating is a crime—period.

The point is that people *need not* be terrified of the IRS simply because a few tax cheaters are convicted each year. People *need not* be afraid to speak out against IRS abuses, or to cry out in opposition to unjust collection practices on the vague threat that jail will result. The facts of life are simply that the IRS cannot possibly prosecute "everybody." Both IRS and Justice

---

[17] Criminal Investigation Division of IRS.

Department attorneys have admitted in federal courts around the country that it is impossible to prosecute all those connected with "illegal" tax practices. Only the most flagrant cases are selected for prosecution. Only those cases which stand to gain the most for the IRS in terms of economic return on investment and media coverage are considered primary prosecution candidates.

PART V—When is the IRS *NOT* Bluffing?

Just as the skilled gambler knows when his opponent *is* bluffing, he must also know what *is not* a bluff. This is also the case with the IRS. Even though many of the statements and demands its agents can and do make have no support in the law, some of the threats can be and are carried out with startling regularity. This is indeed the case with the Collection Division.

Make no mistake about it. The IRS Collection Division has awesome power and all too often, has a twitchy trigger finger. The lien, levy and seizure arsenal possessed by the Collection Division makes the IRS the most powerful federal agency by far. And this fact has been *exploited* by the IRS. The IRS has cleverly used the publicity generated by its own, sometimes tyrannical collection practices, to create a condition of fear in the United States which helps to keep the people whipped into shape. The IRS calls this "encouraging voluntary compliance." These habits go hand-in-hand with those of CID mentioned earlier.

Everybody has seen or heard of an IRS horror story. It is the kind of story which, when told, makes your blood run cold. There have been countless books, articles, and news accounts which reported how the IRS seized businesses, homes, bank accounts and autos, with almost indiscriminate abandon. The impact of such accounts is profound. The publicity has the general public convinced that if one does not turn out his pockets when asked to do so by the IRS, "his house will be seized," or as shown above, "he will go to jail." This kind of publicity has emasculated the public. An overwhelming fear of one's own government has caused him to seek refuge in blind obedience to whatever demand is made, regardless of how arbitrary it may be.

Testimony before the Senate Finance Committee, Subcommittee on IRS oversight, on June 22, 1987,[18] established that the IRS' use of its levy and seizure power *increased* from 1981 to 1986 by 154% and 119% respectively. Conversely, in the same

---

[18] Testimony of Senator Carl Levin.

period of time, delinquent tax accounts rose by only 35%. Indeed, the 1986 Update of *Trend Analyses and Related Statistics*, IRS Document 6011, reports that the overall trend in voluntary compliance is *upward*, with non-business voluntary compliance levels exceeding 90%.[19]

What these figures tell me is that the IRS is out of control, and for no good reason! As a whole, the public is complying with the tax laws. Yet the IRS continues to "enforce" collection in the most oppressive ways. This is a very serious problem, and can be attributed, in large measure, to the fact that the Collection Division has the least in the way of objective guidelines by which it is controlled. Most of the enforced collection practices used by the Collection Division, such as the tax lien and wage levy, can be employed *without* the approval of supervisory personnel.

In fact, I was involved in a case wherein a citizen had his home seized by the IRS for a delinquent tax account which was several years old. While the notice of seizure had been issued, the home was not yet sold. That gave us some time to attempt to work with the revenue officer, to comply with his *legal* demands, the goal being to release the home from the seizure. In early conversations, the officer agreed to cooperate with me to resolve the problems.

We were to get all back tax returns filed, and submit a financial statement. The purpose of the financial statement was to demonstrate that the assessed tax was impossible to pay. The tax returns would show that the assessment was clearly overstated in any event. The revenue officer, based upon my representations to him, initially agreed that the lion's share of the assessment could well be, in his words, "put on the shelf," in light of the true liability as shown on the returns.

"Get the returns filed with the financial statements, and we will release the house," he told me.

After working feverishly for months to submit back tax returns for eight years, and after submitting not one but two detailed financial statements showing both personal *and* business income, liabilities and assets, the revenue officer phoned me with the "bad news."

"We are going to have to go ahead with the sale," he told me in a downtrodden voice.

"Why? We had an agreement!," I said in shock.

---

[19] IRS Document 6011, at Table 2, page 18.

"My manager insists that we go ahead with the sale," he explained.

"But that doesn't make sense," I responded. "We are about to wrap this up!"

He agreed, saying, "I know, but he doesn't think it would be fair to other taxpayers whose houses we have sold if this one is released."

"That is the most absurd statement I have ever heard," I cried. "How can it possibly be *fair* to sell a man's house when he has come into compliance with the law, and is doing everything he can to resolve the situation? Are you telling me that just because other people have been raped by the IRS, that this man must be raped too? This is crazy!" The conversation degenerated from there.

This condition of apparent despair was eventually rectified in favor of the citizen, but not without the need of litigation. The point, however, is that in this case, supervisory personnel stepped in to *stop* a case from being fully satisfied in order that the enforced collection tools of the division could be put to full use.

Rather than having supervisory personnel invoke veto authority when those tools *are about* to be used, it appears that such veto authority is used when those tools *are not* to be used. It seems to me that the circumstances are quite the opposite of what they should be. That would certainly account for the dramatic, seemingly inexplicable increase in the levy and seizure statistics discussed above.

The bottom line is simple: the Collection Division does not bluff. When it states that "enforced collection action will be taken," that is exactly what is meant. Enforced collection *does* mean liens, levies and seizures of property. Any correspondence from Collection *must* be taken seriously and dealt with promptly. We cover these points in more detail in Chapter Six.

CONCLUSION

Senator Henry Bellmon blew the whistle on the IRS 20 years ago, but nobody was listening then. Since then, the IRS has wreaked havoc on the American people in countless, horrible ways. As I stated in the Introduction to this book, the age of taxpayer ignorance is now behind us. The first chapter of this book has covered the principle IRS bluffs which are largely responsible for taking advantage of citizens willing to pay their fair share. But there is more to come, much more.

Chapter Two

10 WAYS TO PROVE DEDUCTIONS AND VERIFY INCOME

Introduction

The idea of an income tax audit is terrifying to most people, and for good reason. The 1987 Internal Revenue Annual Report shows that only *13* of every *100* individual tax returns audited received a clean bill of health.[1] That means that 87% of each of the 103.4 million individual returns filed for 1987 *is wrong!*

What does that tell you? It tells me that something is seriously askew with a tax law which is almost impossible to obey, and that the IRS is *bound* to have a field day when loosed upon such a mass of ignorant and unsuspecting slobs. To further illustrate the point, I refer to two studies which are particularly troubling.

The first was done by *Money Magazine,* and was reported in an article entitled *Even the Pros are Confused this Year.*[2] It was directed at private sector, *professional* income tax preparation firms. In the study, a hypothetical family financial profile was created and this profile was taken to 50 different tax return preparation professionals. The instructions were simple: Prepare a tax return for this fictional family and determine its "fair share" of income taxes payable for the year 1987.

The results were *shocking.* Of the 50 preparers quizzed, *not one* arrived at the same bottom line figure as any other! Each and every answer was different. Mr. and Mrs. America's "fair share" of tax ranged on the low side, from about $7,200 to over $11,300 on the high side. Which of these 50 "fair share" amounts is the correct "fair share," is something that nobody seems to know.

The Government Accounting Office (GAO) did a similar study, though it was pointed at the IRS itself. This study sought to determine the correctness of the answers IRS telephone assisters gave to the public regarding tax problems. GAO researchers, *with the help of IRS officials,* came up with 20 questions which the public would likely ask the IRS via its toll free assistance lines. These twenty questions were posed to assisters in 224 calls around

---

[1] Table 7, page 31, 1987 IRS Highlights.
[2] March, 1988, page 134.

the United States.

The results indicated that the answers given by the IRS experts were wrong 39% of the time. Another 4% of the responses were "correct but incomplete." Does that mean the answer was in fact wrong? I think so. Hence, 43% of all answers given by IRS "assisters" were incorrect.

In its own defense, the IRS disputed the GAO study. Lawrence Gibbs, Commissioner of IRS, proudly reported to the IRS Oversight Subcommittee of the Senate Finance Committee on February 24, 1988, that the telephone assisters were wrong "only 25% of the time." With about 26 million persons expected to phone the IRS for help in the 1987 filing season, (January 1st through April 15, 1988) misleading only 6.5 million taxpayers is, according to Gibbs, "not bad."

Now let us throw in another factor. The IRS believes that *you* are cheating on your income tax return. I am not talking about making a mistake. I am talking about *deliberately* falsifying your return. The IRS claims, in *Income Tax Compliance Research*, Gross Tax Gap Estimates and Projections for 1973-1992[3] that the tax gap for 1987 was $84.9 billion. The phrase "tax gap" is defined in the same treatise as follows:

> "The income tax gap is the amount of tax owed for a given year, but not voluntarily paid. The word 'voluntary' means without actual enforcement action, such as examination, collection, or criminal investigation." (Publication 7285, page 1.)

Who is responsible for "legally owing" but not "voluntarily paying" taxes to the tune of $84.9 billion? Why, *you are*, of course. As you can see from Exhibit 2-1, $56.3 billion, or 66% of the tax gap is directly attributed to *individual filers*. Not corporations. Not criminals. You.

The most interesting thing about the Chart in Exhibit 2-1 is, that of the $56.3 billion blamed on individual filers $48.3 billion, or about 86%, is said to be as a result of *underreported* income, rather than *overstated* deductions and credits. I may be wrong, but I could swear that the IRS and Congress told America it was necessary to begin eliminating itemized deductions so that all of this "flagrant tax cheating" could be brought under control. In fact, is that not why the requirement to obtain a social security

---

[3] IRS Publication 7285, March, 1988.

EXHIBIT 2-1

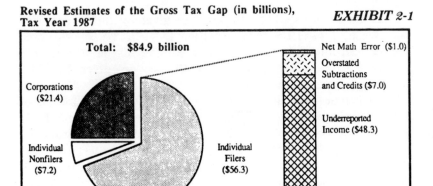

number for minor children was made law?

As it turns out, according to the IRS, that is not the problem at all. Once again, it seems the public was sold a bill of goods by "our government." The simple truth seems to be that itemized deductions are now an endangered species because the IRS and Congress are looking for more ways to take more of your dollars without you getting wise to it. Neat trick, huh?

Here are more facts to consider. Total revenue collected in tax year 1987, from all sources, was $886.29 billion. This was *up* from 1986 by $104.04 billion.[4] We were told, you may remember, that the 1986 Tax Act was "revenue neutral." That is, it would not raise but would merely make tax collection more fair and eliminate cheating, and hence, the tax gap.

If the Act were not designed to raise taxes, then why did tax collections increase by $104.04 billion over just *one year?* And if the Act were designed merely to "make the system fair and eliminate cheating," why then does the IRS *still* report a tax gap of almost $85 billion? The answers seem to be simple. One: The 1986 Tax Act had nothing to do with making the law more simple. The two studies reported earlier prove that. Two: The Act was nothing more than sophisticated legislative sleight-of-hand designed to create the *impression* that taxes were not being raised when in fact they were.

---

[4] Page 24, 1987 IRS Highlights.

The Need For Audits—

From the standpoint of the IRS, it is easy to see why it takes the business of auditing so seriously. It is also easy to see why it is convinced that each audit should result in an increase in taxes and a demand for penalties. In fact, the IRS is so serious about increasing taxes through audits that the *average* 1987 face-to-face audit of 1986 tax returns resulted in a $5,572 *recommended increase* in tax and penalties.[5]

And that just covers the *face-to-face* audits conducted by Revenue Agents. We also know that the IRS service centers conduct regular audits of tax returns by electronically examining the mathematical entries on the forms. That type of examination bagged the IRS another $4,084 in average recommended tax and penalty *increases*.[6] These two figures do not even consider interest which can easily *double* a tax bill.

Yes, the public is afraid of a tax audit. Unfortunately, it seems, it has cause to be. Nobody, including the IRS, knows what the law is. Nobody, it naturally follows, seems to be able to comply with the law. And the IRS, as a knee-jerk reaction, has branded middle-income Americans as tax cheaters. If I did not know better, I'd say it was a jungle out there. Survival of the fittest seems to be the prevailing attitude where application and compliance with the tax laws are concerned.

Understanding The Audit—

The best possible defense to an enemy attack is to know his battle plan; forewarned is forearmed. That the IRS has met with such staggering success in the tax audit arena is surely imputeable to the fact that most taxpayers, (1) have absolutely no idea of what goes on during an audit, and (2) have even less of a notion as to what they are responsible to achieve if selected for audit. That must end, *and now* if the desolation of the American pocketbook by reason of the tax audit is ever to end.

We start by understanding the audit. First, let us define it. The tax audit is nothing more or less than the process by which the correctness of an income tax return is determined. The end is achieved by, (1) determining the accuracy of the math performed on the face of the forms, (2) ascertaining that the taxpayer reported the correct amount of income, and (3) insuring that any

---

[5] Table 7, page 31, 1987 IRS Highlights. See Exhibit 1-2, Chapter One.
[6] Ibid.

subtractions claimed, such as deductions and exemptions, are accurate in amount and, in fact exist. The burden, or responsibility to prove these factors rests squarely upon the shoulders of the citizen. IRS *need not* prove the return is *incorrect* in order to collect additional taxes and penalties.

When considered in an academic sense, all of this may seem rather innocuous. However, we must now interject some intangible factors into the audit environment. First, the IRS *believes* the return is wrong, and knows what to look for and what questions to ask. Secondly, the citizen probably had the return prepared by a "professional" and does not have the slightest idea of what is claimed. And lastly, because the citizen *believes* the first factor to be true, and *knows* the second factor is true, he is terrified.

We can do nothing about the IRS' attitude. Revenue Agents undergo extensive training and are, I am sure, much more familiar with the audit and tax increase statistics than I am. The overall demeanor of the Revenue Agent with whom one is forced to work in a given case is just about the only thing that is non-negotiable. What can be eliminated however, is the cause of the fear: ignorance of one's own tax return.

Understanding the Tax Return—

The general practice is for a person to bring his financial matters to an accountant or tax preparer to have all the required government forms completed. After leaving the material with the preparer, he goes home—and sweats the outcome. When the onerous task is at last completed, the citizen returns to the office, signs the forms, and makes out two checks. One for the IRS, and if there is any money left, one for the preparer. He tucks his copy of the return under his arm and returns home, grateful that yet another year has passed and that he has survived the tribulation. The envelope is stuffed safely in a box marked "Important," which sits on a shelf in the garage right next to six years' worth of back issues of *National Geographic*...also marked "Important."

The mistake is that *no time* was spent with the preparer going over the return. The citizen, despite the fact that he probably prepared and submitted to the accountant a data sheet containing all the raw material, has no idea of how that material was distilled by the tax expert. Take the time to understand your tax return while the information is fresh in your mind! If audited, the examination will take place one or perhaps two or more years after the return was filed. If you are hazy on the facts when the return was filed, you will be hopelessly lost when the return is selected for audit years later.

Use the data sheet the accountant provided you to your advantage. Exhibit 2-2 is an example of a portion of the typical accountant data sheet. Most accountants will keep the original in a file which they maintain. Take a copy of the data sheet and keep it with *your* copy of the return. Before signing and mailing the return, have the accountant take you by the hand and *point out* how each of the totals you provided was computed into the bottom line of the return. Make a note in the margin of the data sheet indicating the specific form and line upon which each total was entered.

For example, the data sheet would ask for the amount you paid in home mortgage interest. You would have entered a total which was then transferred by the accountant to the Schedule A, line 9a. Therefore on the data sheet, next to the total given for the mortgage interest, you would pencil in, "Schedule A, line 9a." See Exhibit 2-2, page two.

Receipts should be kept segregated by subject. A corresponding note should be made on the data sheet indicating which specific return entry applies to that particular pack of receipts. In this manner, your return can be cross-checked with your own records, and more importantly, indexed to your own records *before* it is filed.

Many tax returns have a number of schedules and supplemental forms attached for which there appears to be no logical reason. This is even more true since the enactment of the 1986 Tax Act. (See Chapter Four). As you progress through your tax return with the preparer, on the top or back of each supplemental form, write a complete explanation as to why that form was included with your filing, and how it relates to the 1040. This could prove most helpful later.

The 30 or 40 minutes it will take to accomplish this task will be invaluable. The exercise is *not* limited to those who use a return preparer. Those who prepare their own tax returns can follow the same steps. This will help them to remember how the Herculean task was achieved. Self-preparers should also be careful to save all IRS publications and instructions upon which they relied in the preparation process. They too, may be handy later.

These simple steps will put you in a position to understand your tax return without the necessity of becoming a tax expert.

EXHIBIT 2-2 (page one)

ITEMIZED DEDUCTIONS

List only amounts that have actually been paid during the year. Save all cancelled checks and receipts for a period of at least 3 years. Do not duplicate any entry. You may round off to the nearest dollar.

MEDICAL

Drugs and Medicines	Amount
Prescriptions	53.78
Other General Drugs — *Ins. Reimbursement*	−29.10
Other: *Total Paid*	24.68

Medical Insurance	Amount
Insurance — Paid Directly By You	
Group Health Plans (Deducted from Salary)	45.58
Other:	

Doctors, Dentists, Clinics, Etc.	Paid By You	Other Medical Expenses	Paid By You
Dr. Mark	$170.20	Eye Glasses	
Dr. Ospina	210.00	Hearing Aids & Supplies	
Dr. Leonard	87.50	X-Ray/Lab Fees	
Dr. McCue	140.75	Ambulance	
Dr. Groppolli	59.00	Nurses (Board & Room)	
Dr. Anderson	22.00	Medical Aid Rental	
Total	749.45	Artificial Teeth	
— *Ins. Reimbursement*	(202.76)	Equipment (Prescribed)	
Total	546.69 ✓		
EYE GLASSES			

Transportation: Total number of miles driven for medical reasons during the year.	
Above amounts reimbursed by insurance.	

Comments or explanation:

EXHIBIT 2-2 (page two)

TAXES

Description of Tax		State Located	Amount of Tax
Real Estate Taxes (Home)		minn.	139.08
Real Estate Taxes (Other)			
Property Tax Rebates (If Any)			
Personal Property Tax (If Any)			
Auto Licenses	Number of Licenses Purchased No. 1	Total Cost $	70.00
	Other: Transfer Fees		8.25
Sales Tax	General Sales Tax (Tax Table Used If No Entry)		
	Take Additional Sales Tax For: Auto, Truck, Boat, Motor Home, New Home Building Materials, Natural Gas & Electricity (List Category Below)		
	Additional Tax: Sales Tax on auto		$93.51
State or Local Taxes (Not Listed Elsewhere or on W-2's)			
Other (Explain):			
Comments or Explanations:			

Non-Deductible Taxes: Gasoline, Tires, Telephone, Air Transportation, Tobacco, Alcohol, etc.

INTEREST PAID

Source	Amount	Source	Amount
Home Mortgage - Sch A, iN. 9a	1134.95	Auto Loan	
Other Mortgage		Bank Loan	
Contract For Deed	213.94	Credit Union	
		Personal Loan	
Credit Cards – List	Amount	Installment Loans – List	Amount

Contact lending agencies for amounts of interest paid during year if not shown on end of year statements or reported by mail.

CAUTION: Data sheet shown for illustration only. Do not use for income tax preparation for 1988 or after.

Understanding the tax return is the most important step to success in the audit.

The Starting Point—

All face-to-face audits begin at the same point, with a notice from the IRS. The notice informs you that your return has been selected for audit, and establishes a time and a place for the meeting. See Exhibit 2-3. On the reverse side of the notice is a pre-printed section bearing the heading, "Please bring records to support the following items reported on your tax return." Beneath that heading you will find numerous listings which represent the field of items which may be claimed on a tax return. Turn to Exhibit 2-4. As you see, next to each item is a "ballot box," which if checked, indicates the government's interest in that particular item.

In step-by-step fashion, we will examine the phases of preparation one must undertake to enable him to negotiate successfully in the tax audit.

Step One. Audit defense preparations begin with an analysis of the "documents request" portion of the notice. If you have followed the simple tax return indexing steps outlined above in *Understanding Your Tax Return,* the procedure will be greatly simplified. If you have not, then you must be prepared to spend quite a bit more time on this phase. Peruse the field of possible selections (Exhibit 2-4) to decipher which have been selected in your case.

Step Two. After reviewing the items in question as shown on the notice (Exhibit 2-4), you may now begin to determine two essential facts with respect to each checked item. First, what *in fact* was claimed on the return under the heading flagged by the IRS' notice? And second, are you *in possession* of sufficient proof to verify that the entry made on your return with respect to such item was correct?

Settling on what *in fact* was claimed on the return is a simple matter. One will just look to the form or schedule bearing the entry in question and note the amount shown. An example would be the amount claimed as mortgage interest. *This is the amount that must be proven in the audit.* This is where the data sheet index system (Exhibit 2-2) becomes so helpful. The data sheet is typically organized in a somewhat more logical manner, at least in the eyes of the layman, than is the Form 1040 and its accompanying schedules.

EXHIBIT 2-3   *INFORMATION COPY ONLY*

Internal Revenue Service   Department of the Treasury
District Director

Date: April 26, 1988   Contact Telephone Number:

                                        Appointment Clerk

                                        Auditor:

YOUR NAME
AND ADDRESS HERE

        We selected your Federal income tax return for the year(s) shown below to examine the
items checked at the end of this letter. We have scheduled an appointment for you at the
time and place shown below. If you are unable to keep this appointment, please call the
~~appointment clerk~~ promptly to reschedule a more convenient time.

auditor   **APPOINTMENT INFORMATION**

TAX YEAR(S): 1986   **DAY AND DATE:** Thursday, May 12, 1988
PLACE: Federal Courts Building **TIME:** 1:00 P.M.
        316 North Robert Street
ROOM NO: 300
        St. Paul, MN 55101   auditor
        To avoid any unnecessary repetitive examinations, let the ~~appointment clerk~~ know as
soon as possible if your income tax return was examined in either of the 2 prior years
for the same items and the examination resulted in no change to your tax liability.

        If you filed a joint return, either you or your spouse may keep the appointment.
You may also have someone else represent you; however, if you are not present, you must
furnish your representative with a written authorization. You can get authorization forms
from an IRS office by requesting Form 2848, or for limited authorization, Form 2848-D.
Also, any individual may accompany you as a witness to assist in establishing the facts
in your case.

        We enclosed information guides to assist you in selecting the type of documents
required to substantiate the items checked. It will save you time if you keep together
the records related to each item. Without the requested documents, we will have to proceed
on the basis of available information that may be incomplete. Therefore, we will need
your cooperation.

        The examiner will review your return and records. If we propose any changes to your
tax liability we will explain them as well as your appeal rights. If you agree to the
proposed changes, we will ask you to sign an agreement form. If you do not agree, the
examiner will furnish you with a copy of Publication 5, Appeal Rights and Preparation of
Protests for Unagreed Cases.
                                (over)

316 N. Robert St., St. Paul, Minn.   55101   Letter 889(DO) (Rev. 10-81)

EXHIBIT 2-4   *INFORMATION COPY ONLY*

   If you have any questions, please contact our office at the number shown in the
heading of this letter. When you come in for your appointment, please bring this letter
with you.

   Thank you for your cooperation.

                                       Sincerely yours,

                                       [signature]
                                       District Director

Enclosures:
Information Guides
Publication 876

Please bring records to support the following items reported on your tax return.

☐ Alimony Payments	☐ Employee Business Expenses	☒ Rental Income and Expenses
☐ Automobile Expenses	☐ Energy Credit	☐ Sale or Exchange of Residence
☐ Bad Debts	☐ Exemptions (Child/Children, Other)	☐ Sick Pay or Disability Income Exclusion
☐ Capital Gains and Losses	☐ Income—1099's & 1087's	☒ Taxes – Schedule A
☐ Casualty Losses	☒ Interest Expense – Schedule A	☐ Uniforms, Equipment, and Tools Real-estate a Sales Tax
☐ Child Care Credit	☐ Medical and Dental Expenses	☐
☒ Contributions – Schedule A	☒ Miscellaneous Deductions – Schedule A	
☐ Education Expenses	☐ Moving Expenses	☐

   Please bring all business and personal bank statements. Also, bring canceled checks, accounting ledgers and journals, notes,
agreements, and invoices for the following items:

Schedule C

☐ All Business Expenses	☐ Insurance	☐ Taxes
☐ Bad Debts	☐ Interest	☐ Travel and Entertainment
☐ Cost of Goods Sold	☐ Rents	☐
☐ Depreciation	☐ Repairs	☐
☐ Gross Receipts	☐ Salaries and Wages	☐

Schedule F

☐ All Farm Expenses	☐ Insurance	☐ Repairs and Maintenance
☐ Depreciation	☐ Inventories	☐ Supplies Purchased
☐ Feed and Seed Purchased	☐ Labor Hired	☐ Taxes
☐ Fertilizers, Lime	☐ Machine Hire	☐
☐ Gross Receipts	☐ Other Farm Income	☐

                                       Letter 889(DO) (Rev. 10–81)

Therefore, your margin notes made on the data sheet will direct you quickly and easily to the precise location on the tax return where any particular entry may be found. This will save the necessity of having to pour over every square inch of the form and schedules in search of the troublesome entry. If you used a return preparer, meet with the preparer and go over the return to be sure you understand each of the entries.

Do not proceed to an audit without reviewing the tax return in this manner. If you do, you will have no idea *whatsoever* as to what your burden of proof is on the issues. You will be completely at the mercy of the auditor.

Step Three. After you have isolated each item in question and located each entry on the tax form itself, you must then match your documentary proof to that item to be sure that the two figures coincide. Exactly what types of documentation are considered "sufficient proof" is the main subject of this chapter and is addressed later. For the time being, your preliminary preparation must satisfy this question: Do existing documents, that is, documents currently in your possession or under your control, support the amount of income, deductions or credits claimed on the return? If the answer is "no," then you must, using one of the 10 methods expounded upon in this chapter, supplement your proof so that it is sufficient. If the answer is "yes," then you may proceed to Step Four.

Step Four. After you have answered the question whether your proof is sufficient in terms of dollars and cents, you must now determine whether the proof is sufficient from a *legal* standpoint. This usually involves slightly more effort than just adding receipts and checks with a calculator. It will necessitate, unless you own a copy of the current tax law, a trip to the library.

Most any public library, but certainly every law library will have a copy of the United States Code. The United States Code is a compilation of all the acts of Congress which are currently in effect in the United States. It is, in a word, the body of American law known as "statutes." Statutes within the United States Code are organized by topic. Each topic is assigned a number which is referred to as a "Title."

All Internal Revenue laws are found within Title 26 of the United States Code. This title is commonly referred to as "the Internal Revenue Code." Within Title 26 each separate statute— and there are thousands—is numbered individually, beginning with one. The statute is then referred to as a "section." Hence, the citation "26 USC §6511" is a reference to Title 26 of the United States Code (the Internal Revenue Code), at section 6511.

Paperback copies of the Internal Revenue Code are available from several publishers. They are inexpensive and quite handy. Two companies in particular focus upon publishing materials relative to income taxes, and are practiced with regard to the Internal Revenue Code. These companies are Commerce Clearing House, 4024 West Peterson Avenue, Chicago, IL 60646, and Prentice Hall, Englewood Cliffs, NJ 07632.

The purpose of referring to the code is simple, yet important. Revenue Agents can be expected to assume one of two stances with regard to a given deduction claimed on a return. The first, and most common, can be expected where the citizen's proof does not meet or exceed the numbers shown on the return. "Without further substantiation," you will be told, "I cannot allow the item you have claimed. You are unable to prove satisfactorily that you in fact spent the amount claimed." Hence, down the drain goes the deduction, in whole or in part.

When the proof *does* match the amount claimed, the Revenue Agent will oft-times shift gears. Reverting to Plan B, he claims that while you did indeed spend the amount of money claimed, the *law* does not allow the deduction. "The law is clear," begins the refrain. "A deduction is just not permitted for money spent in this fashion. I am sorry, but I just cannot allow it."

In anticipation of the two-pronged attack, proper preparation for the audit must address both the *factual* (how much was spent, on whom and when) and the *legal* (what the statutes say about money spent in this fashion) aspects of a given deduction. This is especially true in light of the 1986 tax law overhaul. As we have already seen, nobody seems to know the law since the sweeping changes have occurred. With little doubt, we can expect the IRS to try to take full advantage of the newly created, widespread ignorance and confusion.

How to Use the Code—

Using the Code, particularly in paperback form, is very simple. Just refer to the index, under the "key word" in question. For example, suppose you wish to determine the circumstances under which "entertainment" expenses may be deducted in light of the sweeping changes to the law. The index under the general heading of "Entertainment," will point you in several directions. Review the list to see which sub-entry is applicable.

A number will be listed to the right of the index entry. That number is a reference to a code section, not page number, within the tax code. Next to the heading "Entertainment" you will find the reference "274." This is the specific section of the code where one will find the legal authority to deduct entertainment expenses.

We must now read and analyze the pertinent statute. Section 274(a) reads, in part:

> "(a)(1) In General.—*No deduction* otherwise allowable under this Chapter shall be allowed for any item—
> (A) Activity.—With respect to an activity which is of a type generally considered to constitute entertainment, amusement, or recreation, *unless the taxpayer establishes* that the item was directly related to, or, in the case of an item directly preceding or following a substantial and bona fide business discussion (including business meetings at a convention or otherwise), that such item was associated with, the active conduct of the taxpayer's trade or business...(Emphasis added.) IRC §274(a).

At first blush, it appears that someone is trying to confuse you. This is probably because they are! It appears that *no* deduction is allowed. However, upon reading more carefully, we find in subparagraph (A) that an exception is created by the words *"unless the taxpayer establishes..."* The statute goes on to describe what must then be "established."

Specifically, if one can demonstrate that any such expense was "directly related to or associated with the active conduct of the taxpayer's trade or business," then the expense in question becomes deductible under the general terms of §274(a). Only by actually reviewing the particular statute in question is one capable of accurately stating "what the law is" in a given case.

In addition to the Internal Revenue Code where we find the statutes, the body of tax law is made up of other sources of authority. These sources include:

1. Tax Regulations. Regulations are passed into being by the IRS and are *assented* to by Congress. An IRS regulation becomes effective when Congress *fails* to act upon it by expressly voting against its enactment. Through this system of law by default, thousands of requirements are heaped upon citizens by unelected officials.

2. Court Decisions. Court decisions interpret the statutes and regulations on a case by case basis.

3. Revenue Rulings. Revenue Rulings are the IRS' *written opinion* as to how the law is applied in a given set of hypothetical facts and circumstances.

Each of these sources of authority on the law can be helpful to provide support to any single claim made by a citizen.

In The Lion's Den—

The source of most of the difficulty which faces citizens undergoing audit can be traced to the Internal Revenue Code's failure to specifically define the obligations heaped upon American taxpayers with respect to their own records. Under §446(a) of the Code, a taxpayer is required to compute his income using a method of accounting on the basis of "which the taxpayer regularly computes his income in keeping his books." If that statement alone is not confusing enough, consider this: The Internal Revenue Code *does not* define, expressly or impliedly, the "books" which the taxpayer must keep.

Consequently, each citizen and business may have, and often does have, an entirely different method of keeping track of income and expenditures for tax purposes. Add to this the great "discretion" which the IRS has under §446(b), and the potential for abuse is staggering. Section 446(b) reads:

> "(b) If no method of accounting has been regularly used by the taxpayer, or if the method used does not clearly reflect income, the computation of taxable income shall be made under such method as, *in the opinion of the Secretary*, does clearly reflect income." (Emphasis added.)

At the beginning of this chapter I demonstrated that the "opinion of the Secretary" is that most individuals in this country have income beyond that which has been claimed on tax returns. "In the opinion of the Secretary," then, those persons are to have their incomes "adjusted" under such method "as does clearly reflect income." To translate, the IRS adds taxable income, and hence, tax liability, in almost every audit situation. So not only does each audit create a potential danger to one's deductions, his income is equally at risk, standing to be *increased* at the whim of the auditor.

For this reason, one must be prepared to prove that the income shown on his tax return is an accurate reflection of that received by him during the course of the year.

How to Verify Income—

The IRS' Attack—

Success for the citizen in the tax audit game is measured by two specific yardsticks. The first, we all know. It is the deductions test. Have my deductions been disallowed, and if so, to what extent? The second lesser known measure pertains to income. Has any income been *added* to my tax return, and if so, how much?

The initial phase of the audit, by and large, concentrates on the income side of the ledger, with the latter phases focusing upon the deductions side. The IRS uses several techniques for flushing out evidence of additional income. Most of the techniques are concealed in the camouflage of seemingly meaningless questions. For example, refer to Chapter One, Part I(D). Five of the more common methods of determining income which are regularly employed by the IRS, and which have been approved by the courts over the years, are discussed next.

1. *The Bank Deposits Method.* The IRS regularly reviews the records of one's bank account(s). It is quite common for the IRS to request to see all personal and business bank records, including duplicate deposit slips, monthly bank statements, canceled checks and loan documents for a given year.

What do they learn from all of this? A lot! For example, the average man is under the impression that his transactions with a bank are sacred. This is not true. The IRS has ready access to one's bank records, with or without the cooperation of the citizen through the use of IRS Form 2039, Summons. You would be *shocked* to learn just how free-wheeling banks are with supposedly private information.

But believing that the account is private, money or receipts which may not be reported on the tax return are nevertheless deposited to the bank account. When this happens, a discrepancy is created in the amount of the "apparent income" as shown on the tax return versus that which was deposited to the bank account. Let me illustrate:

Suppose you worked for a large corporation during 1988. At the end of the year, the corporation issued a Form W-2, Wage and Tax Statement. The statement, also filed with the IRS, reported the total wages you received during the year.

At the end of the year, your tax records are brought to the tax preparer. Among them is the Form W-2, but you overlooked the fact that you sold that old riding lawnmower to your neighbor.

That money, along with all of the garage sale proceeds, were deposited into your bank account with a paycheck one month. When the IRS auditor totals the deposits to the account, taken from the duplicate deposit slips and monthly statements which you provided, he finds that, for example, $1,200 *more* money appeared in the bank account than was reported as income on your tax return. The difference is determined to be unreported income.

Only in the case of criminals is the failure to report the added income a deliberate act. The common man does not believe that every dime which comes into his possession must be reported to the government on a 1040. Even for one who is most conscientious about reporting everything, truthfully, who remembers to write down *every dime*? Yet, as has already been shown, the IRS believes these "underreporters" to be hiding income intentionally, and when the new tax liability is computed, penalties are naturally included.

2. *Net Worth Increases.* Another method, used less commonly, is the "Net Worth Increase" method. Under this system, the IRS makes a determination of any substantial increase in one's net worth (the value of his assets after taking into consideration any liabilities associated therewith) during a particular year. Once a year-end net worth has been established, it is compared with the net worth as it existed at the beginning of the same year. The difference is then calculated. This figure is then compared to the income shown on the tax return, and the IRS asks itself whether the after-tax income of the citizen was sufficient to account for the increases in net worth. If not, the IRS makes the claim that additional income was earned.

Let me illustrate: Suppose on January 1, 1988, you have a $75,000 mortgage on your home. The home is worth $100,000. If that is your only asset, your net worth is $25,000. Let us further suppose that by December 31, 1988, your home mortgage is paid in full. Without any debt on the home your net worth, assuming no other assets or liabilities, is now $100,000. Your net worth has *increased* by $75,000 in just one year.

Now let us suppose that your 1988 tax return, filed on or before April 15, 1989, discloses that your income was $50,000. The return also shows deductions for such things as contributions and interest in the combined amount of $10,000, making your taxable income $40,000[7]. You must pay taxes on your income, and most, if not all of

---

[7] For purposes of the illustration, we will not consider the value of dependent exemptions which ordinarily would be considered in arriving at taxable income.

that money was collected by the IRS through wage withholding. As the income rate is 28% on the income above $29,750[8] and 15% on the income below that amount, your total federal *income* tax liability would be $7,332.50. Add to that the mandatory social security extractions of $3004.00 taken from your wages,[9] and your *total* federal tax liability would be $10,336.50.

Now we must subtract from gross pay ($50,000) the deductions ($10,000) and the total tax paid ($10,336.50) to arrive at net after-tax income. After these computations are performed, we see that *net* after-tax income is $29,663.50. This is the amount of money you would have had available to spend on all personal living expenses, recreation, investments, etc. As anyone can plainly see, *and so would the IRS*, it is impossible with this amount of money to have paid off the $75,000 mortgage balance on your house. Obviously, the government would have quickly concluded that you had additional income. Equally obvious is the fact that such income was not reported on your return.

The example I just gave of a net worth evaluation was exaggerated and simplified. This is because *all* assets and liabilities must be taken into consideration before any increases can be assumed. It *does* however, depict the process by which such determinations are made. Furthermore, the IRS must *correctly* fix the net worth at the beginning of the year in question before it can be said that the net worth had *increased* by the end of the year. But a thorough investigation would reveal the information necessary to accomplish this. For example, all real estate transactions are recorded and in many cases since the new tax law, are *reported* to the IRS. Similarly, motor vehicle acquisitions are recorded. As we already know, the IRS has speedy access to your bank account and the information which can be mined there.

3. *Cash Expenditures.* TEFRA (my favorite law) added a section to the Internal Revenue Code which requires that all cash transactions in excessof $10,000 be reported to the IRS. The law, §6050I, stipulates that if any person engaged in "a trade or business receives more than $10,000 in cash in one transaction (or two or more related transactions)," that person must supply information to the IRS which includes the name and social security number of the payer, and the date of the transaction.

The IRS uses this information to make evaluations of

---

[8] For a married person filing a joint return.
[9] Computed at the rate of 7.51% on the first $45,000 of income.

unreported income in much the same way as is done in the case of
the net worth assessment. Using the same example as already
expressed above, suppose, rather than paying off the house, the
IRS had information which revealed that you purchased several
expensive furs and diamonds during the course of the year. While
these assets are not "title" assets as an automobile or house, they
are just as easily traceable through the reporting requirements of
Code §6050I.

In addition, the IRS regularly uses Form 4822, *Estimate of
Annual Personal and Family Living Expenses*, to recompute
income. The form, discussed in detail in Chapter One, Part I(D),
asks the citizen to explain to the IRS all of the expenses he paid
during the course of a given year, either by check or with cash. If
the expenses, as delineated on the form by the citizen, seem to
exceed the expendable income available to the citizen, the IRS will
assume additional income was earned and will increase his tax
based upon it.

4. *Bureau of Labor Statistics Estimates.* The Bureau of
Labor annually publishes statistics on the average earnings of
persons in the United States. The statistics cover individuals in
virtually every walk of life. They also take into account the amount
of disposable income necessary to exist in a given community in
the United States.

These data are enlisted by the IRS typically when no income tax
return was filed by a citizen. In the absence of any information
whatsoever, the IRS will make an estimate of one's income based
upon Bureau of Labor Statistics (BLS). Using one's employment
and geographic location as a starting point, the IRS will refer to
the myriad of tables in BLS publications to fix an amount of
income which one "must have received" in order to exist under the
conditions apparent. The statistics will consider whether the
person is a homeowner, whether married and with children, and
other factors which are known or are readily ascertainable by the
IRS.

A BLS estimate will stand up unless the citizen can
demonstrate that the figures are incorrect.

5. *Consumer Price Index Estimates.* The Consumer Price
Index (CPI) marks increases in the cost of living in the United
States from year to year. Moreover, like the BLS tables, these
figures are broken into specific geographic locations. A person in
St. Louis, for example, may not be faced with the same cost of
living increases as, say, a person in San Francisco. The differences

would be reflected in the particular tables compiled within the CPI.

Like the BLS tables, CPI tables provide the IRS with a fruitful source of information upon which to base a tax assessment in the absence of more accurate data or a tax return from the citizen. Commonly when CPI tables are employed, the IRS will pull the last tax return available for the taxpayer, determine his gross income as shown on that return, and merely increase it year to year by multiplying the appropriate CPI ratio to the last known income figure. I will illustrate:

Suppose your last federal income tax return, filed in 1981, disclosed an income of $38,000. Suppose also that you live in Atlanta, Georgia. Let us further suppose that the CPI for Atlanta increased each year by four percent. The IRS will simply multiply $38,000 (your 1981 income) by 1.04 to make the determination that your 1982 income was $39,520. That latter figure will again be multiplied by the 1.04 factor to arrive at 1983 income: $41,000. The procedure will be repeated until each year is accounted for.

6. *Weighted Averages.* The weighted average is a mathematical computation performed by a revenue agent where only partial or incomplete records are available. It works this way: Suppose you have a bank account for 18 months during 1986 and 1987. In July of 1987, the account is closed and you have no further transactions with any bank. As a consequence, the IRS has records of income through bank deposits for all of 1986, but only half of 1987, and none at all for 1988.

To determine income for the last six months of 1987 and the entirety of 1988, the IRS will average the deposits shown in the first 18 months of the period in question. That average will then be projected over the balance of the 18 month period, taking into account the estimated increases in business anticipated from the CPI tables. These averages will form the foundation for IRS' claim of income for the 18 month period in which no bank records existed.

B. How To Counter—

As a taxpayer subject to audit by the IRS at any time, you must be cognizant of what the IRS can and does do on a regular basis to increase the income shown on a tax return. Forewarning of the end permits one to recognize the various means which are used to achieve the end—and to *counter!* In anticipation of the IRS' attack upon your tax return's income revelation, be prepared to counter by rallying one of the proven methods used to verify that your disclosure is correct.

I have distilled four primary techniques which, if used alone or in concert with one another, will allow you to insure that the income portion of your return will remain intact. Each of the techniques, together with a true to life example of how it is used, follows.

1. *Ledgers.* My many years of experience with the IRS has taught me that the most effective way to verify one's income as shown on the tax return is with records made personally and contemporaneously with earning the income. Records which reflect income are commonly referred to as ledgers or journals. Creation of these records by the citizen can be, in the absence of patently contradictory evidence such as enormous increases in net worth or the like, most persuasive in an income dispute.

A case comes to mind where this type of record was the difference between paying tens of thousands of dollars in illegitimate taxes and a *just* conclusion that such a sum of money was truly not owed. Dennis had gone through a tax audit in which he presented to the auditor his bank records and evidence to support his business deductions. Unaware that the auditor was fishing for evidence of unreported income, Dennis candidly answered a barrage of questions about the manner in which he operates his business.

As a piano tuner, Dennis would make house calls to his many customers. Some of the customers paid by check. Many would pay in cash. Naturally, all of the checks were deposited to Dennis' bank account, but for no particular reason, the cash was not. When the IRS audited Dennis' tax return, they reviewed his bank records as is routine. The auditor, a self-styled Sherlock Holmes, believed he had stumbled on to a major discrepancy in Dennis' finances.

The discrepancy was this: Dennis had written off many thousands of dollars in business expenses on his Schedule C. But deposits to his bank account did not even come close to matching the expenses claimed, not to mention other deductions which were claimed on the Schedule A. Even though Dennis had declared sufficient income on the return to account for the expenditure of these funds, it was obvious that Dennis was doing a large part of his business in cash. This fact had caused the auditor to jump to an erroneous and unfounded conclusion that Dennis had underreported his income by many thousands of dollars.

All of this gumshoeing had been done by the auditor without

Dennis' knowledge. Had the agent simply asked, Dennis could have provided ample verification of his income as claimed on the return. Yet the agent did not ask. His concern was rather to place a bill before Dennis and to demand it be payed, right or wrong. And that is exactly what happened.

Some weeks after Dennis had left the audit, he received his 30-day notice with a cover letter from the agent. The cover letter explained that Dennis would be expected to pay the additional tax and penalties promptly in order to avoid further interest. Upon reviewing the examination report, Dennis was shocked to find that the agent had included in the computations thousands of dollars in "unreported income." Flabbergasted by the report, we immediately drafted the necessary paperwork to carry out an appeal.

During the Appeals conference, we presented the ledgers which Dennis had maintained and which were used as the source of the information which eventually found its way on to the income line of Dennis' tax return. Not being an accountant, the ledgers were rudimentary by professional standards, but quite functional for his specific needs. As it happened, they were also more than adequate to establish that his income was reported correctly. Remember, the law does not require that you keep records in a "professional" manner, nor does it require that records be kept in any particular fashion, professional or otherwise. The law requires only that records be kept such as are sufficient to "clearly reflect income."[10]

In form, Dennis' ledger looked something like this:

MONTH/YEAR

Date	Name/Address	Job	Paid

Beneath the heading in each column Dennis would record the data called for by the heading. Where an amount was reflected in the paid column, Dennis would indicate with a check mark whether the amount was paid at the time service was rendered or whether he would have to bill the client. At the end of the month, a

---

[10] See Code §446(b).

statement would be mailed to any person whose name did not bear a check mark in the "Paid" column next to the amount shown. The eventual payment was then recorded in the month in which it was received. At the end of the year it became a simple matter of merely adding the amounts shown in the ledgers which bore a check mark. A total was taken, and that amount was reflected as the gross income on the tax return.

Verifying income at the Appeals level was a less-than-formidable task. We provided copies of Dennis' ledgers together with an explanation as to how they were maintained. Dennis' testimony that these ledgers were made contemporaneously with earning the income was critical. That is to say, they were not concocted in a desperate hope to avoid the additional taxes occasioned by the auditor's zeal.

In the absence of any specific evidence to the contrary, and given the fact that Dennis' explanation was *plausible, reasonable* and Dennis was an *honest* person and clearly *projected* that, the Appeals Officer accepted his proof and recalculated the Examination changes. In the process, all of the phantom income "found" by the revenue agent was dropped.

Many businesses use professional accountants or bookkeepers to establish ledgers or journals which accurately and neatly reflect the daily business of the company. Those without the benefit of such experts should take a lesson from Dennis. One must be careful that he does not fall into the trap of creating ledgers which are too complex and difficult to follow. Unless supervised by an accountant, one's ledgers should be simple and quite to the point. Most importantly, they must be made at the same time the events being recorded occurred. It is important to be able to testify believably that one's ledgers were made at the time the income was *earned*, and *not* on the way to the courthouse.

2. *Bank Records.* Just as the IRS will use bank records to *increase* income, a knowledgeable citizen can use them to cast aside *estimates* of income made by the IRS. Useful tools include the monthly bank statements, and duplicate deposit slips. Between the two sources of data, a person can fix his income quite accurately. In fact, I maintain that the best and most accurate ledger or journal that a person can have is his business bank account. When money is received in the course of one's affairs and deposited to the account, a permanent record is made of the amount and date it was received. If the IRS ever questions the amount of income received in a given year, reference to the bank

records as the full and complete record of one's receipts is virtually unassailable. This of course assumes that the IRS cannot point to large cash expenditures or net worth increases which betray bank account information.

To illustrate this, I point to a case where the IRS had made an estimate of a man's income for two years in the early 1980s. Don did not file income tax returns for the two years in question. Using the BLS tables mentioned earlier, the IRS estimated his income based upon the town in which he lived and his business. Don was a plumber, but not a very successful one. Personal circumstances had caused his business to dwindle and he was working odd jobs to generate money on which to live.

When the IRS issued a notice of deficiency, Don filed a petition in the United States Tax Court challenging both the figures of income asserted by the government, and the amount of business expenses to which he was entitled. BLS statistics, unfortunately, do not take into consideration whether one is successful in business or not. They are, by admission, mere *averages*. In order to have an average, there must of course be a high and low. Don's income was at the low end of the scale. But the BLS tables used by the government put his income over five times higher than it in fact was. With the penalties and interest included, the IRS wanted Don to pay more in taxes for the two years than he earned in income.

Using bank records as the starting point, we set out to determine the *accurate* amount of gross income Don earned during the two years. The bank account in question was in fact owned by Don's wife, Linda. Linda was employed in a job of her own and earned her own money. She also filed her own tax returns and paid her own taxes. But Don was depositing *his* money into *her* account. As she had no obligation to report his income, she reported only her own.

We knew how much Linda earned from her job each month and we knew that she was paid twice each month. A monthly bank statement reflects each deposit and withdrawal transacted in a given month. We carefully reviewed the bank statements and with a red pen, drew a line through those deposits which were identified as Linda's paycheck. In some cases however, a deposit larger than a single paycheck was shown. In that case, we went back to the deposit slip. A deposit slip *identifies* each of the individual items which make up a deposit. By referring to the deposit slips, we were able to focus upon, and mark out each of Linda's paychecks.

The remaining deposits to the account represented money which Don had earned. Having isolated Don's income on each of the bank statements, it was just a matter of adding the total deposits which we could accurately say were his. The total of each of the 12 months was Don's income for the years in question. Our tally was presented to the Appeals Officer, together with *testimony* to the effect that all of Don's receipts were deposited to the account. We also proved that Linda's wages were responsible for the other funds deposited to the account, and showed that Linda had already filed her own return.

With no other evidence that Don had earned the income claimed by the IRS, Appeals personnel were forced to accept the facts as we had presented them. As in the previous example, credible testimony from Don to the effect that all of his income was deposited to Linda's bank account spelled the end for the BLS estimates.

Not all solutions are that simple. Sometimes, bank account analysis is much more laborious and detailed than that necessary in Don's case. Further effort is necessary when the IRS skews figures taken from two or more separate accounts. It happens all the time, and in my judgment, the IRS' acts are deliberate, and I believe, reprehensible. The typical plot unfolds this way:

A small businessman has two (or more) bank accounts.[11] One account functions as a business account, to which he deposits his receipts and from which he pays the business bills. The other account functions as a personal account. The personal account is generally funded by periodic payments from the business account. From the personal account he will then pay personal living expenses.

During the course of an examination, the IRS will review the records of both accounts. The deposits to the business account will be totalled. Then the deposits to the personal account will be totalled. The two figures will then be *added together*, and the sum called "corrected income." It happens too often to be called an error on the part of the IRS, and unfortunately, this process just as often handcuffs the citizen.

Let us look at what such a trick does to one's gross income. Suppose total deposits to the business account in a given year were $200,000. Suppose further that the owner of the business takes a "draw" or self-imposed salary of $3,000 per month, which he pays

---

[11] One man with whom I dealt in 1978 had *13* accounts.

to himself in a check drawn on the company account. In the typical sole-proprietorship type business, all the income of the business as well as its expenses are reported on Schedule C. The difference between company receipts and all of its expenses is considered personal income to the owner. With very few exceptions, that difference is manifested exclusively by the "draw" or salary.

Under our example, the yearly income of our hypothetical proprietor is $36,000 ($3,000 per month). The $36,000 is taken *from* the $200,000 gross, it was not received *in addition* to the $200,000 gross. Yet when the IRS, in its wisdom, adds together the total deposits of *each* account, it concludes that the gross was $236,000, not $200,000. Worse than that, since there appears to be no additional *expenses* to offset the apparent unreported income, the *net* income to the proprietor is recomputed to be *$72,000*— exactly *twice* what in reality was earned. I trust I do not have to explain what that does to one's tax liability.

So, what is the cure? In one very similar case, we explained to the agent that the funds he called "unreported income" were in fact redeposits from the business account. We further explained that the money was *already* accounted for on the Schedule C. Sitting back in his swivel chair, he cracked a devilish smile and glibly said, "prove it." So we did.

Beginning with the canceled checks written on the *business* account, we shuffled through them individually. Anytime we happened upon a check written to the citizen or his wife, we set it aside. After unearthing each such check, we unfolded the bank statements from the *personal* account. The amounts of specific deposits to the personal account were compared with the checks written on the *business* account. In this manner, we were able to trace the money from its source in the one account to its destination in the other. A yellow highlighter marked the particular line of the monthly statement where one could find a "redeposit." When finished, we were able to follow each personal deposit to its origin in the *business* account. The conclusion we correctly reached was that no money had come into the personal account from any source other than the business.

At the same time, we tallied the deposits to the business account by reference to the monthly statements. That number was then compared to the one shown on the Schedule C as gross receipts for the year. As anticipated, the two matched.

Back for a second meeting with the examiner with proof in hand, I reiterated the steps we had taken. Pointing first to the canceled checks drawn on the business account, and then to the monthly statements for the personal account, I insisted that the evidence plainly showed the sole source of funds in the personal account to be redeposits from the business account.

Next, I waived the business account's monthly statments in the air, together with a calculator tape which depicted the total of the deposits. Gesturing then to the Schedule C, I made the point that there was no "unreported income" as originally alleged by the agent. In the face of this presentation, the agent was forced to alter his posture. He assented to the proposition that all income had been correctly reported.

Bank records do not lie. For that reason, they can often times be extremely helpful in verifying one's income. This is particularly true where bank records are the only source of certifiable intelligence on the question.

3. *Information Returns.* An information return contains data compiled by a third party and transmitted to the IRS. The information, usually in the nature of a Form W-2 or 1099, communicates to the IRS how much a person was paid by an employer, a bank, etc. In the absence of any contradictory evidence, an information return can be the last word on the question of income.

An Appeals Officer once told me that in his experience, information returns were incorrect about 30% of the time. Usually, they *overstate* the income received. As a result, the IRS will "adjust" one's tax return to match the income shown on the information return. For that reason, it is always a good idea to compare one's paycheck stubs with the W-2 or 1099 to ensure the latter's correctness.

Assuming, however, that the information return is indeed correct, it is a helpful tool when the IRS attempts to increase income for some reason. In one audit situation, George had claimed several thousand dollars in "unreimbursed employee business" expenses on his tax return. As an employee of an automobile dealership, he participated in a program with other salesmen whereby appreciation gifts were purchased for those customers investing in new cars. The gift purchases were handled by the employer but George and his fellow salesmen had a fixed amount of money deducted from their respective checks each month to pay the costs. As George never saw the money thus taken from his check, he deducted the charges as unreimbursed employee business expenses.

The audit called into question the verity of the employee expenses. The auditor claimed that the funds were somehow reimbursed by the employer and consequently, they could not be deducted by George. George insisted that they were not *reimbursed*, and adamantly clung to his position that they were therefore deductible.

But the agent did not waiver. She demanded some kind of proof that George did not receive from the employer a refund of the money expended in the appreciation program. George inquired as to the kind of proof she had in mind. Thoughtfully, she responded by saying that a statement from the employer would be sufficient.

George inquired of the agent whether it was not true that a Form W-2 was "statement from the employer." She had to agree that it was, as it had been prepared by the employer from the employer's records pursuant to federal law. George pointed to an entry on the form W-2 under the heading "Wages, tips and other compensation."

"This was, according to my employer's statement, my gross pay," he explained. "There is no question about that, is there?" She agreed there was not. He went on, "These other entries are for subtractions from the gross pay, aren't they?" Again, she agreed.

In a space on the form purposefully left blank by the government so that employers could apply it to their own designs was a figure which matched exactly that which George had claimed as employee expenses. The company computer created a heading for the blank, which it called "Spiffs," a word used by salesmen to refer to funds paid to others in appreciation for business referrals.

Now arguing the case, George explained, "The amount shown as a deduction in the 'Spiffs' column was, according to the W-2 *deducted* from my pay. According to the form itself, which was prepared by my employer, I never got reimbursed for the money. If I had, the space for 'Spiffs' would be blank. It is obvious, according to my employer, that I paid the money and did not get reimbursed."

Looking carefully at the form, she wrinkled her brow and pulled at her ear nervously. It was plain from her actions and lack of words that she was without the capacity to gainsay the arguments presented. She had earlier demanded a statement from the employer to verify George's position. On the spot, she was presented with a "statement from the employer," in the form of the W-2. It contained all of the information she demanded.

We knew the issue had been put to rest when, without comment, she moved on to the next point of the contention. George was able to use the Form W-2 to his distinct advantage because he was quite familiar with the information it contained. Information returns can be quite helpful in this respect.

Forms W-2 and 1099 can also function effectively as a person's method of tracking his own income. Many people who receive wages or are commissioned salespersons do not necessarily keep a journal reflecting their periodic receipts. For this reason, until the Form W-2 or 1099 is received, they have no idea what they have earned in a particular year. This makes them prime targets for the IRS to arbitrarily *increase* their income. This precise thing occured in the case of a commissioned jewelry salesman.

Paul was audited for tax year 1985. His return claimed income from sales in the amount of $18,300. The auditor could not believe that Paul was able to survive on that "little amount of money." Agreeing with the auditor, Paul said, "I couldn't! That is why I had to find a new job!" But in her mind, the auditor was convinced that Paul's income as stated in the form was "just too low."

"That is all I made," he assured her.

"Well, then I would like to see your bank account statements for the year" she replied.

"I didn't have a bank account," Paul popped. "There is nothing to show you."

When the audit report issued, the agent had included in her recomputation an amount of income which was determined by "using the cash transactions method." She had arbitrarily assumed that Paul needed an additional $3,900 in which to live (ignoring his paltry living habits and expenses) and thus, *added that much to his declared income.*

Later, we presented a statement in the form of a 1099 from the person for whom Paul sold jewelry. The form showed the same amount of money Paul claimed as income having been paid as income. In addition to the form, Paul submitted a statement from the employer to the effect that such was all he earned during the year. Furthermore, Paul provided his own testimony to the effect that he did not earn any more money than was claimed on the return. As there was no bank account for the year, these uncontradicted statements were, as they had to be, accepted as the true reflection of Paul's income.

In the absence of specific evidence to the contrary, information returns and similar statements can be the best way to verify income.

4. *Testimony.* The area of testimony is the most misunderstood aspect of the federal income tax audit process. Is testimony acceptable, and if so, under what conditions? Who may provide the testimony? These questions are often unanswered by tax professionals and ignored by the IRS. In fact, with precious few exceptions, I have, in nearly 14 years of experience with the IRS, never met an agent who fully understood the role which testimony plays in the tax audit.

Contrary to popular belief, not only is testimony a useful adjunct to the other methods of verifying income, in some cases, it is the *only* method. The IRS has, over the years, become quite adept at putting citizens on the defensive with regard to their tax returns. Indeed, the IRS is practiced at painting people into corners from which there is no apparent escape.

Let me offer an example: In the previous section, I related a case where the IRS arbitrarily increased by $3,900 Paul's earnings for 1985 on the theory that "he could not live very well on what he earned." Nobody suggested that he could. In fact, *he* pointed out the details of his limited lifestyle.

But without bank records, Paul was not in a position to prove with "extrinsic" evidence that he did not earn the additional $3,900. Furthermore the auditor chose to ignore the statement from the employer on the topic. So what was Paul left with in the way of proof? His only remaining option was to provide testimony which would shed light on the subject. Still, is the IRS bound to accept "his word" on such an important issue? I submit that it is, and over the years, several court decisions have agreed.

Let us first understand the posture into which the taxpayer is thrust. Under these circumstances, one must "prove a negative." Since the IRS' changes to a tax return are "presumed to be correct," the burden rests with the citizen to prove that such determination is *incorrect.* You must therefore prove that you did not earn the income the IRS attributes to you. You must, in essence, prove that you cannot fly, something we all know is difficult, if not impossible to do.

The IRS does not make this task any simpler. It usually maintains that whatever testimony you may offer to support your "negative" position is "inadequate" or (and this is their favorite phrase) "self-serving." Without corroborating documentation, suggests the con, testimony is unacceptable. However, this concept has been expressly rejected by the courts.[12] As a matter of fact (believe it or not) *the opposite is true!* What I mean is this, when the IRS makes an affirmative claim with regard to income,[13] that claim must be supported by some "foundation of substantive evidence" before the burden will shift to the citizen to disprove receipt of that phantom income.[14] Stated another way, without the IRS itself presenting some kind of tangible proof that you had additional income, your testimony that you did not have such additional income will be completely sufficient to defeat their claim.

One court put it this way, "So long as the taxpayer found himself unable to prove a negative," the IRS could not rely upon the "presumption of correctness" in connection with its claim. The *IRS*, not the citizen, would be forced to present evidence to prove the receipt of unreported income. Without such evidence, the court would "readily reject" the IRS' claim.[15]

Thus we see that the IRS, not the citizen, has the burden to present "extrinsic" evidence on the question of income. Without it, one may fully and legally rely upon testimony to combat such a claim.

Still, much difficulty remains in the ability of the individual to communicate the notion that he did not receive what the IRS claims he received. The IRS will almost always demand "records to prove" whatever may be your stated position. But what happens when no records are kept? As you will recall, Paul did not keep a bank account to which all of his income was deposited. Was he therefore stuck with the determination, albeit arbitrary, that he in fact *had* additional unreported income? I think not.

In one Tax Court case, the absence of records was explained most suitably by the Petitioners. In that case, the IRS maintained that two ministers had substantial unreported income for several years. To justify its estimate, the IRS pointed to the BLS tables for the city in which the two lived. Both men lived exclusively upon gifts from their family and members of their congregation. Under the IRS Code, gifts are expressly delineated as non-taxable. As such, neither man filed a tax return or kept records of how much was received by them in a given year.

---

[12] Carson v. United States, 560 F.2d 692 (5th Cir. 1977); Demkowicz v. Commissioner, 551 F.2d 929 (3rd Cir. 1977); Herbert v. Commissioner, 377 F.2d 65 (9th Cir. 1966); Adams v. Commissioner, 71 T.C. 477 (1978). This list could go on and on.

[13] This rule *does not* apply where deductions are concerned.

[14] See Weimerskirch v. Commissioner, 596 F.2d 358 (9th Cir. 1979).

[15] See Carson v. Commissioner, cited above.

The government argued that the two ministers failed to prove that they did not have sufficient income to require a tax return. In its brief to the court, the IRS attorney stated that the Petitioners:

> "...did not place in evidence any books and records that reflected that they did not receive taxable income during the years at issue."

This obviously ridiculous argument was countered with the following diatribe:

> "First of all, why would one keep records to prove there was no need to keep records? Section 6001 of the Code provides in part:
>> 'Every person *liable* for any tax imposed by this title, or for the collection thereof, *shall keep such records*, render such statements, make such returns, and comply with such rules and regulations as the Secretary may from time to time prescribe.***'
>
> "If one is not 'liable for any tax imposed' by the Code, one is not required, by virtue of that very Code, to keep records. We have seen that §102 and 107 specifically exclude from "income" the only two types of payments received by the Petitioners during the years in question. Why should they keep records of these payments when the law imposed no tax upon such payments, and thus, no duty exists to record them?
>
> "The idea that one would record a negative is superfluous. When was the last time this Court saw a contract written by two parties solely for the purposes of proving there was no contract between them? What would such a document say?
>
> "If there is no contract, then there would be no written instrument between the parties. Similarly, if there is no income, there naturally and logically would be no records. A record, by its nature, evidences a happening, an event, an historical occurrence. One cannot record that which does not occur. We do not record the fact that *no* children were born to a family. We record those that *are*. We do not record automobiles that *are not* purchased, we record those that *are*. And we do not record the home that *is not* purchased, we record the one that *is* purchased. So too, we do not record income which is *not* received, we record only the income which *is* received. The Petitioners had nothing to record. Hence, no recording was carried out." (Emphasis in original.)

As argued, it is utter nonsense to suggest that one should create and maintain records to prove a negative. Yet the IRS will make a person believe that without such proof, he is stuck with whatever contrary conclusion the agent may wish to concoct. As we have already seen, such is *not* the law.

What then must one's testimony consist of in order that the IRS' arbitrary decisions with regard to income may be overcome? Court cases[16] which have addressed the issue provide substantial guidance to us in this regard. From them, we learn the following:

1. Testimony must be very particular as to the issue. In this regard, "unequivocal denials" of having received the additional income are quite compelling. Any testimony which tends to be unclear or somehow without conviction as to the subject matter would not dissuade the court from the IRS' point of view.

2. Testimony must be believable and reasonable, not "improbable, unreasonable or questionable."[17] To this end, whether one's testimony is credible and believable depends to a large extent upon his personality, his attitude and demeanor in the eyes of the court. A person who "appears" to be lying may communicate to the court that his testimony is unbelievable. On the other hand, one who testifies with a knowledge of the facts and is not vague or evasive with his testimony, and who is capable of explaining to the satisfaction of the court the details of any transactions in question, will generally be held by the court to be credible and believable.

3. Testimony should be "uncontroverted." If not uncontroverted, one should be able to cast such doubt upon the contrary evidence that the court finds the *contradiction*, and not your *testimony*, to be lacking in credibility. In this respect, if one insists that he did not have the additional income alleged by the IRS, he would do well to be sure that the IRS does not present bank records or substantial purchases with cash to controvert the testimony. Similarly, "surprise witnesses" who appear at the last minute to testify that one was skimming large amounts of cash from a business tend to discredit oral testimony. That is not to say that such contrary evidence is the last nail in one's testimonial coffin. If a reasonable and plausible explanation, or an outright impeachment of the witness disarms the impact of the damaging "evidence," the court could very well elect to disregard the

---

[16] Two cases in particular are **Demkowicz** and **Herbert**, cited above.
[17] **Lovell & Hart, Inc. v. Commissioner**, 456 F.2d 145 (6th Cir. 1972).

contrary evidence. This result is more likely to occur if the testimony offered is otherwise believable and convincing.

Perhaps the most important lesson learned from the case law on the subject is this: "...we believe that the taxpayer was not required to 'corroborate' his testimony in order to meet his burden..."[18] Stated another way, one need not keep records to prove a negative. He need not have "documents" or other writings in order to substantiate that he did not receive unreported income.

If the courts have ever "come clean" on anything, it is the notion that it is impossible to "document" a negative. Even more difficult is the task of anticipating the negatives one may be called upon to prove at some time in the future, and then to undertake a recordkeeping sojourn to satisfy those unknowns. The very idea is not only preposterous, thinking about how one would accomplish such a task gives me a headache.

How to Prove Deductions—

I have taken strides to illustrate that where the IRS attempts to challenge the income shown on a tax return, in a very real way, the burden of proof rests with the IRS, at least to the extent that it must demonstrate that any claimed addition to income is based upon *some* foundation of substantive evidence. In the absence of specific proof that one had received yet failed to report income in a given year, the citizen cannot be required to "prove a negative."

Not so in the case of deductions. The courts are fond of pointing out that "deductions are a matter of legislative grace,"[19] and that one wishing to avail himself of the benefits of a deduction bears the burden to "point to some specific statute to justify his deduction and establish that he comes within its terms."[20] One is not "inherently entitled" to claim deductions. Without sufficient proof, the deduction *will not* be allowed.

To this end, the earlier section of this Chapter entitled *How to Use the Code* will prove quite valuable. Many people are bluffed out of deductions because Revenue Agents tell them that their proof is legally insufficient, or that because of certain language in the law, the deduction cannot be allowed. All of this is taken by the ignorant citizen at face value, as precious few have even *seen* a copy of the Internal Revenue Service Code, much less actually

---

[18] See **Demkowicz**, cited above.
[19] **Roberts v. Commissioner**, 62 T.C. 834 (1974).
[20] Ibid.

read a provision or two. One writer put it this way, "It ain't what a man don't know that makes him a fool, but what he does know that ain't so."[21]

In this section, we will examine the six accepted ways in which deductions may be proven. They are field-tested and proven techniques.

It can be said that certain standards apply in the area of proving deductions. Without exception, one must be prepared to prove the following elements with regard to any payment claimed as a deduction:

1. That the money was paid in the year claimed;
2. That the amount claimed on the return was in fact paid;
3. That the character of the payment is recognized by the the Code as a deductible expense; and
4. That the amount claimed does not exceed any statutory limits.

A. Canceled Checks—

Some people deal exclusively with banks and checkbooks. I have known persons who, rather than carry any cash at all, would write a check for such a miniscule sum as $1.58. As this is a routine practice, all evidence which such a person possesses is in the form of canceled checks.

This is not all bad. Canceled checks provide a most handy tool to prove deductions. On the face of one document an auditor will find the date the bill was paid, the amount paid, to whom paid, and if the check writer is careful, a notation as to the purpose of the bill. All of this information is necessary if one is to establish his entitlement to a deduction.

The difficulty with canceled checks is that people have a tendency to become lazy. For example, one may write a check payable to William Jones, rather than to Dr. William Jones. The check written to William Jones contains no proof on its face that William Jones is a physician and that the payment was for deductible medical expenses. Because of the omission, additional evidence would have to be submitted to prove that William Jones was indeed a practicing physician at the time the check was written to him.

The lower left corner of the check blank contains a space for

---

[21] The Complete Works of Josh Billings, 1919.

recording bits of information relative to the payment. Use it! This space will help greatly in establishing the nature of the payment and the fact that such payment meets the requirements of a deductible expense. This is especially true with small businesses. Many times the proprietor of a small business will write checks which appear from their face to be for personal purposes. Checks to "Bill's Supermarket," or "Stan's Repair" may be for purely business purposes and fully deductible, but without supplemental data on the check, they may be classified as a personal expense and disallowed by the auditor. A notation in the memo portion of the blank will help to put any such questions to rest.

B. Cash Receipts or Invoices—

The cash receipt or invoice functions in much the same way as the canceled check, but is susceptible to much more looseness than is the check. The reason is that store and shop proprietors who make out the receipts generally are even more abbreviated than those writing checks. Usually in a hurry, the operator will scribble the amount and sometimes a description of the item purchased. As often as not, the date is missing and usually, the description of what was purchased is so sketchy as to defy a third party to figure out what it was.

When making a cash purchase, be careful to have the receipt completed in a manner sufficient to plainly communicate what was purchased, the date it was purchased, and the amount paid. It is not improper for you as the purchaser to make your own notes on the back of the receipt. Notes made contemporaneously with the purchase are quite helpful to trigger one's recall during an audit several years later. You may wish to note in your own terms, rather than in the retailer's product number, the item purchased. You may also note how the item was put to use. This information will be most helpful to establish the deductible nature of your purchase.

It is not uncommon for one to combine a canceled check with the cash receipt or invoice. This is very helpful for the simple reason that between the two documents all necessary information will typically be found.

A word of caution about the invoice: an invoice is a *bill* mailed or presented to one for payment on goods or services. Unlike a statement, the invoice is not by itself proof that anything was paid. For example, telephone bills are invoices. The bill contains no independent proof that the amount demanded was in fact paid.

For this reason, one must be careful that such proof *does* accompany an invoice when being presented to the IRS.

C. Year-End Statements—

A year-end statement communicates information compiled by a third party. The most common example of a year-end statement comes from the mortgage company to whom one makes a house payment. The document states how much of the payment was applied to interest, principal and taxes during a given year. The statement is indispensible because even though a person can prove that payments were made to the mortgage company each month, he generally cannot prove how the payment is applied to interest and principal. Of course, only the interest and real estate taxes portion of such a payment is deductible. For these reasons, one will be greatly handicapped in efforts to prove these items without the statement.

In many cases, year-end statements are the only available method to prove one's entitlement to certain deductions. This is often the case where one has invested in a limited partnership or other investment type arrangement which is managed by a third party. An example is the audit of Larry's 1985 income tax return. On Schedule E he showed gross royalty income from a limited partnership of $23,592. On the same schedule his expenses associated with the business were reported to be $15,080. The profit was computed and carried over to the 1040 Form.

The company in question sent to Larry a statement which spread on a month by month basis the income and expenses associated with his share of the investment. Totals were shown in two areas. They were identified as "Gross" and "Expenses." These two totals were placed upon the appropriate lines of the Schedule E.

During the audit, Larry was asked to provide support for the expenses claimed on Schedule E. He mailed a copy of the year-end statement to the auditor. After reviewing the statement, the auditor wrote asking for further proof that these expenses were incurred by Larry. I responded to the letter and explained that, "The year-end statement was prepared by the authorities of the company based upon their own records. As you can see, most of Larry's share of the proceeds were applied to the expenses of earning the income. The specific records are not available to Larry, as he did not keep them. The company was responsible for keeping the records, which they did; and to report to Larry at the end of the year, which they did. His return is based upon these reports. All documentation in his possession proves that he incurred the expenses claimed."

The agent replied by asking for a copy of the company's tax return. "We do not have the return," I wrote. "Furthermore, we do not have access to the return. We have a statement prepared by the company reflecting Larry's expenses. We are entitled to rely upon that as proof of his expenses."

In Larry's case, the IRS would accept the year-end statement as proof of the expenses. The fact that we were careful to point out that the statement was prepared by the company based upon company records led to the conclusion that the proof was valid with respect to those expenses.

To the greatest extent possible, year-end statements are a good habit to develop from the standpoint of a citizen. The reason is that they take *all* of the guess-work out of proving deductions. This is because all of the information necessary to prove a deduction is contained in one document prepared by a third party, not the citizen himself.

For example, a year-end statement from a church or other charitable organization would be prepared by the secretary or treasurer of the organization itself, not the citizen. It would be on the letterhead or similar document of the organization, it would state the year in which the sums were paid, and the total amount paid. With such a statement, it becomes unnecessary to sift through the hundreds of canceled checks compiled during a given year in an effort to segregate those paid to the organization. Furthermore, the statement of a third party tends to be more credible in the eyes of the auditor than one's own records. I do not mean to suggest that one's own records are inadequate. They of course are not. I mean only to suggest ways to simplify the task.

D. Log Books—

A log book is a ledger or diary which is made by the citizen as the event being recorded occurs. It is common to keep a log of two primary expenses, those being automobile mileage and related costs, and travel and entertainment (T&E) expenses. The log is either a separate book unto itself, or can be incorporated into an appointment calendar or other similar device.

The law is rigid on the type of information which must be shown in order to substantiate travel and entertainment expenses. For this reason, logs are quite helpful. For example, Code §274(d)

requires that in order to prove entitlement to such a deduction, one
must show:

1. The amount of the expense;
2. The time and place of the travel or entertainment, etc.;
3. The *business purpose* of the expense; and
4. The *business relationship* to the persons entertained.

It is easy to see that such a detailed bit of information is most
readily kept in a log made contemporaneously with the travel, etc.
Without a log book, one must go back to reconstruct all of the
necessary information needed to fit through the eye of the needle.

CAUTION: IRS Agents Lie! The most common bluff used on
unsuspecting taxpayers rears its ugly head in this very area of logs
and T&E expenses. IRS auditors will tell you that unless your logs
were made *contemporaneously* with having incurred the
expenses, the deduction absolutely will not be allowed.. And this is
absolutely *not true!* Log books are *helpful* to organize and prove
one's T&E expenses, but they are no longer *mandated* by law.

With the Tax Reform Act of 1984, a provison was placed in the
law which mandated that all T&E expenses be substantiated with
a contemporaneous log. This provision was expressly *repealed* in
1985, when President Reagan signed Public Law 99-44. The 1985
legislation did, among other things, the following:

1. Revoked the contemporaneous substantiation
requirement *as though it had never been enacted;*

2. Provides that T&E claims may be supported by
"adequate records" or by other "sufficient evidence" *which does not
have to be written,* to corroborate one's claims of entitlement to the
deduction;

3. Repealed the IRS's regulations which implemented the
contemporaneous record-keeping rules;

4. Eliminates the requirement that tax return preparers
advise their clients that all T&E expenses must be verified by
contemporaneous records; and

5. Repealed the so-called "no fault negligence penalty"
which was imposed when the contemporaneous record-keeping
requirement was not met.

I like logs because they can make the job easier. But in the
absence of logs, one is still in a very strong position to verify his
deductions using any one or more of the other methods. *Do not be
misled!*

E. Reconstructions—

Reconstructions are used where there are no supporting documents upon which a claimed deduction is based. It is perhaps the least known method of proving deductions. The reason is that the IRS has its prey convinced that without a piece of paper supporting the claimed expense, the expense will not be allowed. This is just not true. Reconstructions are done all the time and when done correctly, are every bit as valid as the other methods of proof.

The following history will demonstrate just how reconstructions are useful. Kathy was a traveling sales representative for a firm which imported women's clothing. She traveled all across five midwestern states and did so for three years. Often using her American Express card, she would go from town to town peddling her wares. As an independent contractor, she was responsible to pay all of her own costs of doing business, including her travel and related expenses. These expenses climbed into the tens of thousands of dollars for each year she was on the road due to the high volume of travel she did.

For some reason, her personal records were lost. When called in for an audit of the tax returns which claimed the greatest amount of travel and related business expenses, she did not have one scrap of paper to document a trip around the block, much less across the region several times. Without sympathy for her hard luck story, all of the business expenses, of which travel represented the lion's share, were disallowed.

A notice of deficiency was issued and Kathy took an appeal to the Tax Court. The case was assigned to an attorney for litigation and we began the process of reconstructing three years of her life. As a starting point, we had her address book in which she recorded the names and addresses of the various retailers who purchased her wares and upon whom she called, whether or not they ultimately purchased. We also knew that Kathy used her American Express card quite often while on the road.

A letter was sent to American Express requesting their copies of the monthly bills sent to Kathy during the three years. As you may know, charge card slips are itemized with the name, address and date of the item charged. Most hotel and meal charges, we reasoned, could be shown on the slips.

When the American Express material was returned several months later, the long process of retracing Kathy's steps was undertaken. The first charge slip showed that Kathy had spent a night in Fargo, North Dakota. Looking then to her list of actual and prospective customers, she determined and listed on a separate sheet each of the retailers she had called upon in Fargo and its immediate area. When we were able to pin down the specific amounts spent on food and fuel, they were noted. When we were unable to do so, the amounts were estimated on the basis of reason and common sense.

This process was followed for each of the 36 months at issue in the three year period. When we had completed the painstaking task, we were able to document most, if not all of the expenses which Kathy had incurred during the periods in question. Where there was a gap in time or place due to the incompleteness of the American Express records (the card was not used 100% of the time) we supplemented the estimates with testimony which, in conjunction with the address book, proved the likelihood that Kathy had been where she said she was at the time she said she was there. The reconstructions were allowed—to the penny.

By their nature, reconstructions are estimates and to the best extent possible, attempt to recreate a picture of reality as it was in years past. Because they are not "self-contained" as are canceled checks or cash receipts, they must be supported with oral testimony. For example, in many cases Kathy's charge slips showed a hotel expense evidencing that she had spent the night in a distant town, but did not show any cost of food. Common sense dictates that one must eat on a daily basis, but the IRS does not always fly with common sense alone. For that reason, we were careful to provide *testimony* to the effect that food was purchased on those days when no food charges were shown.

When used in conjunction with oral testimony, reconstructions are as valid a method of proving deductions as exists.[22]

F. Testimony—

Testimony is nothing more than the oral representations and assurances by the citizen to the effect that the amounts claimed were in fact paid. When such proof is offered to a Revenue Agent, the most common response is something such as, "Well, I am sure you are telling the truth, but I cannot take your word for it. I must have some kind of proof."

This statement assumes that your word is not "proof." The courts have taken a completely different view of your word,

---

[22] See **Hernandez v. Commissioner**, T.C. Memo. 1982-327.

however. Courts regularly allow deductions when the only proof offered by the citizen is testimony—his word. How is that so? Simple, provided the testimony is plausible, believable and credible, the court cannot refuse to consider it. Testimony which meets these criteria is just as valid as any piece of paper I can name.

Let me prove it. Tom was a regular church-goer. Every Sunday, he and his family would attend weekly services at the local Baptist church. Every Sunday, Tom would put money in the collection plate. For spiritual reasons, Tom would not put the money in an envelope or otherwise associate his name with the contribution. He would give cash, usually $40, each Sunday.

At the end of the year, Tom deducted $1,980 from his income tax return as a charitable contribution. He was later audited. As you may have guessed, the auditor requested to see substantiation that Tom had given $1,980 to the church during the year at issue. He did not have any substantiation as he gave only cash. But he did explain to the agent what his practices were, why he engaged in the practices and that without a doubt, he did give the money.

The auditor was not impressed. After resolution of all other issues, Tom took an appeal on the question of his deductions. His case ended up before the Tax Court. During the trial, Tom testified to the judge as to his practices and the reasons for them. The judge kindly asked Tom questions about his habits and how he was able to determine how much money he had given. Tom's answers were direct and to the point. His answers were sensible and believable. All in all, Tom was honest and forthright with the judge during the trial.

In addition to his own testimony, Tom presented the testimony of the church pastor who corroborated the fact that Tom was present at church each Sunday. The pastor also backed up Tom's position that he always tithed with cash rather than by check. The pastor's attitude and demeanor reflected the same attributes as did Tom's.

At the conclusion of the trial the court ruled in Tom's favor, upholding his claim of $1,980. Specifically, the court held that the deduction was supported by his testimony and that of the church's pastor.

You may be thinking that a trip to court probably is not worth the few dollars in additional tax liability one would incur if the measly $1,980 were disallowed. That is subjective. Each person will answer differently. My answer is that the IRS' rules and regulations, and even some statutes recognize that testimony is an *acceptable* means of proving deductions. For example, Code §274(d), the travel and entertainment section we discussed above, contains the following language:

> "No deduction or credit will be allowed. . .unless the taxpayer substantiates by adequate records or by sufficient evidence corroborating *the taxpayer's own statement*. . ."

The express language of the law allows one to prove these touchy deductions with oral testimony. Furthermore, an Internal Revenue News Release[23] issued in 1986 stated that, with respect to the business use of a motor vehicle, the IRS would not require contemporaneous logs to prove the deduction. Rather, the citizen could substantiate such use "with any type of evidence, including the taxpayer's own oral statements corroborated with no more than circumstantial evidence."

Circumstantial evidence is evidence which tends to make a particular fact more (or less) probable. It is not direct evidence such as that of an eyewitness, or in this case, a canceled check. Circumstantial evidence can consist of countless different types of proof which, when considered in the context of the case, make your claim of expenses more probable.

To be effective, oral testimony must be specific. Qualified claims and vague recollections will not carry the day. Be sure that all explanations are seasoned with as many hard facts as is humanly possible. Specificity leads to believability. To illustrate, one citizen recently provided testimony to an auditor on the issue of church contributions which was sufficient to justify the amounts claimed on the return in the absence of records. The auditor asked several questions about how much money was put into the collection plate and how often.

As people generally do, Tammy was giving answers that were not sufficiently specific to satisfy the auditor's curiosity. But the auditor was not making this known to Tammy. I could see this, so I cut in and began the questioning. I asked, "How often do you go to church?" She answered, "Every week." That information gave us the *multiplier* to use in computing her total contributions.

Next I asked, "If you had to state an *exact* figure which you gave

---

[23] Ann. IR-86-37 (March 28, 1986).

each week, what would that figure be?" Tammy quickly replied, "$15 per week." That answer *completed* the equation: $15 per week multiplied by 52 weeks per year; total: $780. Tammy had claimed $750 on her return. Thus, the figure was plausible under the circumstances.

Lastly, I asked how it was that she always seemed to have cash on Sunday. She answered that she would receive her check on Friday and take it to the bank. She would deposit half the check and take the remaining amount in cash. She would then go to the grocery store to stock up for the next week. When finished, she would have spending money for the weekend, which included money for the church collection plate. As before, this information was direct, to the point and made sense. Clearly it was not a concocted line which one could smell coming a mile away. On the basis of this showing, her contributions were allowed at the audit level—without a single scrap of paper to support them!

Conclusion—

The most important thing to keep in mind with respect to an audit is the need for preparation. Even if you intend to employ a tax professional to help with the details, you and you alone must run down the proof necessary to carry the day. If the task is approached systematically and with sufficient tenacity, there is no reason to leave the audit with less money than what you had when you went in.

Chapter Three

14 SECRETS TO EFFECTIVE COMMUNICATION

Introduction

Much of the confusion which swirls around the IRS begins with communication. There are literally hundreds of letters which the IRS regularly sends to the public. They routinely make phone calls, and yes, even house calls from time to time. In my years of experience with the IRS and disgruntled citizens, I can say that the lion's share of bad experiences began with *miscommunication.*

In the typical scenario, we see the IRS sending a letter which the recipient does not understand, and which he does not seek guidance in resolving. Stumbling along with no information, or misinformation regarding the communication is generally the catalyst which starts what often turns out to be the most bleak period in one's life. Once the trouble has started, one will frantically attempt to patch together the hull of what is now a sinking ship by phoning the nearest IRS office. This does nothing but enhance the frustration and the feeling that the "left hand does not know what the right hand is doing." within the IRS.

The reason is that generally, there is no central IRS office that has control of, or monitors those cases pending within a district. The handling of IRS cases is quite decentralized, and will be controlled by the *division* of the IRS, either locally or at a Service Center level, which is currently processing the case. For example, the Examination Division will have no knowledge of the progress, or even presence of a case being handled by the Collection Division. While there are exceptions to this general rule, the key to effective communication begins with accepting this premise as *given,* and proceeding from there.

This Chapter contains a panoply of ideas which will greatly assist in insuring that your case never gets out of control.

1. *Maintain a **current** mailing address—*
Does this seem to simple? It probably is, but on the average, Americans will move every 18 months. Postal regulations currently provide that mail be forwarded for one year after a change of address is given to the Post Office.

There was a time when the Post Office made a concerted effort to forward and re-forward mail for a postal customer who has moved more than once in a short period of time. *They no longer do this!* Once the forwarding order is expired, mail will be *returned* to the sender. It may *or may not* bear a tag which indicates the correct address of the addressee. Moreover, the IRS may *or may not* feel obliged to remail their letter once the first has been returned due to insufficient address or because a forwarding order has expired.

This seemingly insignificant problem becomes overwhelming when the IRS letter is a notice of deficiency. The notice of deficiency is the IRS' final administrative determination that an additional tax is due for the period stated. The time limitation for response is 90 days. The IRS will send the notice of deficiency to the last *known* address of the citizen, and that is where its legal obligation *ends.* If the notice is returned as undeliverable, the amount of tax, interest and penalty claimed in the notice will be assessed at the end of the 90-day period. At that point, the amount due will become immediately payable. Now watch how fast they find you!

This fact is best illustrated by a case involving a man who moved three times in five months during 1985. Mike originally lived in New Brighton, Minnesota. In April of 1985, the IRS mailed a notice of deficiency to him there, which to the IRS, was his last *known* address. However, Mike had moved to Los Angeles before the notice was sent. The IRS was informed of the move by the Post Office so it remailed the letter to Mike at his Los Angeles address. By the time the letter had reached Mike's address in L.A., he had moved again, this time to Glendale, a suburb north of L.A. Then for good measure, he moved once more to Clearwater, Florida.

The IRS untypically attempted to remail the notice each time it had learned of a new address, but apparently had given up by the time it realized Mike had headed for Florida. The IRS demanded over $3,400 in its deficiency determination. By November of 1986, Mike had relocated in St. Paul, Minnesota, and had started a new job. The IRS traced Mike through his social security number and Mike began receiving notices and demands for payment of the tax.

Over a year and one half had gone by and Mike had no idea the IRS was attempting to get in touch with him. You can imagine his chagrin when the IRS levied his bank account in an effort to satisfy the debt. By the time the IRS did catch up with him, interest and penalties had escalated the bill to over $8,000.

This pattern of movement is *not* unusual for many Americans. Since the Post Office will forward mail for just one year after a change has been filed, steps must be taken to insure that your correct address is known to the IRS. This is vitally important because any notice of deficiency or notice of levy which is mailed to the last known address—whether or not correct—*is valid.*[1] However, where the IRS knows or has reason to know that such address is incorrect, then the notice is *invalid.*

The term "last known address" as used here has been interpreted by the courts to mean the address shown on the tax return filed *for the year in question.*[2] The implications of this rule are staggering. Suppose you are to be audited for the year 1987. It is now 1989, two years later. All communications regarding the audit, including perhaps the notice of deficiency, will be mailed to the address shown on the '87 return. Statistics show however, this address is invalid.

Equally important is the rule which states that the *citizen* has the burden, or responsibility, of providing the IRS with notice of a new address.[3] In the absence of such a notice, the IRS is legally entitled to rely on the "last known address"—that which is shown on the return for the year under audit.

For these reasons, I believe it is imperative that one keep the IRS apprised of any changes to his permanent mailing address. I do not say this because I have a hidden desire to make the tax collector's job easier. You cannot avoid the IRS and its collection machine just by moving from Minneapolis to Denver. Especially, if once in Denver, you get a job, open a bank account, buy a car or house, and generally continue life "business as usual." In the time it has taken you to read this paragraph, the IRS can trace you through your social security number. You would have given that number to your new employer, your new banker, and to whomever else becomes financially involved in your life. On the other hand, if you plan to escape all reality by moving to Tahiti and becoming a beachcomber for the rest of your natural life, perhaps you can ignore the remainder of this treatise.

The change of address notice should be sent by *certified mail* to the Internal Revenue Service Center to which your tax return is mailed. The notice must include your name, social security number, the *old* address, and of course, *the new address.* The notice should also state to which type of tax the address-change relates.

---

[1] IRC §6213(a) and 6331(a).
[2] **Weinroth v. Commissioner,** 74 TC 430 (1980).
[3] **Alta Sierra Vista, Inc. v. Commissioner,** 62 TC 367 (1974).

An example of this is where one involved with a corporation or partnership maintains a business address apart from his home address. If the *home* address is to change but the business address is to remain constant, the notice would inform the IRS that the change is applicable to *personal* income taxes. If the *business* address were to change, the notice would state that the change applies to corporate taxes, partnership taxes, etc.

Running from the tax collector does not solve tax collection problems. It can only escalate them. I knew one man who would write "Deceased—Return to Sender" on the face of all mail received from the IRS. Another man I knew would write "I don't do business with gangsters" whenever he received the infamous brown envelope. The letter would then be mailed back to the IRS. As cute and clever as both these men believed they were, their problems were not solved by the whimsical quips; they were worsened.

Little problems become big ones when ignored, or when some type of fail-safe system is not installed in the machinery. Where your personal income tax situation is concerned, the fail-safe mechanism is a correct address on file with the IRS. You cannot hope to defend yourself against the IRS if you do not know what they are doing. It is much like boxing with a blindfold. You can swing away all you want, but your chances of hitting anybody are remote at best.

2. *Take delivery of all **certified** letters—*

The rule which commands the IRS to mail its correspondence to the "last known address" *says nothing* with regard to whether the correspondence *is actually received* by the person in question. As long as it can be shown by the government that its notice was mailed to your last known address, the fact that you may not have received it is irrelevant.[4]

I know of many people whose only defense to IRS claims is that they refused to accept the certified mail left for them at the post office. "That'll teach 'em," one man boasted. "They can't harass me if I don't accept their junk mail." While it may well be true that by refusing IRS mail you may not *feel* the "harassment," it is *not* true that the "harassment" ends. It merely takes another form. Whether such "different harassment" is harassment at all depends entirely upon your perspective.

---

[4] United States v. Ahrens, 530 F.2d 781 (8th Cir. 1976).

For example, a mosquito buzzing next to my ear all night is "harassment." However, a rhinoceros chasing me through the jungle is a bit more serious than "harassment." In fact, it is life-threatening.

When you ignore letters—especially certified letters—the mosquito goes away, but the rhino appears, and he is angry! Failure to respond to certified letters—whether or not they were received—leads to a tax assessment as we saw in Mike's case. Assessments lead to liens and levies against wages and bank accounts, and that indeed goes far beyond mere harassment. It moves into the realm of a life-threatening situation.

3. *Respond in a **timely** manner*—

Nearly every essential communication which comes to mind is dated, and requires a response within a certain period of time. You cannot begin to negotiate your position with the IRS on a given issue if you fail to respond in a timely manner to an adverse determination.

Some of the most common errors made in this regard are: (1) failure to petition the United States Tax Court within *90 days* of receiving a notice of deficiency,[5] (2) failure to demand abatement within *60 days* of a tax assessment made under the mathematical recomputation rules,[6] and (3) failure to respond within *30 days* to a notice and demand for payment of assessed taxes.[7] Some communications (the mathematical recomp notice is an example) do not specifically state that a time deadline for responding applies. One must be prepared to determine exactly what the communication means, and whether a time deadline does apply. Only by responding within the time frame established by law can your negotiation position be preserved.

The following is a list of 11 of the more common written communications received from the IRS. With each letter is a brief description of what it means, how long one has to respond, and the consequences of failing to do so within a timely manner.

a. *Audit Notice.* Informs the citizen that his return has been selected for audit and establishes a time and place for the conference. A response date is generally set out in the body of the letter. Failure to respond will lead to either a disallowance of all deductions claimed, or the IRS may issue a summons demanding

---

[5] IRC §6213(a).
[6] IRC §6213(b).
[7] IRC §6331.

that your records be produced. An example of an audit notice is found in Chapter Two, Exhibit 2-3.

   b. *Examination Report/30-Day Letter.* This notice will issue after an audit has been completed. It reports the changes which the IRS intends to make to your income tax return. The changes typically involve the disallowance of deductions or increase in taxable income. The letter points out that if one wishes to take issue with the IRS' determination, a written protest must be filed within 30 days of the date of the notice. Failure to respond in any way will lead to the issuance of a Notice of Deficiency. See Exhibit 3-1 for an example of a 30-day letter.

EXHIBIT 3-1 (page one)

Internal Revenue Service
District Director

Department of the Treasury

Date:

APR 1 4 1988

Tax Year Ended:
 December 31, 1985
Person to Contact:

Contact Telephone Number:

Contact Address:
 3rd Avenue South & Washington
 Minneapolis, MN 55401

Dear Taxpayers:

   Enclosed are two copies of our report explaining why we believe adjustments should be made in the amount of your tax. Please look this report over and let us know whether you agree with our findings.

   If you accept our findings, please sign the consent to assessment and collection portion at the bottom of the report and mail one copy to this office within 15 days from the date of this letter. If additional tax is due, you may want to pay it now and limit the interest charge; otherwise we will bill you. (See the enclosed Publication payment details.)

   If you do not accept our findings, you have 15 days from the date of this letter to do one of the following:

   1. Mail us any additional evidence or information you would like us to consider.

   2. Request a discussion of our findings with the examiner who conducted the examination. At that time you may submit any additional evidence or information you would like us to consider. If you plan to come in for a discussion, please phone or write us in advance so that we can arrange a convenient time and place.

   3. Discuss your position with the group manager or a senior examiner, if an examination has been held and you have been unable to reach an agreement with the examiner.

(over)

316 N. Robert St., St. Paul, Minn. 55101

Letter 915(DO) (Rev. 3-85)

EXHIBIT 3-1 (page two)

If you do not accept our findings and do not want to take any of the above actions, you may write or call the telephone number shown above within 30 days from the date of this letter to request a conference with an Appeals Officer. The Appeals Officer will be someone who has not examined your return and will contact you regarding the time and place for the conference. However, if the examination was conducted entirely by mail we would appreciate your first discussing our findings with one of our examiners. If we do not hear from you within 30 days, we will have to process your case on the basis of the adjustments shown in the examination report.

The enclosed Publication 5 explains your appeal rights.

If you write us about your case, please write to the person whose name and address are shown in the heading of this letter and refer to the symbols in the upper right corner of the enclosed report. An envelope is enclosed for your convenience. Please also provide your telephone number, area code, and the most convenient time for us to call, in case we find it necessary to contact you for further information.

If you prefer, you may call the person at the telephone number shown in the heading of this letter. This person will be able to answer any questions you may have. Thank you for your cooperation.

Sincerely yours,

District Director

Enclosures:
Examination Report (2)
Publication 5
Envelope

---

c. *Notice of Deficiency/90-Day Letter.* This letter is your legal notice that the IRS has made a final determination with regard to your tax liability. Generally, it sustains, in whole or in part, the disallowance of deductions or increase in income as set out in the 30-day letter. To protest the determination, one must file a petition in the United States Tax Court within *90 days* of the date stamped on the notice. Failure to file a petition within that period *will lead* to assessment of the tax and penalties claimed due, and eventual collection. A sample 90-day letter is shown in Exhibit 3-2.

EXHIBIT 3-2   ***INFORMATION COPY ONLY***

Internal Revenue Service   Department of the Treasury
District Director

Date: JUL 2 5 1988

Social Security or
  Employer Identification Number:

Tax Year Ended and Deficiency:

See Details - Page 2
Person to Contact:
  ESP:STP
Contact Telephone Number:
  (612) 290-3100

Certified Mail

Dear Mr. and Mrs.

    We have determined that there is a deficiency (increase) in your income tax as shown
above. This letter is a NOTICE OF DEFICIENCY sent to you as required by law.
The enclosed statement shows how we figured the deficiency.

    If you want to contest this deficiency in court before making any payment, you have
90 days from the above mailing date of this letter (150 days if addressed to you outside
of the United States) to file a petition with the United States Tax Court for a
redetermination of the deficiency. To secure the petition form, write to United States
Tax Court, 400 Second Street, NW., Washington, D.C. 20217. The completed petition form,
together with a copy of this letter must be returned to the same address and received
within 90 days from the above mailing date (150 days if addressed to you outside of the
United States).

    The time in which you must file a petition with the Court (90 or 150 days as the case
may be) is fixed by law and the Court cannot consider your case if your petition is filed
late. If this letter is addressed to both a husband and wife, and both want to petition
the Tax Court, both must sign the petition or each must file a separate, signed petition.

    If you dispute not more than $10,000 for any one tax year, a simplified procedure is
provided by the Tax Court for small tax cases. You can get information about this
procedure, as well as a petition form you can use, by writing to the Clerk of the United
States Tax Court at 400 Second Street, NW., Washington, D.C. 20217. You should do this
promptly if you intend to file a petition with the Tax Court.

    You may represent yourself before the Tax Court, or you may be represented by anyone
admitted to practice before the Court. If you decide not to file a petition with the Tax
Court, we would appreciate it if you would sign and return the enclosed waiver form.
This will permit us to assess the deficiency quickly and will limit the accumulation of
interest. The enclosed envelope is for your convenience. If you decide not to sign and
return the statement and you do not timely petition the Tax Court, the law requires us to
assess and bill you for the deficiency after 90 days from the above mailing date of this
letter (150 days if this letter is addressed to you outside the United States).

    If you have questions about this letter, please write to the person whose name and
address are shown on this letter. If you write, please attach this letter to help
identify your account. Keep the copy for your records. Also, please include your
telephone number and the most convenient time for us to call, so we can contact you if we
need additional information.

    If you prefer, you may call the IRS contact person at the telephone number shown
above. If this number is outside your local calling area, there will be a long distance
charge to you.

    You may call the IRS telephone number listed in your local directory. An IRS
employee there may be able to help you, but the contact person at the address shown on
this letter is most familiar with your case.

    Thank you for your cooperation.

cc: Sincerely yours,
    Universal Tax and Financial
    Systems, Incorporated   Lawrence B. Gibbs

                                     Commissioner
                                     By *Louann Davies*

Enclosures:
Copy of this letter
Statement
Envelope

Letter 531(DO) (Rev. 1-87)

d. *Notice of Tax Due.* This letter is a computer printout generated by the Service Center or Automated Collection. It is a statement of one's account balance with the IRS. It makes a demand for payment, with interest and penalties, of any outstanding balance. It points out that enforced collection action can be taken by the IRS if payment is not immediately forthcoming. There is no specific time period set out in the notice for response, but as a general rule, any such notice should be responded to within 60 days. Failure to do so will lead to enforced collection action. See Exhibit 3-3 for an example of a notice of tax due.

EXHIBIT 3-3   *INFORMATION COPY ONLY*

342226316 0A 30 8712   8820
                           880530   0000   07221-124-03400-8   208244 49

Department of the Treasury   Date of this notice: MAY 30, 1988
Internal Revenue Service   Taxpayer Identifying Number
ATLANTA, GA 39901   Form: 1040   Tax Period: DEC. 31, 1987

                                    For assistance you may
                                    call us at:
                                    354-1760   LOCAL JAX.
                                    1-800-424-1040 OTHER FL

                                    Or you may write to us at
                                    the address shown at the
                                    left. If you write, be
                                    sure to attach the bottom
                                    part of this notice.

OVERPAID TAX APPLIED TO
OTHER FEDERAL TAXES OWED

     OUR RECORDS SHOW YOU OWED OTHER FEDERAL TAXES, SO $6,686.71 OF THE OVERPAID TAX ON
YOUR TAX RETURN FOR THE ABOVE YEAR HAS BEEN APPLIED TO THE UNPAID AMOUNT. THE FIGURES
BELOW SHOW THE AMOUNT OF ANY REFUND DUE YOU.
     YOU MAY HAVE RECENTLY MADE A PAYMENT ON THE TAXES YOU OWED AND IT WAS NOT CREDITED TO
YOUR ACCOUNT WHEN YOUR OVERPAID TAX WAS APPLIED, OR YOU MAY STILL HAVE A REFUND DUE FOR THE
ABOVE TAX YEAR. IF SO A CHECK WILL BE SENT TO YOU FOR THE TOTAL AMOUNT DUE YOU IF IT IS
MORE THAN $1. HOWEVER, IF THE AMOUNT DUE YOU IS LESS THAN $1, IT WILL BE SENT TO YOU ONLY
IF YOU ASK FOR IT.

                         TAX STATEMENT

          YOUR OVERPAID TAX ON RETURN................. $6,818.00
          AMOUNT OF OVERPAID TAX APPLIED.. $6,686.71
          AMOUNT OF INTEREST APPLIED...... $.00
          TOTAL AMOUNT APPLIED (SEE BELOW)............... $6,686.71

          AMOUNT TO BE REFUNDED TO YOU................... $131.29
          (ANY INTEREST DUE YOU WILL BE ADDED)

               HOW YOUR OVERPAID TAXES WERE APPLIED

FORM(S)	TAX PERIOD(S)	AMOUNT(S) APPLIED	BALANCE REMAINING
1040	DEC. 31, 1986	$6,686.71	0.00

To make sure that IRS employees give courteous responses and correct information to taxpayers, a second IRS employee sometimes listens in on telephone calls.
Keep this part for your records   Overlay 5 Form 8489 (Rev 11-8)

Return this part to us with your check or inquiry

Your telephone number	Best time to call
( ) -	

342226316 0A 0000 30 0 8712

INTERNAL REVENUE SERVICE
ATLANTA, GA 39901

e. *Final Notice Before Seizure/30 Day Letter.* This is also a computer printout, usually generated by Automated Collection. It is the follow-up to the previously mentioned Notice of Tax Due. It is mailed when previous notices and demands have not been answered. In its pointed and unmistakably bold language, it informs the citizen that unless the tax is paid within 30 days, enforced collection action will be taken. Failure to respond will lead to liens and levies of wages and bank accounts. See Exhibit 3-4 for an example of a 30-day letter.

EXHIBIT 3-4   *INFORMATION COPY ONLY*

```
                              000404  518  4801         RPT              ACR
        Department of the Treasury
        Internal Revenue Service   P 902 785 024    If you have any questions, refer to this information:
                                                    Date of This Notice: 07-25-88    504    8833
        Past Due                                    Taxpayer Identifying Number:              KB
        Final Notice (Notice of Intention to Levy)  Form     Tax Year Ended   Document Locator
        Read Carefully                                                            Number
                                                    1040A     12-31-84      18254-561-64035-8
        lll.ll..lll.ll..ll.l.l.ll.l.l.ll..ll.l.ll.ll..lllll

                                                    Call:   1-800-424-1040
                                                    or
                                                    Write:  Chief, Taxpayer Assistance Section
                                                            Internal Revenue Service Center
                                                            AUSTIN, TX  73301

                                                    If you write, be sure to attach the bottom part of this notice.
```

THIS IS YOUR FINAL NOTICE. YOUR FULL PAYMENT OF THE FEDERAL TAX SHOWN BELOW HAS *
STILL NOT BEEN RECEIVED. IF FULL PAYMENT IS NOT RECEIVED WITHIN TEN DAYS FROM THE DATE
OF THIS NOTICE, WE WILL BEGIN ENFORCEMENT PROCEEDINGS.

A NOTICE OF FEDERAL TAX LIEN MAY BE FILED, WHICH IS A PUBLIC NOTICE THAT THERE IS A
TAX LIEN AGAINST YOUR PROPERTY. AS PROVIDED BY SECTION 6331 OF THE INTERNAL REVENUE
CODE, YOUR PROPERTY OR RIGHTS TO PROPERTY MAY BE SEIZED. THIS INCLUDES SALARY OR WAGES,
BANK ACCOUNTS, COMMISSIONS, OR OTHER INCOME. REAL ESTATE AND PERSONAL PROPERTY SUCH AS
AUTOMOBILES, MAY ALSO BE SEIZED AND SOLD TO PAY YOUR TAX.

TO PREVENT THIS ACTION, SEND FULL PAYMENT TODAY BY CHECK OR MONEY ORDER PAYABLE TO
INTERNAL REVENUE SERVICE. WRITE YOUR TAXPAYER IDENTIFYING NUMBER ON YOUR PAYMENT.
INCLUDE THE BOTTOM PART OF THIS NOTICE WITH YOUR PAYMENT SO WE CAN QUICKLY IDENTIFY AND
CREDIT YOUR ACCOUNT.

WE HAVE CALCULATED PENALTY AND INTEREST AMOUNTS TO TEN DAYS FROM THE DATE OF THIS
NOTICE. IF PAYMENT IS NOT RECEIVED BY THEN, ADDITIONAL INTEREST AND PENALTIES WILL BE
CHARGED. THE FAILURE TO PAY PENALTY INCREASES FROM ONE HALF PERCENT PER MONTH TO ONE
PERCENT PER MONTH AFTER THIS NOTICE.

IF YOU RECENTLY PAID THE AMOUNT DUE, OR IF YOU CANNOT PAY THIS AMOUNT IN FULL,
CONTACT THE OFFICE SHOWN ABOVE TODAY.

TAX FORM NUMBER	1040A
TAX PERIOD ENDED	12-31-84
BALANCE OF PRIOR ASSESSMENTS	$18,549.39
LATE PAYMENT PENALTY	$45.32
INTEREST	$106.73
TOTAL AMOUNT DUE	$18,701.44

ENCLOSURES: Reply within 10 days *
ENVELOPE   to avoid enforcement action
                            and additional penalties.

If you have any questions, you may call or write -- see the information in the upper right corner of this notice. To make sure IRS
employees give courteous responses and correct information to taxpayers, a second employee sometimes listens in on telephone calls.
See back of this notice for more information including the notice about backup withholding.
        ▼ DETACH HERE ▼   Keep this part for your records   Form 8125 (Rev 8 8F)

The 10-day period was changed to 30 days by the Taxpayers' Bill of Rights Act.

f. *Notice of Levy.* IRS Form 668 is the Notice of Levy. This form is used by the IRS to seize the property of a delinquent taxpayer. See Exhibit 3-5. The Form 668-W is a levy against wages, salary and other employee type income. Section 6334(a)(9) *exempts* from levy certain wages and salary, but the burden is on the citizen to file with the employer a *Claim for Dependent Exemption.* (Rev. Reg. §301.6334-5.) This must be done within three (3) days of the levy. Failure to file the form will prevent the citizen from availing himself of the exemption under §6334(a)(9). Exhibit 3-6 is a claim for dependent exemption.

EXHIBIT 3-5   *INFORMATION COPY ONLY*

Form **668-W** (Rev. September 1986)	Department of the Treasury — Internal Revenue Service 2128 126
	Notice of Levy on Wages, Salary, and Other Income

Date: December 29, 1987   District: St. Paul, Minnesota   Telephone number of 612-334-4239
IRS Office IRS ATTN: COLLECTION
6040 Earle Brown Drive Rm 400
Brooklyn Center, Mn 55430
Name and Address of Taxpayer

TO:

REPLY:

Identifying Number(s)

Kind of Tax	Tax Period Ended	Unpaid Balance of Assessment	Statutory Additions	Total
1040	12/31/82	4,482.72	700.66	5,183.38
1040	12/31/83	4,150.49	649.86	4,800.35
			Total amount due ▶	9,983.73

Interest and late payment penalty have been figured to_____.

As required by the Internal Revenue Code, notice and demand for the above amount were made on the taxpayer, who neglected or refused to pay. The amount is unpaid and still due. Chapter 64 of the Internal Revenue Code provides a lien for the tax and statutory additions. Items levied on to pay this are: (1) all wages and salary for personal services of this taxpayer that you now possess or for which you become obligated, from the date you receive this notice of levy until a release of levy is issued, and (2) other income belonging to this taxpayer that you now possess or for which you are obligated. These wages, salary, and other income are levied on only to the extent that they are not exempt from levy under Code section 6334 as shown in the instructions. Demand is made on you to pay the total amount due.

EXHIBIT 3-6   *INFORMATION COPY ONLY*

Form **668-W** (Rev. January 1983)	Department of the Treasury — Internal Revenue Service **Statement of Exemptions**

Name and Address of Employer

┌   ┐

Statement to be completed by taxpayer named below

A Notice of Levy on Wages, Salary, and Other Income was served on my income. To help figure the amount of my income the law exempts from levy, I certify that the persons named below receive more than half of their support from me.

Name *(Last, first, middle initial)*	**Relationship** *(Spouse, son, daughter, etc.)*

I further certify that no one named above is my minor child to whom *(as required by law)* I make support payments that are already exempt from levy. I understand that the information I have provided above is subject to verification by the Internal Revenue Service. Under penalties of perjury, I declare that this statement of exemptions is true and correct.

Your signature	Date

Name and Address of Taxpayer

┌   ┐

└   ┘

Part 5 — To be returned to Internal Revenue Service by employer   Form 668-W (Rev. 1-83) *g. Mathematical Recomputation.* This notice is what I have repeatedly called in *The Naked Truth*, the "arbitrary notice." It is computer-generated and claims that an error has been found in one's tax return. The form recomputes the tax liability, but without explanation. Further, it adds interest and penalties and demands immediate payment, similar to the Notice of Tax Due. In fact, it very closely resembles the notice of tax due with the exception that it contains none of the explanations used in the former. Upon receipt of the arbitrary notice, one must respond within 60 days by demanding an abatement of the liability. Failure to do so will result in assessment and collection of the amount claimed. See Exhibit 3-7 for an example of the arbitrary notice.

EXHIBIT 3-7　　　　　　　　　　　*INFORMATION COPY ONLY*

880704

1　　0000　18254-561-64035-8　39854 22A

Department of the Treasury
Internal Revenue Service
AUSTIN, TX 73301

Date of this notice:　　JULY 4, 1988
Taxpayer Identifying Number
Form: 1040A　　Tax Period:　DEC. 31, 1984

I.....II.I.III...I...II....I.IIII.I...........I.I.I.I.I.....IIII.I

For assistance you may
call us at:

291-1422　MNPLS.-ST. PAUL
800-424-1040　　OTHER MN

Or you may write to us at
the address shown at the
left. If you write, be
sure to attach the bottom
part of this notice.

STATEMENT OF CHANGE TO YOUR ACCOUNT

   WE CHANGED YOUR TAX RETURN TO CORRECT YOUR ACCOUNT INFORMATION.

                  STATEMENT OF ACCOUNT

ACCOUNT BALANCE BEFORE THIS CHANGE	NONE
INCREASE IN TAX BECAUSE OF THIS CHANGE	$13,522.00
CREDIT ADDED -- TAX WITHHELD	4,457.00CR
FILING LATE PENALTY ADDED - SEE CODE 01 ON ENCLOSED NOTICE	2,266.25
ESTIMATED TAX PENALTY ADDED - SEE CODE 02 ON ENCLOSED NOTICE	500.00
NEGLIGENCE PENALTY ADDED - SEE CODE 06 ON ENCLOSED NOTICE	2,393.84
INTEREST CHARGED - SEE ENCLOSED NOTICE - CODE 09	4,324.30
AMOUNT YOU NOW OWE	$18,549.39

    YOU MAY AVOID ADDITIONAL INTEREST AND PENALTIES IF YOU PAY THE AMOUNT YOU OWE
BY JULY 14, 1988. PLEASE MAKE YOUR CHECK OR MONEY ORDER PAYABLE TO THE INTERNAL REVENUE
SERVICE. WRITE YOUR SOCIAL SECURITY NUMBER ON YOUR PAYMENT AND RETURN IT WITH THE BOTTOM
PART OF THIS NOTICE. AN ENVELOPE IS ENCLOSED FOR YOUR CONVENIENCE. THANK YOU FOR YOUR
COOPERATION.

To make sure that IRS employees give courteous responses and correct information to taxpayers, a second IRS employee sometimes listens in on telephone calls
Keep this part for your records

h. *Summons for Personal Records.* Form 2039 is used by the IRS to obtain personal and third party records. The personal summons will direct the individual to respond much the same way as does an audit notice. You will be required to produce your personal tax records to an agent at a stated place and time. Failure to properly respond could lead to court enforcement of the summons and possible fines. See Exhibit 3-8.

i. *Summons for Third-Party Records.* A summons, Form 2039, to a third-party such as a bank, must be responded to within 20 days if one wishes to prevent the IRS from obtaining these records. To take *action*, a suit must be filed in the district court for the judicial district where the *third-party* is located. Failure to do so will result in the IRS gaining access fo the records without further notice. In form, the summons to a third-party record-keeper is identical to that issued to an individual. See Exhibit 3-8. The difference is that the latter is directed to an official within the organization summonsed, rather than to the citizen.

EXHIBIT 3-8   *INFORMATION COPY ONLY*

Form 2039
(Rev. Aug 1986)

Summons

Department of the Treasury
Internal Revenue Service

In the matter of _____ Brooklyn Park, MN _____ Minneapolis, MN _____

Internal Revenue District of __ St. Paul _____   Periods 1983, 1984 and 1985   Calendar Years:

The Commissioner of Internal Revenue

To __ Norwest Bank Camden, NA __ Installment Loan officer
4141 Lyndale Avenue North
At __ Minneapolis, Minnesota __

You are hereby summoned and required to appear before ____ Special Agent Daniel T. Nye ____
an officer of the Internal Revenue Service, to give testimony and to bring with you and to produce for examination the following books, records, papers, and other data relating to the tax liability or the collection of the tax liability or for the purpose of inquiring into any offense connected with the administration or enforcement of the internal revenue laws concerning the person identified above for the periods shown.

SEE ATTACHMENT A

Business address and telephone number of Internal Revenue Service officer named above:

Room 135, Federal Building, 210 Third Avenue South, Minneapolis, MN 55401

Place and time for appearance:

at __ 4141 Lyndale Avenue North, __

on the _____ day of __ March __, 19 87 at __ 11 __ o'clock __ A __ M.

Issued under authority of the Internal Revenue Code this 13th day of February, 19 87

_____
Signature of Issuing Officer   Special Agent
                                    Title

__ Not Required __
Signature of Approving Officer (if applicable)   Title

Original to be kept by IRS   Form 2039 (Rev. 8-86)

j. *Minimum Bid Worksheet.* This notice, Form 4585, is mailed to the citizen after the IRS has seized property and is preparing to sell it at auction or by sealed bid. The form computes the value of the property and sets the minimum amount the IRS will accept as payment for its purchase. If one objects to the amounts shown on the form, a response is required within *five* days. Failure to respond will allow the IRS to sell the property for the amount shown on the form. See Exhibit 3-9.

EXHIBIT *3-9*   *INFORMATION COPY ONLY*

Form **4585** (Rev. February 1981)	Departme the Treasury — Internal Revenue			☒ Initial ☐ Revised
	Seizure and Sale Worksheet			
1. Taxpayer's name *(from TDA's)*				2. Serial number
3. Liability *(including unassessed amounts)*			$ 35,094.54	
4. Estimated expenses of sale			$ 62,040.00 200.00	**Amount**
5. Property value				$ 62,040.00
6. Property value reduction			25 %	$ 15,510.00
7. Forced sale value *(Line 5 minus Line 6)*				$ 46,530.00
8. Percentage of forced sale value			70 %	$ 32,571.00
9. Reduced forced sale value *(Line 7 minus Line 8)*				$ 13,959.00
10.	**Prior Claims**			
Name and Address of Claimant	Nature of Claim	Date		Balance Due
NONE				$ - 0 -
11. Total of prior claims			▶	- 0 -
12. Minimum bid price *(Line 9 minus Line 11)*				$ 13,959.00

13. Remarks   HIGH FORCED SALE VALUE REFLECTS EXPECTED LIKELIHOOD OF INABILITY TO MARKET PROPERTY OR SOLICIT BIDDERS DUE TO CLOUDED TITLE.

14. Reason for revised minimum bid price *(Continue on attachment if more space is needed)*

15. Revenue Officer's signature		Date 7/15/87
16. Approval signature	Title Group Manager	Date 7/15/87

Part 2 — Taxpayer's Copy   Form **4585** (Rev. 2-81)

k. *Notice of Jeopardy Assessment.* This notice is mailed when there is a finding that the citizen is either somehow removing his assets from the reach of the government, is preparing to leave the country, or is otherwise taking strides to sidestep normal tax collection procedures. The notice immediately assesses the tax shown due and renders it immediately collectable. To protest, one must file a petition for administrative review within 30 days of the notice. If denied, he can then file suit in the district court within thirty days of the denial. Failure to protest will give the IRS full collection rights and leaves as your only option, the right to petition the Tax Court for a redetermination of the liability. In the meantime the tax is collectable. See Exhibit 3-10 for an example of a jeopardy assessment.

EXHIBIT 3-10 (page one)   *INFORMATION COPY ONLY*

Internal Revenue Service   Department of the Treasury

District   Mailing Address: Attn: E:R:30D
Director   P.O. Box 0000
                                           New York, New York 00000
                                           June 1, 1981
▸Mr. and Mrs. John Doe
 1 Main Street
 New York, New York 00000

Dear Mr. and Mrs. Doe:

NOTICE OF JEOPARDY ASSESSMENT AND RIGHT OF APPEAL

Under Section 6861 of the Internal Revenue Code, you are notified that I have found you appear to be designing to depart from the United States or to conceal yourself; or appear to be placing your property beyond the reach of the Government either by removing it from the United States or concealing it or by transferring it to other persons thereby tending to prejudice or render ineffectual collection of income tax for the period ending December 31, 1978. Accordingly, based on information available at this time, I have approved assessment of tax and additional amounts determined to be due as reflected in the attached computations which do not reflect interest due to the date of payment:

Taxable Period	Tax	Penalty
7812	$125,000.00	$41,500.00

Under section 7429 of the Internal Revenue Code, you are entitled to request administrative and judicial reviews of this assessment action.

For an administrative review, you may file a written protest with the District Director within 30 days from the date of this letter, requesting redetermination of whether or not:

EXHIBIT 3-10 (page two)   *INFORMATION COPY ONLY*

1. the making of the assessment is reasonable under the circumstances, and
2. the amount so assessed or demanded as a result of the action is appropriate under the circumstances.

A conference will be held on an expedited basis to consider your protest. Your protest will be forwarded to the Regional Appeals Office where a conference will be held.

If you submit new information or documentation for the first time at an Appeals conference, the Appeals Office may request comment from the District Director on such evidence or documents.

Enforced collection action may proceed during any administrative appeal process unless arrangements are made regarding collection of the amount assessed. To make such arrangements, please contact:

Revenue Office Richard Roe
P. O. Box 0000
New York, New York 00000
Tel: (000) 000-0000

You may request a judicial review of this assessment by bringing a civil suit against the United States in the U.S. District Court in the judicial district in which you reside, or in which your principal office is located. However, in order to have this action reviewed by the District Court, you must request administrative review within 30 days of the date of this letter. Such suit must be filed within 30 days after the earlier of (1) the day the Service notifies you of its decision on your protest, or (2) the 16th day after your protest. The Court will make an early determination of the same points raised in your protest to determine whether the making of the assessment is reasonable under the circumstances, and whether the amount assessed or demanded is appropriate under the circumstances. The Court's determination is final and not reviewable by any other court.

Appeal to the Courts in Case of Income, Estate, Gift and Certain Excise Taxes

If an agreement is not reached with the Internal Revenue Service, a notice of deficiency is required by law to be issued within 60 days from the date of jeopardy assessment made under section 6861 of the Internal Revenue Code. You will then have 90 days (150 days if outside the United States) from the date the notice is mailed to file a petition with the United States Tax Court.

Very truly yours,

/s/

District Director

4. *Respond to the **appropriate** office—*

The Internal Revenue Service is as decentralized a bureaucracy as exists. As a case progresses from stage to stage in the evolution of tax administration, the file changes hands from one compartmentalized office to another. No division of the IRS necessarily knows or cares what any of the others are doing—or not doing—in a given case.

If your case is in the Appeals Division, a response directed to the Examination Division will fall on deaf ears. If the case is before the Tax Court and in the hands of District Counsel, any time expended writing letters to Appeals will be wasted.

Communications from the IRS will be on letterhead stationery which discloses the particular division presently handling the case. Identification of this particular division will enable you to do two important things. First, it will tell you where your case is within the system, and secondly, it will enable you to commence or continue negotiations under procedures appropriate within that division.

When a communication does not bear a specific letterhead identifying the division with which you are to negotiate, the *signature* upon the letter will often give the title of the person writing the letter. The typical titles which may appear in a given case, and the division to which the title corresponds is as follows:

Title	Division
Revenue Agent	Examination
Revenue Officer	Collections
Appeals Officer	Appeals
Special Agent	Criminal Investigation
Attorney	District Counsel
SPS Advisor	Special Procedures
Researcher	Automated Collection
Chief-Taxpayer Assistance	Service Center

To determine the correct division to which your response must be directed simply match the title on your letter to the above list.

As I have stated, most IRS communications bear a letterhead of the Department of Treasury. On the letterhead is a pre-printed portion which contains much information about the specific communication. It will tell you the year in question, the date of the letter, your social security number (as though you had to have somebody tell you what that is) and most importantly, an entry next to a heading: Person to Contact. You will also generally see a "mail stop" or "room number" next to this person's name. See Exhibit 3-1 for an example of the IRS letter.

Once you have determined from whom your communication has been sent, *by all means*, respond to the appropriate person within the appropriate office.

5. *Make all communications in writing—*

All of your communications with the IRS should be in writing. You must be able to refer to a date and time when you said what to whom. There is no better way of keeping a record of what was said.

All letters to the IRS should be mailed via certified mail with a return receipt requested. A photocopy of the letter should be maintained in your personal file. Attached to the photocopy should be the receipt for certified mail, and the signature card returned to you by the Post Office. The signature card bears the signature of the recipient of your letter. It constitutes positive proof that the letter you claim was mailed was indeed *received* by the IRS. That can be very important in many situations, such as when the date of filing a Tax Court petition is called into controversy.

6. *Do not respond to verbal contacts—*

It is not always possible to instigate every communication with the IRS in writing. It is not unusual for the IRS to make phone calls or personal visits to initiate contact. Through the use of the phone and personal appearances, the IRS routinely makes various kinds of requests of individuals and businesses.

Recently, two IRS Revenue Officers[8] appeared at the offices of a local business. They barged into the room and demanded that the secretary point them to the file cabinet where they might find copies of federal income and payroll tax returns. "Vee vaunts to see zem," barked the officer. One agent flashed some kind of badge, but was so quick about it that the secretary was unable to determine the identity of the agent.

The boss was out of the office but just happened to phone at the instant this was transpiring. "Who are they? What do they want?" These questions bounced off the terrified secretary like rubber balls. Either the agents were not making themselves very clear (possible) or the secretary was too shook up to make sense of it (probable). The instructions given to the secretary by her boss were simple: "Send them away and have them put whatever it is they want in writing. I will respond to them promptly."

Even the fear-stricken secretary was able to carry out these simple instructions in the face of what she believed to be great adversity. Due to the apparent saber-rattling and grandstanding by the agents while in the office, they had the secretary so spooked she could barely remember her name. So that a correct response to

---

[8] **Revenue Officers** are charged with the duty of collecting unpaid tax accounts.

the visit could be written, I questioned the secretary after the event took place.

"What were their names?" I asked.

"I don't know," she said. "They didn't say."

Surprised, I said, "Didn't you ask?"

"No. They just said they wanted to see the files."

"What files were they talking about? Did they tell you what they wanted to see?"

"No," she said. "The one lady just kept saying something about tax returns."

"Can you remember what type of returns she was talking about?" I queried.

"No. She just kept telling me that the forms had to be mailed to her right away."

"Did you ask for her address?"

"No."

When I asked why such a basic question was not asked, she squeaked defensively, "I didn't know I was supposed to ask for one. I didn't know what to do."

What this dialogue shows is that it is very easy to become scared and disoriented when IRS personnel appear unexpectedly and begin to make demands. For this reason, it is wise to know in advance what one will do under those circumstances.

Since there was no tangible information upon which to base a reply, the decision was made to not do *anything*. After all, one cannot write a letter when you have no name or address which to write. And what do you say when you have no idea who appeared or even why they appeared at your door? I felt that if the contact were genuine, the IRS itself would follow up with written correspondence since, (1) the agent was asked to, and (2) she did not receive anything tangible from the visit.

Within just a few days, a letter did appear at the office. After we calmly read the request, it was determined that the IRS had somehow misfiled the company's employment tax returns under an erroneous identification number, and thus had no record of them being filed. All that was necessary to settle the dispute was to supply copies of the requested documents.

In retrospect, I can see no legitimate reason why the IRS had to come barging into the office demanding to see documents "now." If they had a concern as to whether the forms in question were filed in a timely fashion, a letter would have been much more efficient. As it turned out, a letter was required in any event.

More importantly, it was good that the boss was not present when the IRS did arrive at the door. He may have been inclined to provide the IRS with all kinds of documents and access to much more, not having any idea why the agents were demanding these things.

The presence of mind to send the agents away with a request that they put their demands in writing helped in many valuable respects. First, and perhaps most significantly, it eliminated the tension of the moment. It allowed everybody involved, particularly the poor secretary, to catch their breath and actually think before reacting out of pure fear. Secondly, it put the onus on the IRS to make a *specific demand* for a specific item, rather than permit it to continue to rely on the shotgun approach taken by the agents in the office. The IRS would not have unchecked access to "the file cabinet." Lastly, once the *written* demand was received by us, we were able to fully analyze the request in light of the history of the company and its filing practices. We were then able to determine the best, most effective and least risky way of settling the dispute. None of this is possible when responding spontaneously to verbal demands made without prior warning.

I once asked a Special Agent[9] why they make it their routine practice to call upon the targets of criminal investigations without any prior warning or notice of *any* kind. For example, it is common practice for the IRS to arrive at the home of a citizen at 7:30 in the morning, just as the man is getting out the shower. After *reading a Miranda warning* to the shocked citizen, they begin asking one question after the other about tax-related events which took place three, maybe four years ago. "Why?" I asked. "Where is the sense of fair play in this type of tactic?"

The agent's response was that an unannounced interview "encourages spontaneity" on the part of the citizen, and that "spontaneous answers tend to be more accurate." That answer may be impressive to the uninformed citizen, but my experience has shown that there is in fact an entirely different, and if you will, more *sinister* reason for "encouraging spontaneity."

Consider this: You have been surprised by a Special Agent quite early in the morning. Prior to this, you had no idea the IRS was even interested in you, much less concerned about criminal conduct. After having been read your *Miranda rights* at 7:00 a.m., you are bombarded with questions concerning transactions and events which occurred many years ago.

---

[9] **Special Agents** conduct criminal investigations for the IRS.

You have not given a moment's thought to any of these events since they occurred. You are confused. You are scared. You do not know why the IRS is asking you these questions. When you do try to get a little information of your own, the agents sandbag you. "We can't tell you that," they say. "We are asking the questions here."

The result is that you make statements and give information which is *not accurate*. No other result could reasonably be anticipated under the circumstances. Later, after you have had a chance to review your records and files and to consult counsel, you find that the statements you made were indeed wrong. The difficulty is that you can never *change* information you have already given to the IRS. All you can do is *supplement* that information with information you *believe* to be correct.

What is important at this juncture is not *whether* the latter material is indeed accurate, but that it *contradicts* that which was first given in response to the questioning.

Contradictions do not bode well with the IRS. Moreover, this tactic is deliberate and carefully calculated, not to obtain correct information, but rather to cause the citizen to make contradictory statements regarding the facts.

For these reasons, I insist that all correspondence with the IRS be in writing. If the initial contact is made via phone or in person, one can politely send the agents away asking that they follow up with a written request. At the same time, it is good practice to make careful notes of conversations you have with the IRS and to maintain those notes in a file. The notes should be of an "I said—he said" character. They should also bear the time and date of the conversation, together with the names of the parties involved.

These types of notes, referred to as Memoranda of Interview, are *always* kept by the IRS. The notes will then form the basis of: (1) a follow up letter summarizing the points of the conversation, and (2) a future reference by which to reconstruct obligations *made* and agreements *reached* during the course of the negotiations. The steps mentioned in this paragraph should always be followed where any conversations have taken place.

7. *Take careful **notes** during all face-to-face discussions—*
During the course of an audit, it should come as no great surprise that much is said by both parties on many issues. Unless you are an extremely unusual person with a superb memory, it will be difficult, if not impossible to recall all the points made during the audit. This handicap is overcome through the exercise

of the skill I mentioned above: take notes!

As hard as this may be to believe, most people enter an audit with all or part of the books and records demanded by the IRS, but without blank paper and pencil with which to take notes! "I didn't know I could—or had to—take notes," one man told me after his audit. I was questioning him about the additional information the IRS agent said was needed to support certain deductions claimed. He just simply could not remember what was said. Certainly a follow up letter solved the problem, but there are no doubt countless citizens who lose the benefit of a deduction because they did not take notes during the audit and were unable to respond in the fashion required under the circumstances.

For example, it is a regular occurrence during an audit for the IRS to request additional information or further proof of certain deductions. One audit involved several issues where follow up documentation was necessary. We needed additional proof of business miles claimed, uniform deductions taken, and the rental property expenses deducted.

I did two things during the audit to assure that the citizen's interests were protected. First, I took *careful* notes of my own during the course of the interview, recording what items on the return were fully verified and those which needed additional documentation. Secondly, at the end of the interview I asked the agent to provide an *Information Document Request*, Form 4564. This form is a written request for additional information needed to verify the items mentioned earlier.

I compared the agent's request for additional information with my own notes. This allowed me to verify the items which were *lacking* in proof, but more importantly, it allowed me to verify the items which were *fully* proved. When the additional proof was mailed to the agent, I sent a cover letter which itemized the documents contained in the package. Also, based upon my own notes *and* the document request, I itemized the issues which were *fully proven* and over which no further controversy existed. This acted to prevent the agent from later saying these additional items had not been proven and thus, were disallowed.

Exhibit 3-11 is IRS Form 4700. This form is used by Revenue Agents during the course of an audit. It helps them to keep in perfect order all of the issues discussed at the audit. Particularly, paragraph D, under the heading *Items to be considered, explored, verified*, contains the subheadings "Year, Per Return (amount claimed), Corrected (amount verified), Adjustment (amount of

EXHIBIT 3-11

Page ____ of ____

Examination Workpapers		Year(s)

Taxpayer's name, address, SSN (Use pre-addressed label or show changes)	Examiner	Date
	Grade	Taxpayer
	Reviewer	Home -
		Work -
	Representative - Power of Attorney	☐ Yes ☐ No
	Name	Phone number
	☐ CPA ☐ Attorney ☐ Enrolled agent ☐ Witness ☐ Other (Sepcify)	

A

Initial Interview History

1. Appeared for interview
   ☐ Taxpayer   ☐ Spouse   ☐ Representative
2. Change of address   Yes   No
3. Appeal rights explained   Yes   No
4. Privacy Act explained   Yes   No
5. Current employer _____
6. Current occupation _____
7. Current filing status _____
8. Continue on Form 4700 Supplement

Address

B

Closed No Change

Issue:
☐ Letter 590   ☐ Letter 1156   ☐ Other

Examiner

C   **Reminders**

Examination Items

1. Proforma Worksheets utilized where applicable
2. W-2 math verification
3. Inspection of prior and subsequent year returns. IRM 4215
4. Probe for unreported deductions and credits
5. Scope of Examination. IRM 4253.2
6. Automatic adjustments resulting from AGI change(s)
7. Minimum tax
8. Income averaging
9. Restricted interest
10. Penalty consideration

Case Processing

Fraud Cases
Forms 2297 and 3363
Information Reports (IRM 4219)
Form 5346
FICA, Self-Employment or Tip Income Adjustments

SAMPLE

D

→ (Items to be considered, explored, verified)	Year	Per Return	Corrected	Adjustment	Workpapers Index

E

	Year	Per Return	Corrected	Adjustment	Workpapers Index

Form **4700** (Rev. 8-84)   Department of the Treasury — Internal Revenue Service difference), Workpapers Index (location of computations)."

When complete, each of these figures allows the Revenue Agent to see at a glance all that was accomplished during a given audit. He can see what items were reviewed and whether and to what extent it may have been adjusted. The blank spaces beneath the heading allows the agent to record any appropriate comments, such as whether additional proof will be supplied on a given item.

One can easily adapt a version of this form to his own use. It would consist of paragraph A where we find the year in question, the date of the audit, the name of the examiner, etc., and paragraph D and E, repeated as many times as possible on an 11-inch sheet of paper. Duplicated in blank, such forms will make it virtually impossible to take incomplete or insufficient notes during an audit.

8. *Be sure you are always dealing with a **person**—*

It is very common for the IRS to send computerized notices and letters which do not bear the signature of a person. Although I have mastered the microwave, I have not yet been able to negotiate successfully with a computer.

The most fateful difficulty in attempting to resolve matters brought on by form letters or computer notices is the inflexibility of the notice. One of the most glaring examples of this lies in demands for payment sent by the Automated Collection Service (ACS). The notice states that you owe an amount of money, with interest and penalties, and will demand that it be sent immediately. See Exhibit 3-3. If you respond by calling the 800 toll free number with your questions, the operator will reply by passing on to you all that the "computer" says you owe. Similarly, any written inquiries will be answered with another computer letter demanding payment of the sum of money mentioned in the initial correspondence. Repeated questions, regardless of the forcefulness with which they are asked, will lead only to frustration.

Unsigned communications must be responded to promptly, and with a demand that an *agent*—that is, a living person—be assigned to handle your case forthwith. I was working with a man in Memphis who had received a letter from the local IRS office. The letter requested that the man appear at the IRS office on a certain date, "between the hours of 8:30 a.m. and 4:30 p.m." His 1985 income tax return was to be audited. There was no name on the bottom of the letter, and information in the letterhead did not indicate that any particular agent had been assigned to the case.

I wrote to the IRS office which had generated the correspondence. My request was simple: "Please assign an agent to this case so that pre-conference discussions might resolve as many of the issues ahead of time as possible." As my letter went unanswered for some time, I phoned the office and asked for the "appointment clerk," as such a person was mentioned in the original IRS letter. The appointment clerk informed me that she had indeed received my letter and request for an agent assignment, but that none had been assigned. "When do you expect to assign one," I asked.

"We will not be assigning an agent until the taxpayer comes in to the office," she responded.

"You may have misunderstood my letter," I replied. "We won't be coming into the office *until* an agent is assigned."

Rather huffy, she explained, "Our policy here is not to assign an agent until the taxpayer arrives."

"I have several good reasons why an agent should be assigned now," I stated. "For example, the audit notice does not indicate which specific items on the return have been called into question. I will have to speak with an agent to determine which items of proof we will need to prepare before our arrival at the meeting. Secondly, it is my policy to at least *talk* with the agent before the meeting to establish the ground rules under which the audit will take place. I will not be coming into the office before the assignment of an agent with whom I can discuss these matters."

Further discussion took place, after which the appointment clerk agreed to consider my request. I wrote a follow up letter based upon my notes of the conversation. In the letter I summarized the facts and restated my reasons for having an agent assigned. I repeated my specific request for the assignment of an agent, and informed the clerk that we *would not* be appearing without an agent being preassigned to the case.

After the passage of several more weeks, I received a phone call from Martha, a Revenue Agent in the Memphis office. She had been assigned to the case, and was calling to inform me. We discussed the audit over the phone and agreed upon the procedure that would be followed in this case. Again, I followed up the conversation with a letter to verify the agreements we reached.

It is even more important to have an agent assigned when you are dealing with ACS. The ACS sites around the country, some 21, are charged with the duty of collecting overdue tax accounts. This is done through the computer—generated use of payment demands, liens and levies on bank accounts and wages. The first notice you will see from ACS will be a demand stating words to the effect of, "The tax shown on this form is past due. This is notice to you that if you do not pay the amount shown on this form within 30 days of the date of this notice, enforced collection action will be taken." See Exhibit 3-3. The form will not necessarily tell you what the enforcement action is, but trust me, it is most uncomfortable!

Upon receipt of a demand for payment, *resist the temptation to ask questions.* Whether you write a letter laced with questions, or phone the 800 number in an hysterical tirade, you *will not* get satisfaction. "I'm sorry, Mr. Jones," will be the refrain. "The computer shows your account is past due for 1986 income taxes. You owe $4,593. You will have to pay that amount."

ACS personnel are humorless people. I had one lady from the Buffalo office phone to ask whether I was still the power of attorney for a couple from Anoka, Minnesota. "Yes, I am," I responded, "How can I help you?"

"Well, Mr. Pilla," she sighed, "we have here an outstanding balance for your clients in the amount of $854,837.54. When may we expect payment?"

When may we expect payment? As if we could send them a check for eight hundred thousand dollars just like that! "Ah, honey? Have you made the deposit yet? We have an unexpected bill this month!"

I quickly responded by saying, "I'm sorry. My client cannot make that payment. He only has $854,800 in his account!" There was dead silence on her end of the phone. Sarcastic humor is not one of their strong points.

The lady I spoke with was not interested in my explanations. Before I could expect any real progress in the matter, the case would have to be transferred to the *local* Collection office. There, I would have the opportunity to talk with a Revenue Officer with whom the necessary steps could be taken to ensure that the case would be handled in the most beneficial manner. Without a transfer, collection is fully automated and insensitive to the problems and particularities of the individual involved.

Transfer from ACS to the local office is *not* a routine matter. Collection of delinquent accounts *will be* handled by ACS in the typical case. Where the account can be handled from the remote locations at which ACS offices are housed, and where it is apparent that collection can be accomplished through the harshness of liens and levies, the account will not be transferred.

Any request for transfer *must* come from the citizen. Without a transfer to the local Collection office, it will be very difficult to effectively communicate on such matters as the correctness of the tax liability or the ability to pay the amount demanded. Unfortunately, because many people do not understand the role of ACS and the necessity to have the case transferred, they end up stonewalled in their communication efforts.

The Internal Revenue Manual[10] specifies that a case will be transferred to a Revenue Officer when the "taxpayer requests a transfer..." The manual goes on to state that requests for transfer must be supported by the facts of the case and meet the requirements of manual part 5521(15). Manual part 5521(15) states that the IRS will *not* honor requests for transfer "based merely on taxpayer preference for personal contact where the facts do not justify the transfer."

The manual is silent as to what exactly constitutes "facts justifying the transfer," but it does suggest that transfer is appropriate where "taxpayers say they are currently working with a field employee on other cases, or where the case seems unusually complex." Further guidance on the matter may come from manual part 5534.5. It is entitled *Cases Requiring Special Handling.* There are six subtitles within this manual part which, if raised by the citizen, require that ACS personnel jump through certain specified hoops. They are:

   a. Taxpayer Claims Liability is Paid;
   b. Taxpayer Claims Tax is Not Owed;
   c. Taxpayer Requests Explanation of Balance Due;
   d. Taxpayer in Bankruptcy;
   e. Levy on State Income Tax Refunds Paid Tax;
   f. Taxpayer out of Business.

In order to transfer a case out of ACS into the local Collection office, communicate with specifity the particular facts of your case, alleging that the complexity necessitates a transfer. Be sure to raise one or more of the above arguments, where appropriate to further justify the need for a transfer. This should be done as soon as you receive *any* correspondence from ACS. It is important to be as specific as possible when stating the facts.

---

[10] Chapter 5500, section 5548.2(2)(a)1.

9. *Establish* **ground rules** before your meeting—

Them most common error made in connection with efforts to communicate and negotiate with the IRS is to walk into a meeting or conference blind. The advantage is decidedly with the IRS if you are ignorant as to the purpose of the meeting in which you are about to participate. For your own good, establish the ground rules under which *you will operate* during the meeting before hand.

Three specific examples of how this works come to mind. The first involved a routine audit which raised complex questions regarding equipment purchases and installation. The IRS contended that the equipment, for a number of reasons, did not qualify for certain business deductions and credits. During the audit, we intended to do two things which to the IRS, are generally looked upon with disfavor. First, we intended to bring witnesses to the audit who would give testimony regarding the nature of the equipment and its uses. Secondly, we intended to tape-record the audit to capture that testimony for later use if necessary.

The IRS does not like to have "unauthorized persons" present during any meeting where one's private tax affairs are discussed. Under the auspices of Code §6103, the "disclosure" statute, the confidential tax information of a given person cannot be disclosed to another. The IRS will often times take unfair advantage of this "right of privacy," actually using it against the citizen. This circumstance is discussed in detail in Chapter One, Part I (F).

My "ground rules" letter had to inform the IRS that we would be presenting witnesses, and that I would expect the Revenue Agent to respect the right of my client to present evidence through witnesses, which would tend to prove the correctness of the claims made on her income tax return. I informed the agent that we would be prepared with IRS Form 2848D, Authorization and Declaration,[11] for each of the witnesses in the event that written authorization became necessary.

Since it was our intention to tape-record the audit, I had to inform the agent. It has been my experience that if one presents an unannounced tape recorder at an audit conference, the IRS will quickly and forcefully "terminate the conference," and disallow all deductions. For some reason, it just does not want its audits recorded. This adverse effect is eliminated when the agent is forewarned of your intention to use the device.

---

[11] See Chapter One, Part I (F).

The third example of a ground rule that should be pre-established grew out of a case involving an income tax return preparer who had come under attack by the Criminal Investigation Division. In an effort to build a case against the preparer, the IRS had pulled for audit, each of the tax returns he had prepared for his clients for two years.

A number of audits with the various clients themselves had taken a course quite wide of that followed by the typical audit. Rather than focusing upon the correctness of the income tax return of the *client*, the auditor asked a myriad of questions relating to the *preparer*. Obviously, the IRS was using the audit process as a means of gathering evidence and information to use against the preparer.

The client with whom I was working did not intend to be used by the IRS as an unwitting source of information against the preparer. The ground rules letter informed the agent ahead of time those issues we would, and *would not* discuss at the audit.

Specific items which may be addressed in a ground rules letter include:

a. The time and place of the meeting;
b. The presence of witnesses;
c. The specific issues in question;
d. What will and will not be discussed;
e. The nature of evidence for and against you;
f. Disclosure of appeal rights;
g. Use of tape or other recording devices;
h. Representation by counsel;
i. The probable result of failure to cooperate;
j. The IRS' legal authority to demand the meeting; and
k. The uses to which information they obtain from you could be put.

This list is not intended to be exhaustive. I have found that it varies from person to person, depending upon the facts and circumstances of each case. The idea is to be aware of your right to establish basic rules which you—and which you expect the agent—will follow in your face-to-face meetings. By doing this, you stand to accomplish two very important goals. First, you eliminate the unknown aspects of the conference. You will learn exactly why the meeting is to take place, and the circumstances under which it will be conducted, and you will learn—indeed helped to establish—the latitude that each party will be permitted at the conference.

Secondly, by playing a major role in setting ground rules early on, you communicate the important message that you are an informed citizen, and that you have a full understanding of your rights. Having sent this message, the IRS will be less likely to attempt to take advantage of you during the course of the meeting.

10. *Do not ask questions, make* **demands**—

The IRS has quite an effective way of dealing with requests. The answer is generally pretty simple: "No!" For that reason, I have long since abandoned the idea of making requests for treatment of one kind or another. Rather, I have found that making specific demands, politely and professionally, are much more effective. For one thing, there is no question about what you want when you affirmatively state your position. When you mealy-mouth around without taking a clearly defined stand, it is more difficult for the IRS to *understand* what you are seeking, and more simple to pursue the course of its own choosing without regard to your needs.

The most flagrant example of where the "request" works to the distinct disadvantage of the citizen is where the IRS mails the so-called "mathematical" recomputation. Under the law,[12] the IRS is allowed to recalculate one's income tax liability if the recalculation is based upon a mathematical error on the return. However, the IRS is obligated to abate its assessment if, within 60 days of receiving the notice, the citizen objects in writing.

The typical response to the mathematical recomp is for a citizen to write ACS, from whom the notice is usually generated, and to *inquire* as to the nature of the bill. "Please tell me what error I committed on the form," they ask. "I do not understand why you have included penalties in your notice," they complain. "Please respond to my questions at your earliest convenience," they beg. Nothing in the way of a specific demand is ever made, and consequently, the IRS does not feel obligated to take any action.

On the other hand, this statement is more effective: "I have reviewed your bill and find that I disagree with the amount you claim is due. Please abate this tax immediately. If you feel I owe the tax, I demand a hearing on this matter." This very specific statement is difficult to misunderstand. And in the event that it is ignored, it would be infinitely easier to convince a court or other higher authority that your request was made plainly.

---

[12] Code §6213(b).

Keep in mind that the law which binds you also binds the IRS. The Internal Revenue Code (passed by Congress) and the tax regulations (written by the IRS and assented to by Congress) are the law which binds us. The IRS manuals, though extensive on every aspect of IRS procedure, *are not* law. The manual procedures set out the basic road map which the IRS will follow in a given case. For IRS purposes, it may well be binding. It is not, however, binding upon citizens. It serves as a guideline for us to follow, but it is not the *final* authority.

The point is that while the IRS would like you to believe that its "procedures" or way of doing things is the law, indeed it is not. Statements such as "you must appear when I tell you to," and "you cannot have witnesses with you," find no support in the statutes or regulations. As long as your request does not expressly depart from settled statutory principles, you are entitled to have that request honored.

That is not to say, however, that the IRS will necessarily roll over to your every whim. They are not likely to do so. However, where you make a legitimate demand, such as that an audit take place on a given date or time and the agent refuses to honor the request, he is powerless to cause any adverse effects to accrue to you as a result. He may threaten, he may huff and puff, and he may become openly hostile or irate, but the plain truth is that he can do nothing about it.

As an example, I refer back to the case of the harassed tax preparer. You will recall that I sent a ground rules letter to the agent informing her that we would not discuss matters which involved my client's conversations, or the character of the association with the tax preparer. When we arrived at the audit, the agent adamantly insisted that we discuss these matters, despite my letter. I repeated our position: We would not discuss them. "We are here to prove the correctness of the items claimed on the return," I said. "That is where this meeting will begin and end." After some heated discussion, the audit proceeded on the issue of the tax return. We did not answer the other questions and regardless of her snarling, we could not be forced to do so.

11. *Focus on **agreements**, not disagreements—*

An IRS Appeals Officer once told me during the course of settlement negotiations that, "If we can agree on the major issues, the small ones have a way of falling through the cracks." What he was telling me is that in any multi-issue negotiation, some of the issues are "litigation points," and others are "bargaining chips."

The litigation points are those issues which neither party wishes to concede. The bargaining chips are those which one is willing to trade in order to prevail on a litigation issue.

I do not like to trade anything. In the real world, however, it is not always possible to maintain such a puristic attitude. The give and take of life requires that one be prepared to "surrender" on some of the world's minor points, while at the same time, "sticking to your guns" on the issues which shape your values, morals and beliefs. Where the IRS is concerned, the litigation points are those which most profoundly affect the *pocketbook*, both theirs and yours. It is with respect to these issues that you will most want to remain tenacious.

At the same time, *it is* possible to negotiate in such a manner as to *minimize* the number of issues which must be placed on the table as bargaining chips. In the *most successful* negotiation, none of your issues will be surrendered as bargaining chips. In the *realistic* negotiation, some (but not all) of your bargaining chips will be passed across the table in exchange for success on the litigation points of your case. Whether and to what extent you are successful depends in large measure on *technique.*

In my judgment and experience, the most beneficial manner in which to *bring about* overall agreement in a tax dispute is to start by discussing the agreements *which already* exist on the minor points of the case. This has a profound psychological benefit, as well as many practical benefits. Psychologically speaking, the IRS audit and administrative procedures environment is quite adversarial in nature.

When the typical person walks into an IRS office, he is usually ranting and raving about the ridiculous bill he has received, or the arbitrary way in which the IRS has disallowed his deductions. Although some may doubt this, IRS agents and employees *are human,* and the human tendency is to *defend* one's actions—right or wrong—in the face of an all-out, frontal assault.

Consequently, when you begin negotiations with such an attack, all defense mechanisims are immediately summoned and your adversary goes to "red alert, battle stations." You are faced with a bitter fight on each and every point. Not only are you arguing the merits of your litigation points but you find that your bargaining chips have also been thrown into the ring. Before you know it, you stand to lose on all issues.

On the other hand, if one begins to negotiate with a less acrimonious attitude, he is less likely to meet with resistance on all fronts. A less adversarial environment is created, and it naturally becomes much easier to reach agreement on critical issues. I am not saying that one become milktoast, or that he allow himself to be swept away in the current of change encouraged by the IRS representative. On the contrary, my formula, if allowed, will create—not *react* to—the circumstances which dictate the overall direction of the negotiations.

To put the technique into effect, whether it be in an audit or during an appeal, I like to begin negotiations by *identifying the issues* in question. While apparently simple and non-productive, one would be surprised how many tax appeals fail simply because the taxpayer did not understand exactly what he was arguing, never mind *proving* his point.

You will learn what the issues are by reference to your ground rules letter, the IRS audit notice, or if an audit has already taken place, the IRS' examination report. The examination report details the items that have been changed by IRS action. This is the agency's statement on the issues in question, and becomes your guide to pinning down the IRS representative on those points.

Using the examination report or audit notice as your guide, proceed issue by issue seeking the agent's assent to the proposition that such point is an issue in the case. By reading from the IRS' document, it will be difficult for the agent to suggest that matters *not stated* in the document are issues in the case. By the time you reach the end of the document, you have not only gotten the agent to agree with you several times (creating the favorable atmosphere discussed earlier), you have accomplished the important task of *fixing* the points which you will not address one at a time.

Moving into the first issue, always begin by discussing those aspects of the issue to which there is or can be no reasonable disagreement; that is, focus upon the *agreements*, not disagreements. Let me give you an example of how it works in practice.

I recently helped a woman remove a federal tax lien from her home. Marilyn was going through a divorce and had her home, which she owned jointly with her husband, up for sale. The IRS had obtained a large tax judgment against her husband after he ignored a notice of deficiency. However, the assessment was *not* recorded against Marilyn. Moreover, the IRS had not sent her a notice of deficiency for any tax year. In short, Marilyn owed the IRS nothing.

The Revenue Officer assigned to the case was quite belligerent and would not allow the sale to close without full payment of the tax owed. The problem was that the tax was in excess of $22,000, and the equity on the home was just $18,000, half of which was Marilyn's. The Revenue Officer had the closing company convinced that the entire lien would have to be paid at the time of closing before it would be released and clear title given to the buyers.

Marilyn's position was that the most the IRS could get was *one half* the equity. Marilyn's interest in the home, it was argued, could not be touched as she had no tax liability, and her money could not legally be taken to satisfy the separate debt of her husband. But all of the pleadings of her attorney had fallen on deaf ears insofar as the Revenue Officer was concerned. Without full payment, the lien would not be released, and without a clear title to pass to the buyers, the company would not close the sale.

When I contacted the Revenue Officer, her opening words were, "What do you want from me?" It did not take a palm reader to know that she was not very interested in working out the problem. After just a couple of minutes of initial headbutting over my request to allow the house to close, I quickly determined that this "hard case" would have to be taken very slowly and deliberately. I began to focus on the most basic of points to which I knew we could agree.

I took a deep breath and began. "Pat, I said, "you will agree with me, won't you, that there is no assessment against Marilyn?" She did.

"And you will agree, won't you, that without an assessment, the IRS cannot file a lien against Marilyn?" She did.

"And you will also agree, won't you, that without a valid assessment, the IRS cannot collect any money from Marilyn?" She did.

"And you will also agree, won't you Pat, that before the IRS can get an assessment, certain administrative procedures have to be followed?" She did.

"Now Pat, you will follow all established IRS administrative procedures with regard to Marilyn and her obligations with the IRS, won't you?" Of course, she agreed with that!

"Then you must also agree that you cannot legally seize any of the money which Marilyn is entitled to from the sale of the house, don't you?" She did.

Having gotten an *agreement* on the basic underlying facts, I had moved the Revenue Officer into a position where it would be impossible for her to *disagree* with me on the ultimate issue in the case. The next question I asked was, "Then there is no legal reason not to lift the lien and allow the home to be sold, is there?" She was forced, based upon the previous agreements, to *accept* this premise. I followed up the conversation with a letter and the house sale went ahead as scheduled. Marilyn got her full share of the money from the title company and the buyers got a clear title to the property.

In most cases, it is not necessary to resort to such basic statements of fact in order to get an agreeent from the IRS. It was necessary in this example because of the hard-headedness of this particular Revenue Officer. What is necessary, however, is that you begin the process with the simpler issues, moving up to the more difficult or controversial issues. Proceeding in this fashion enables you to: (1) obtain as many agreements as possible before reaching the pivotal issues, and (2) having reached the major issues, or litigation points, you would have surrendered *as few bargaining chips as possible* under the circumstances.

Beginning with the larger issues and moving backwards means that the agent always has the ability to negotiate your litigation issue by cashing in some of your bargaining chips. Since I do not like to surrender on any point, I do not like moving in a backwards direction. Also, by moving from lesser points to litigation issues, it becomes *more difficult* for the agent to *retract* a previous agreement in order to negotiate a litigation point. He becomes more or less committed to any previous concession.

This point is illustrated by a case which was recently settled in the Tax Court. The citizens were involved in several farm-related businesses during the early 1980s. One business involved the installation of a mechanical heating system in veal barns which enabled the farmer to capture the body heat from the veal calves and with it, actually heat his barn. My clients had purchased the heating system from the manufacturer and leased it to several veal producers in the central Wisconsin area.

Rowena, the citizen, received a notice of deficiency for several years during which this, and numerous other business ventures were pending. Many of the points raised by the IRS in its notice were nuisance items, but a major issue revolved around the character of the leases. The IRS took the position that Rowena and her partnership had purchased *paper* (written lease contracts) from the manufacturer of the heating system. Rowena insisted that she had purchased *equipment* rather than paper, and had then leased the equipment to the individual *farmers*.

The difference was substantial. If the IRS were to prevail in its view, then Rowena would be denied over $10,000 in investment tax credits claimed on her 1981 income tax return. The tax credit applied to purchase of equipment only, and not leases.

In negotiating the settlement, the IRS Appeals Officer had made it clear that he was willing to trade several of the lesser issues in exchange for the major lease question. I quickly realized that the IRS would be willing to "surrender" on the more minor points if we were willing to exchange them for the more important litigation issue.

Having foreseen this eventuality, I determined to head it off at the pass. Just as I described above, I presented proof to the IRS District Counsel attorney and the Appeals Officer on each of the *minor* points, or bargaining chips. One at a time, canceled checks, receipts, and testimony were offered to the satisfaction of the IRS officials. After all proof on *an individual* item was presented, I was careful to seek *and receive* from the Appeals Officer agreement that such proof was sufficient to eliminate the point as an issue in the case. If there were further questions, each question was resolved to the satisfaction of the officer *before moving to the next point.* I went down the list of issues until I reached the major lease issue.

As I anticipated, we could not reach an agreement on the lease question. The IRS held to its view of the facts and the law, and we stuck to ours. The result was an impasse and each party threatened to go to Tax Court to resolve the question in his or her favor.

As is its wont, the IRS then threatened to take the case "back to ground zero" if we were to go to Tax Court. See Chapter One, Part II(B). "All bets are off if you litigate," said the IRS lawyer. Each of the issues raised in the notice of deficiency will be litigation points, he claimed. Expecting this ploy, I responded to the lawyer by pointing out that he had seen all of the proof we offered, and more importantly, *he agreed* that such proof put those items to rest! "You cannot, in good faith," I asserted, "litigate issues which you already agreed have been proven. The Tax Court will not look favorably upon it, and the whole purpose of the meetings we held was to *narrow* the issues in the case."

After several minutes of bantering, he agreed that if we were to litigate, the only point of the trial would be the matter of the leases.

The technique I just explored worked to carve tens of thousands of dollars worth of bargaining chips out of the case, allowing Rowena to make a decision whether to litigate based solely upon the probability of success on the key issue alone, without risking the loss of the several, lesser issues.

12. *Negotiate the **deduction**, not the tax—*

Perhaps the most significant mistake a person can make when dealing with the IRS is to attempt to negotiate points which are not negotiable. After receiving a bill for $1,700 in taxes at the completion of an audit, a man asked me whether he could, "offer 'em $850 to settle the whole thing?" Like buying a used car, one's first reaction to an IRS bill is to attempt to "talk them down." While the technique may be successful when responding to a classified ad, it often meets with failure when dealing with the IRS.

The Examination and Appeals Division do not concern themselves with the process of paying taxes. The only function of these two divisions is to determine whether the correct tax has been assessed. Collection of those taxes is then a matter left exclusively to the wisdom of the Collection Division. For this reason, both Examination and Appeals will be unimpressed with an offer to settle a case "for half what you say I owe."

But the function of these two divisions as I have just described them gives us a major clue as to how one may approach a negotiation problem with them. As I said, the function of each division is to determine *liability*. This is done by taking into consideration all of the deductions, credits and exemptions to which one is entitled under the law. It is also done by determining one's total income in a given year. If either the amount of income is *increased*, or a deduction, credit or exemption is *decreased*, the ultimate tax liability will *increase*. The process is as simple as that.

Hence, rather than attempting to negotiate the bottom line liability, one can look forward to some measure of success by negotiating the deduction which has been disallowed. Let me give an example: Suppose you claimed a charitable contribution deduction on your tax return of $5,000. During the audit, the agent disallowed the entire deduction. When presented with the bill, you are asked to pay an additional $1,500 in taxes, penalties and interest.

Your first instinct may be to "offer" the agent $750, or half, to settle the case, but we know this will not work. The agent will likely respond to such an offer by saying, "Mr. Smith, I understand that $1,500 is a lot of money, but that is how much you owe. There is nothing I can do about that."

On the other hand, in negotiating the deduction, you might approach the problem this way: "Mr. IRS Agent, I claimed $5,000 on the return. You disallowed the entire amount. But surely my receipts prove that I gave $2,500 to charity. I feel this evidence entitles me to the benefits of at least one half the deduction, or $2,500." Provided you can prove that you gave at least $2,500 to charity using one or more of the techniques we discussed in Chapter Two, the agent would have to oblige. You would be given credit for one half of the total amount claimed. The result is that the ultimate tax is cut in half!

Remember, when a tax bill reflects deductions which have been disallowed, the process of adding those items back into the return will lead to a corresponding cut in the tax liability. For this reason, when dealing with Examination or Appeals, one should always concentrate on negotiationg the deduction, not the tax liability.

Just as one should avoid negotiating the tax liability, you should also avoid making offers of settlement to Examination or Appeals which are based upon the "nuisance" value of the case. Litigation is expensive, both for the government and private citizens. In cases which do not involve the government, attorneys routinely settle cases based upon the concept of the "nuisance" value which a case has. The nuisance value is the cost of litigation which will have to be borne by a party if the case were to go to trial, whether or not that party eventually wins.

Litigants have a tendency to bring nuisance values into tax negotiations believing that the IRS is interested in keeping tax administration costs down. Based upon this theory, it is often suggested to the IRS that, "I believe my settlement offer is fair and that it should be accepted. After all, if I decide to take this case all the way to Tax Court, your costs of litigation will exceed anything you may stand to gain even if you win the case."

Be advised that the IRS *will not* consider offers of settlement which are based upon the nuisance value of a case. Offers of settlement must be based upon the law and facts as they have been developed in the case. They must represent a *good faith* effort on your part to settle the case in a manner which fairly represents the interests of both parties. For this reason, any offer of settlement must be buttressed with solid references to the record created in the case, and to the settled law which governs the issues in the case.

An offer based upon anything else, particularly the nuisance value, will be readily rejected.

13. *Always ask for a **hearing** date—*

Many times, communication with the IRS begins with a phone call or letter. Under these circumstances, a face-to-face meeting is not usually in the IRS' plan of action with respect to your case. Since most people tend to shy away from face-to-face meetings, the IRS, is, in a general way, geared to resolve problems and cases through the mail or over the phone. The protection offered by distance allows the IRS, in my judgment, to be more arbitrary and capricious in a given case than it might otherwise be if faced with the victim of its intended iniquity.

For that reason, it is a good practice to always demand a face-to-face meeting, or hearing on the merits of any claim you may make. An example is where a written protest letter is made with regard to a tax claimed due by the IRS. In fact, it is especially important to make such a claim where the IRS is demanding additional taxes. We learn this from Revenue Regulation §601.105, entitled *Examination of Returns, and claims for refund, credit or abatement; determination of correct tax liability.* In the absence of a specific request for a hearing, the case is not likely to be assigned for hearing.[13]

14. *Enlist the aid of **outside** offices—*

It is not unusual for communications, and hence, negotiations with the IRS to stall or completely break down. This is particularly true where a collection case is stuck in ACS and letter after letter or call after call requesting a transfer has fallen on deaf ears. ACS often times just ignores the facts of a case and proceeds—right or wrong—to collect taxes where it can do so freely and easily.

Under these circumstances, the lines of communication can sometimes be re-established by appealing to one of two "outside" offices. The first such appeal could be taken to the Problems Resolution Office. This is a division of the IRS which is *not* charged with the duty of enforcing the tax laws as such. The function of the PRO is to get to the bottom of and sort out disputes with the IRS where communication with the division in charge has failed to produce results.

In one case, a citizen filed a claim for refund with the IRS regarding excess taxes collected for several years. The claim, once

---

[13] Rev. Reg. §601.105(b)(2).

submitted to the IRS, became what appeared to be *lost.* The Revenue Officer to whom the claims were submitted sent them to the Service Center which was responsible for processing the claims. Under ordinary procedures, the claims would have come back to the district office for review and a determination of their merits. In this case, however, nobody in the IRS district office or at the Service Center seemed to know what had happened to them.

Letters to the Service Center were answered with pattern responses and generalities which shed no light whatsoever upon the problem. The Revenue Officer's only input was, "I sent them to the Service Center. It's their baby now."

After several months of waiting, a letter was written to the Problems Resolution Officer in the district. It asked his assistance in tracking down the claims and expediting disposition on them. Within a matter of days, the PRO had located the refund claims. It seems they had been routed to Special Procedures for a determination on a unique procedural issue that was inherent in the claims. Once we knew where they were, we were able to correspond directly with the persons responsible for making a decision on the matter, and to provide such additional information and proof as was necessary.

The next "outside" office which can be of valuable assistance is that of your Senator or Congressman. In some circumstances, determined prodding by a conscientious Representative may lead to favorable results in your tax case.

Take care however, to see that your Representative is informed of all of the facts of your case, and begins communication at the appropriate level of the IRS, usually with the District Director. One problem which has hampered Congressional inquiries in the past is that the IRS is forbidden by law from releasing one's tax return or *return information* to any unauthorized individual. Generally, one's position as a Senator or Congressman *is not* an exception to this rule *per se.* I have seen the IRS stonewall Congressional inquiries on this basis.

To avoid the problem IRS Form 2848D, *Authorization and Declaration,* should be prepared, signed and deliverd to your Representative. He or she can then submit it to the IRS, together with the request for help or action. The 2848D is written authorization by the citizen directing the IRS to release confidential tax return information to the person named in the form. This effectively prevents the IRS from holding back the information sought by the Congressional inquiry.

I started this Chapter with the story of Mike who had moved so many times not even the IRS could catch up with him. That is, until it was too late. Because of his several moves, the IRS' notice of deficiency did not find Mike before the 90-day period for petitioning the Tax Court had expired. Long after having expired, and after having moved back to Minnesota, the IRS did find Mike and began enforced collection action.

We argued to the local Collection Division, and later to ACS, that since he never had an opportunity to contest the IRS' claim, that Mike was entitled to an audit reconsideration.[14] Letters were written, demands were made and documents were mailed, but after months of contention, no results were obtained. Finally, after the IRS had levied Mike's bank account, we turned to a local Congressional figure for help.

The full story was laid at the feet of the Congressman together with a Form 2848D to prevent possible IRS sandbagging. After several letters to local IRS authorities, Collection Support personnel within the IRS finally agreed to reopen the case. That allowed Mike the opportunity to prove his disallowed deductions, something he did not do earlier because of his many moves.

Not all Congressional inquiries obtain results. The main reason they fail seem to be: (1) Congressmen or Senators may be unwilling to push the IRS hard enough to get the desired results, (2) failure on the part of the citizen to communicate all of the facts to the Representative, or, as was the situation in one case, communication of false details in the hopes that somebody would be misled, and (3) lack of legal justification for the demands made by the Representative.

Of the three reasons cited, I have seen a lack of willingness to aggressively pursue resolution of tax problems as the most prevalent reason Congressional inquiries fail. For this reason, I have adopted a policy to follow when seeking Congressional support when IRS negotiations have stalled.

First, I always submit to the Representative a written description of the legal problem, citing Code sections and where appropriate, case authorities. This eliminates the need for the Representative or more likely, his staff, to do all kinds of research on the problem. The truth is, if such information is not provided, I do not believe you can expect your Representative to seek it out.

---

[14] This procedure is discussed in detail in Chapter Four, Part 1.

Next, a written procedural history of the case should be prepared and submitted. This evidences that all administrative remedies have been pursued and exhausted without satisfaction.

By placing this kind of file before the Representative, you have communicated the idea that *you* have done your homework, and *he* will not be made a fool of after shooting off his mouth in your favor. This is important. Most Congressmen and Senators are concerned *first* about their image and re-election, and *then* about helping people.

Once a Congressional inquiry has begun, the IRS will respond in writing to any letters, and will generally send a copy to the citizen. The typical first response you will receive from the Congressman goes something like this: "Enclosed is a copy of the correspondence we received from the Internal Revenue Service in response to the inquiry of this office. Please review it to determine whether it is satisfactory."

The letter is a form letter. And since only you can determine whether the IRS' response—if a response at all—"is satisfactory," *do not* leave the Representative on his own. A quick response pointing out the inadequacies of the IRS' offer or solution gives the Representative something tangible with which to counter.

In the final analysis, the effectiveness of this kind of appeal is directly related to your ability to provide ammunition from the background. Remember, it is your case that is in question, and you—*not the Representative*—know all the facts and must live with the results.

Conclusion—

On July 3, 1988, the Government Accounting Office released the findings of a study done with regard to the notices the IRS mails to citizens. The GAO said that of all the letters mailed by the IRS, 50% contain information which is either *wrong,* or is simply *incomprehensible!*

I have heard the term "communication" defined by psychologists as "the transmission and reception of understandable messages." If this is an accurate definition of the term, the IRS fails miserably in its efforts to communicate with the public. Sadly, those who eventually pay for this ineptitude are the very persons with whom the IRS *attempts* to communicate.

Recognizing the problem is just the beginning. Employing the secrets which I have disclosed here will help greatly to bring this problem to an end.

Chapter Four

11 FORMS THAT SNAKE-BITE TAXPAYERS

Introduction

Caution: Do Not Sign Another Tax Form
Until You Read This Chapter!

The tax forms dispensers we all see in bank and Post Office lobbies are just the tip of the federal paperwork iceberg. The vast majority of taxpayers responsible for the annual income tax paperwork blizzard have no idea how many different forms are *routiney* used by the IRS and demanded from citizens. I must confess, until I did a little legwork myself, I tended to *understate* the number of IRS forms in existence.

As part of my research on this book, I phoned the IRS office in Washington, D.C., responsible for the development of all tax forms. I spoke with a section chief in the Forms Development Division, whose job it is to oversee the preparation of a particular class of federal tax form. I asked the man if he would be willing to answer a trivia question. "I'll try," he said politely.

"Here goes," I warned. "How many different tax forms are there?" A long silence enamated from his end of the phone. Then he abruptly asked, "Who are you?" I told the man my name and chuckling, repeated my request: "I want to know how many different forms the IRS uses for tax purposes."

Now that he had a clearer understanding of what I wanted, he replied, "How many stars are there in the sky?" After my laughter subsided, I asked whether there was a master catalog of some kind (my catalogs are woefully incomplete) which would provide the information I was seeking. He replied, "Are you smoking some good stuff, or what?"

After some further jocularities, we got down to business. He reported to me that there are between two and three *thousand* tax forms used by the IRS. These include the "major tax forms," such as 1040, Schedule A, etc., and all other forms generated for "public use" by the IRS. After trying to pin him down on a total, he said, "If I ever find out how many are out there, I'd probably commit suicide!"

Of the two to three thousand, only 531 are considered "major tax forms." Have you ever wondered how many forms you as an individual taxpayer could be responsible to complete correctly and submit to the appropriate IRS office at the appropriate time? The answer is this: 112. Corporations are responsible for 153 different forms, and there are 126 which relate to the so-called conduit organizations such as trusts and partnerships. All of this is topped off with 140 *miscellaneous* forms. The Form W-4 falls into this category.

I asked the man whether he could tell me how many forms were changed by the new tax laws. After a deep sigh, he said, "God only knows how many of them there are. A heckuva lot." Now remember, the 1986 Tax Act was supposed to *simplify* the law, making it easier for each citizen to comply!

Next I asked how many *brand new* forms the recent legislation was responsible for creating. Another long sigh, and then he said, "Wait. Let me count some of them." Paging through a catalog of some kind, he was counting under his breath: "Two, four, six, ten, fifteen..." When he finished, he reported that "at least 40" *new forms* were born as a result of Congress' love affair with obtaining information form the public.

With nearly 3,000 tax forms flying around the countryside in the tornado of "information reporting," it is no secret that taxpayers are quite often confused by some of the more obscure forms with which they may come in contact. It is bad enough that people have to keep track of such things as W-2's, W-4's, 1040's and 1099's. But what about forms such as 4822, 870 and 2751? Who knows what these forms are, much less what they say and the implications of signing such a form?

While this Chapter is by no means exhaustive (how could it be?), I have endeavored to compile several of the more routinely used tax forms which all have one thing in common. Each has its own peculiar way of coming back to haunt the one who signs it. Some of the forms you will undoubtedly recognize, such as the 1040. Some you may not, such as the 433. To be sure, you will never look upon any of the listed forms in the same light as you may once have done. To be sure, you never want to sign another such form until you read this Chapter!

The following information is provided for reference purposes. Not every reader will have an immediate need to know the "bad news" about each of the listed forms. You may, however, take comfort in knowing that if you are ever presented with such a form and a demand for a signature, there is a place to turn for the truth about the form, something you are not likely to receive from the IRS.

1. Form 433 — *Statement of Financial Condition and Other Information*

The Form 433, *Financial Statement,* is the first thing a Revenue Officer will demand from a citizen burdened with an unpaid tax bill. This financial statement is probably the most detailed package of information one could ever present to the IRS. It contains much more information than does the Form 1040 and its supporting schedules. The Form 433 is *partially* reproduced in this work as Exhibit 4-1. I say, "partially" because the document is *eight* pages long. Two pages are included in this work.

As can be seen from page one, the form requires disclosure of the typical name and address information, as well as the nature and amounts of tax liability which are at issue. Page two begins to get much more personal. The IRS wants information on all assets owned by the citizen, the asset's cost and fair market value.

On page three (not reproduced), the form asks for the disclosure of all life insurance policies one may own. It also seeks a complete listing of all accounts and notes receivable, together with amounts and persons from whom these are due. Page four asks for merchandise or inventory owned by the citizen with values, all real estate owned with values, all furniture and fixtures with values, and all trucks and automobiles with values.

Page five seeks disclosure of all securities, such as stocks and bonds, together with values. It also asks for disclosure of the names and addresses of any persons who have judgments against the citizen. Page six is where the citizen is required to disclose his monthly income, and the sources from which that income is derived. Unlike the tax return which seeks only totals, the Form 433 seeks a line by line breakdown of the income, including income from wages, dividends, interest, income from a business or profession, partnership income, etc. Page six also asks the citizen to disclose all of his living expenses, including taxes deducted from his pay, medical expenses, interest and mortgage payments, etc.

Page seven does not apply to individuals.

Lastly, page eight asks you to disclose all assets you have *disposed of* since the beginning of the year in question. You must list the property you have sold or transferred, the date this was accomplished, and the consideration received for transferring the property. Page eight also asks whether or not you have an interest in any trust or estate. If so, all information relative to the trust or estate is sought on the form.

EXHIBIT 4-1 (page one)

Form **433**
(Rev. Feb. 1982)

Department of the Treasury — Internal Revenue Service

Statement of Financial Condition and Other Information

(Please file in duplicate with offer in compromise)

Please furnish the information requested in this form with your offer in compromise, if the offer is based in whole or in part on inability to pay the liability. If you need help in preparing this statement, call on any Internal Revenue office. It is important that you answer all questions. If a question does not apply, please enter N/A. This will speed up consideration of your offer.

1a. Name(s) of Taxpayer(s)	b. Social Security Number	c. Employer Identification Number

d. Business Address	e. Bus. Tel. No.	2. Name and Address of Representative, if any

f. Home Address	g. Home Tel. No.	

3.	Kind of tax involved	Taxable period	Amount due	Amount offered
a.				
b.				
c.				
d.				
e.				

4. Due and unpaid Federal taxes, *(except those covered by this offer in compromise)*

	Kind of tax	Taxable period	Amount due
a.			
b.			
c.			

5. Names of banks and other financial institutions you have done business with at any time during past 3 years—

	Name and address		Name and address
a.		b.	
c.		d.	

e. Do you rent a safety deposit box in your name or in any other name?
☐ No   ☐ Yes *(if yes, give name and address of bank)*

6. If income withholding or employment tax is involved, please complete 6a through f

a. Were the employees' income withholding or employment taxes, due from employees on wages they received from employment, deducted or withheld from the wages paid during any period shown above?   ☐ Yes   ☐ No

b. If so, was the tax paid or deposited to the Internal Revenue Service?   ☐ No   ☐ Yes

c. If deducted but not paid or deposited to IRS, how did you dispose of the deducted amounts?

d. Has business in which you incurred such taxes been discontinued?   ☐ No   ☐ Yes

e. If so, on what date was it discontinued?

f. How did you dispose of assets of discontinued business?

---

7. Offer filed by individual

a. Name of Spouse	b. Age of Spouse	c. Age of Taxpayer

d.	Names of dependent children or relatives	Relationship	Age
(1)			
(2)			
(3)			
(4)			
(5)			
(6)			
(7)			

Page 1

Form 433 (Rev. 2-82)

EXHIBIT 4-2 (page 2)

Please furnish your most recent financial information. In the columns below, show the cost and fair market value of each asset you own directly or indirectly. Also show all your interests in estates, trusts, and other property rights, including contingent interests and remainders.

8.   Statement of assets and liabilities as of _____
                                          (date)

a.	Assets	Cost*	Fair market value
(1)	Cash	$	
(2)	Cash surrender value of insurance (See item 9)		
(3)	Accounts receivable (See item 11)		
(4)	Notes receivable (See item 11)		
(5)	Merchandise inventory (See item 12)		
(6)	Real estate (See item 13)		
(7)	Furniture and fixtures (See item 14)		
(8)	Machinery and equipment (See item 14)		
(9)	Trucks and delivery equipment (See item 15)		
(10)	Automobiles (See item 15)		
(11)	Securities (See item 16)		
(12)			
(13)			
(14)			
(15)			
(16)			
(17)			
(18)			
(19)			
(20)			
(21)			
(22)			
(23)			
(24)			
(25)			
(26)			
(27)	**Total assets** ▶	$	$

b.	Liabilities	Amount	
(1)	Loans on insurance (See items 9 and 10)	$	
(2)	Accounts payable		
(3)	Notes payable		
(4)	Mortgages (See item 13)		
(5)	Accrued real estate taxes (See item 13)		
(6)	Judgments (See item 17)		
(7)	Reserves (Itemize)		
(8)			
(9)			
(10)			
(11)			
(12)			
(13)			
(14)			
(15)			
(16)			
(17)			
(18)			
(19)			
(20)			
(21)			
(22)	**Total liabilities** ▶	$	

(*Less depreciation, if any)   Page 2   Form **433** (Rev. 2-82)

Finally, in addition to a column which asks for "Any other assets" as though the previous seven pages were not sufficiently probative, one must sign the form "under penalty of perjury," stating that all information is "true, correct, and complete," and that no other assets are owned "either directly or indirectly," and that you have no other income "of any nature other than as shown in this statement."

How it Bites. The Revenue Officer who asks for the completed Form 433 will state that unless the form is filled out and submitted, the IRS will be unable to accept less than full and immediate payment of the outstanding tax. The "con" suggests that if one were to fill out the form and disclose the information sought, the agency will be able to determine and accept an "adequate monthly payment." Without the information, the Revenue Officer will suggest that the IRS is unable to determine whether and to what extent installment payments are justified.

Under the pretext of determining the citizen's ability to pay, the IRS is in reality using the Form 433 as a ruse to uncover potential *levy and seizure* sources. In fact, IRS Manual Part 5500 relating to Automated Collection Functions, provides repeatedly throughout the manual and particularly in subpart 5534, that IRS employees are to "secure levy sources" by questioning the citizen about his assets under the guise of determining his "ability to pay." At one point in the manual, the statement is made that the IRS employee should:

> "Explore borrowing possibilities with the taxpayer and use the opportunity to *obtain levy sources.* Suggest that the taxpayer try to borrow at his/her credit union (ask for employer data) or at his/her bank (ask for names/addresses." (Emphasis added.) IRS Manual Part 5534.31.

Extreme caution should be used whenever one provides to the IRS the kind of detailed information as that which is sought on Form 433. Many Revenue Officers and other Collection representatives will deliberately lead one to believe that they are asking these kinds of questions to help resolve the problem. See the Manual quotation above. In fact, they are often surreptitiously probing for assets which can be seized at the earliest possible time.

Make no mistake! The IRS *does not* routinely look for ways in which a delinquent citizen may make comfortable payments to the IRS. The IRS does not consider itself a bank or indeed, even a creditor. When one owes money to the IRS, they want it—now! When fishing for information of the kind here discussed, that information is wanted to enable the IRS to *seize* the assets disclosed. There are very few exceptions to this rule.

2. Form 870 — *Waiver of Restriction on Assessment and Collection*

Form 870 is the form which Revenue Agents will routinely ask—or demand—that citizens sign at the conclusion of an audit. In fact, you will note that in Chapter One, Part I(G), Bud was told by his tax auditor that he was *required* to sign this document. The Form 870 appears in full as Exhibit 4-2.

The form is generally prepared by the Revenue Agent who handled your audit, and will accompany his examination report. The examination report is the detailed analysis of how the additional tax and penalties were computed. The Form 870 will state the years in question and the amount of the increase, or in rare instances, decrease in taxes as determined by the audit. A signature on this form is the citizen's *acceptance* of the conclusions reached by the auditor.

Quite often auditors will *demand* that this form be signed at the conclusion of an audit. Even more often, auditors will conveniently overlook or otherwise fail to explain one's appeal rights with respect to the auditor's findings. In this regard, the form is treated in a very matter-of-fact and perfunctory way. A cover letter written by the auditor and which accompanies the examination report will treat the act of signing the form as a routine "next step" in the process. "Please sign and return the form," you will be asked calmly. Rarely will an agent explain the ramifications of signing the form, and even more rare is the honest statement that one *need not* sign the form.

How it Bites. The term "waiver" is legally defined as "the intentional or voluntary relinquishment of a known right."[1] The right which one "voluntarily relinquishes" by signing Form 870 is the right to appeal the findings of the Revenue Agent. By signing the form, the citizen *consents* to the assessment of the additional tax claimed to be due. Thus, the entire bill, with added interest and penalties, is *fully collectable.* One should not sign the form if he disagrees with the agent's conclusions.

---
[1] Black's Law Dictionary, Fourth Edition, page 1751.

Signing the Form 870 will deprive you of an opportunity to take the issue of the additional tax assessment into the United States Tax Court where it can be contested without the necessity of prepayment. Once the form is signed, the IRS will undertake to collect the tax with its full tax collection enforcement arsenal.

EXHIBIT 4-2

Form **870** (Rev. June 1980)	Department of the Treasury — Internal Revenue Service **Waiver of Restrictions on Assessment and Collection of Deficiency in Tax and Acceptance of Overassessment**	Date received by Internal Revenue Service

Names and address of taxpayers (Number, street, city or town, State, ZIP code) John and Mary Doe 1 Main Street New York, New York 00000	Social security or employer identification number 123-45-6789

Increase in Tax and Penalties

Tax year ended	Amount of tax	Penalty
1977	$ 4,500	$
	$	$
	$	$

Decrease in Tax and Penalties

Tax year ended	Amount of tax	Penalty
	$	$
	$	$
	$	$

Examiner's Signature	District	Date

Remarks *(If additional space is needed, use back of form)*

Instructions

General Information

If you consent to the assessment of the deficiencies shown in this waiver, please sign and return the form in order to limit any interest charge and expedite the adjustment to your account. Your consent will not prevent you from filing a claim for refund *(after you have paid the tax)* if you later believe you are so entitled. It will not prevent us from later determining, if necessary, that you owe additional tax; nor extend the time provided by law for either action.

If you later file a claim and the Service disallows it, you may file suit for refund in a district court or in the United States Court of Claims, but you may not file a petition with the United States Tax Court.

We will consider this waiver a valid claim for refund or credit of any overpayment due you resulting from any decrease in tax

and penalties determined by the Internal Revenue Service, shown above, provided you sign and file it within the period established by law for making such a claim.

Who Must Sign

If you filed jointly, both you and your spouse must sign. If this waiver is for a corporation, it should be signed with the corporation name, followed by the signatures and titles of the corporate officers authorized to sign. An attorney or agent may sign this waiver provided such action is specifically authorized by a power of attorney which, if not previously filed, must accompany this form.

If this waiver is signed by a person acting in a fiduciary capacity *(for example, an executor, administrator, or a trustee)* Form 56, Notice Concerning Fiduciary Relationship, should, unless previously filed, accompany this form.

Consent to Assessment and Collection

I consent to the immediate assessment and collection of any deficiencies *(increase in tax and penalties)* and accept any overassessment *(decrease in tax and penalties)* shown above, plus any interest provided by law. I understand that by signing this waiver, I will not be able to contest these years in the United States Tax Court, unless additional deficiencies are determined for these years.

Signatures	/s/ John Doe		Date 1/15/80
	/s/ Mary Doe		Date 1/15/80
	By	Title	Date

Form **870** (Rev 6-80)

If one *agrees* with the findings of a tax auditor, the Form 870 should be signed and the tax paid as soon as possible to avoid the accumulation of additional interest. Once the form is signed, the only remaining mode of appeal is to pay the tax and file a claim for refund. If the claim for refund is denied by the IRS, the citizen has the right to file a suit for refund in the United States District Court.

3. Form 870-AD — *Waiver of Restrictions on Assessment and Collection of Deficiency in Tax and Acceptance of Overassessment*

The Form 870-AD is much the same as Form 870 discussed above. For this reason, a reproduction of the form is not provided. The 870 however, is used by the Examination Division, whereas the 870-AD is preferred by the Appeals Division. Upon completion of the Appeals process, a Form 870-AD will be prepared by the Appeals Officer and presented to the citizen for signature. Just as with Form 870, once the 870-AD is signed, one's right to any review of the decision, before being forced to first pay the tax, will have evaporated.

If one is in agreement with the proposed liability, the Form 870-AD is an effective way to dispose of the matter because of the finality it brings to a case. The 870-AD is a *bilateral* agreement, whereas Form 870 is a *unilateral* agreement. The difference is significant. Signing the Form 870 *does not* prevent the IRS from re-opening a case. However, the 870-AD is more in the nature of a closing agreement. It is signed not only by the citizen, but also on behalf of the Commissioner of Internal Revenue. Thus, it is not only an agreement by the citizen to accept the assessment of the additional tax liability, but is an agreement by the IRS to *not* re-open the case unless there is present either fraud, malfeasance, concealment, misrepresentation of a material fact, or an important mistake in a mathematical calculation. Even then, it can *only* be re-opened with the approval of the Assistant Regional Commissioner for the Appeals Division.

How it Bites. Unlike the Form 870, the 870-AD operates to *prevent* the citizen from prosecuting a suit for refund of the taxes covered by the waiver. Once the waiver is signed, the tax liability for the year in question is a *dead issue.* All that remains is for the tax liability to be paid.

However, if the form is not signed, a notice of deficiency will be mailed allowing the citizen the option of petitioning the Tax Court without the need of pre-paying the tax.

4. Forms 872 and 872A - *Consent to Extend the Time to Assess Tax*

Form 872 is also a waiver of one's rights. In the case of the Form 872, one is waiving the protections of the statute of limitations on assessment of additional taxes. Under ordinary circumstances, the IRS has just three years from the date the return is filed to make changes to the tax liability shown on the return.[2]

Like most waivers, the form is usually not explained to the citizen, nor are the consequences of signing. Rather, the form is presented as a "no option" requirement which the citizen is bound to accept. But the citizen has an option. The right created by the statute of limitations belongs to you, the citizen. It can therefore only be waived by you voluntarily and with knowledge of the implications of the act.

Form 872 is the so-called "fixed date waiver." See Exhibit 4-3. The form will be prepared by the Revenue Agent who examined the return in question and will seek to extend the statute of limitations to a *fixed date*, usually a year or 18 months beyond the time the statute is set to expire. That extension of the limitations period allows the IRS to conduct an examination into the return and to make such adjustments to the return as it deems appropriate.

Form 872-A (not reproduced) is identical in form and substance to the Form 872, with one important exception. It is an *open-ended* waiver. Unlike the Form 872, it does not fix a new date on which the statute of limitations will expire. The open-ended waiver eliminates altogether the application of the statute of limitations with respect to the particular year stated on the form. This gives the IRS *carte blanche* to hold the case open as long as it feels necessary in order to audit the return.

How They Bite. Quite simply, waiving the statute of limitations gives the IRS power which they might not otherwise have. That power is manifested in the form of additional time in which to delve into and develop a case to a point well beyond which it might otherwise be able to do. Before the examination is complete, the Form 872 or 872-A will be presented to the citizen with a demand that it be signed.

---

[2] See Code §6501. The statute contains some exceptions to the normal three-year rule.

If the form is not signed, the IRS will generally issue a notice of deficiency which arbitrarily disallows deductions or otherwise makes an unsupported stand with regard to the return. This result is *not* automatic, but if the IRS is reasonably sure that something is not right with the return, the notice will issue. This puts the

EXHIBIT 4-3 (page one)

Form **872** (Rev. January 1980)	Department of the Treasury — Internal Revenue Service **Consent to Extend the Time to Assess Tax**	In Reply Refer To: SSN or EIN

John Doe and Mary Doe
_____
(Name(s))

taxpayer(s) of 1 Main Street, New York, New York   00000
_____
(Number, Street, City or Town, State, ZIP Code)

and the District Director of Internal Revenue or Regional Director of Appeals consent and agree to the following:

(1) The amount of any Federal income tax due on any return(s) made by
(Kind of tax)
or for the above taxpayer(s) for the period(s) ended December 31, 1977

may be assessed at any time on or before December 31, 1982 . However, if
(Expiration date)
a notice of deficiency in tax for any such period(s) is sent to the taxpayer(s) on or before that date, then the time for assessing the tax will be further extended by the number of days the assessment was previously prohibited, plus 60 days.

(2) This agreement ends on the earlier of the above expiration date or the assessment date of an increase in the above tax that reflects the final determination of tax and the final administrative appeals consideration. An assessment for one period covered by this agreement will not end this agreement for any other period it covers. Some assessments do not reflect a final determination and appeals consideration and therefore will not terminate the agreement before the expiration date. Examples are assessments of: (a) tax under a partial agreement; (b) tax in jeopardy; (c) tax to correct mathematical or clerical errors; (d) tax reported on amended returns; and (e) advance payments. In addition, unassessed payments, such as amounts treated by the Service as cash bonds and advance payments not assessed by the Service, will not terminate this agreement before the expiration date.

This agreement ends on the above expiration date regardless of any assessment for any period includible in a report to the Joint Committee on Taxation submitted under section 6405 of the Internal Revenue Code.

(3) The taxpayer(s) may file a claim for credit or refund and the Service may credit or refund the tax within 6 months after this agreement ends.

(SIGNATURE INSTRUCTIONS AND SPACE FOR SIGNATURE ARE ON THE BACK OF THIS FORM)   Form **872** (Rev. 1-80)

citizen in the position of being able to petition the Tax Court to
correct the *arbitrary determination* made by the IRS.

The probable result of failing to sign the form begs the question,
why should I not sign if all I achieve is a notice of deficiency
requiring a trip to the Tax Court? The answer, while not

EXHIBIT 4-3 (page two)

MAKING THIS CONSENT WILL NOT DEPRIVE THE TAXPAYER(S) OF ANY APPEAL RIGHTS TO WHICH THEY WOULD OTHERWISE BE ENTITLED.

YOUR SIGNATURE HERE ➤ /s/ John Doe   9/30/80
                                                       (Date signed)

SPOUSE'S SIGNATURE ➤ /s/ Mary Doe   9/30/80
                                                       (Date signed)

TAXPAYER'S REPRESENTATIVE
SIGN HERE ➤   _____
                                                       (Date signed)

CORPORATE
NAME ➤ _____

CORPORATE   ┌ _____   _____
OFFICER(S)   │   (Title)   (Date signed)
SIGN HERE   └ _____   _____
                     (Title)   (Date signed)

DISTRICT DIRECTOR OF INTERNAL REVENUE   REGIONAL DIRECTOR OF APPEALS

BY /s/ _____   _____
          (Signature and Title)   (Date signed)

Instructions

If this consent is for income tax, self-employment tax, or FICA tax on tips and is made for any year(s) for which a joint return was filed, both husband and wife must sign the original and copy of this form unless one, acting under a power of attorney, signs as agent for the other. The signatures must match the names as they appear on the front of this form.

If this consent is for gift tax and the donor and the donor's spouse elected to have gifts to third persons considered as made one-half by each, both husband and wife must sign the original and copy of this form unless one, acting under a power of attorney, signs as agent for the other. The signatures must match the names as they appear on the front of this form.

If this consent is for Chapter 41, 42, or 43 taxes involving a partnership or is for a partnership return, only one authorized partner need sign.

If this consent is for Chapter 42 taxes, a separate Form 872 should be completed for each potential disqualified person, entity, or foundation manager that may be involved in a taxable transaction during the related tax year. See Revenue Ruling 75-391, 1975-2 C.B. 446.

If you are an attorney or agent of the taxpayer(s), you may sign this consent provided the action is specifically authorized by a power of attorney. If the power of attorney was not previously filed, please include it with this form.

If you are acting as a fiduciary (such as executor, administrator, trustee, etc.) and you sign this consent, attach Form 56, Notice Concerning Fiduciary Relationship, unless it was previously filed.

If the taxpayer is a corporation, sign this consent with the corporate name followed by the signature and title of the officer(s) authorized to sign.

Form **872** (Rev. 1-80)

applicable in every sense, is generally that an arbitrary notice of deficiency is much easier to defeat in the Tax Court than a case in which the IRS is well prepared.

Surely, permitting the IRS to rummage through your life with the luxury of a limitations waiver in existence gives them "all the time in the world" to build a case which will most certainly be more difficult to overcome in Tax Court later. Bear in mind that unless you accept the findings of the Revenue Agent (which usually are that you owe more taxes) a Tax Court proceeding is inevitable *anyway*. The only legitimate question then is, who will be in the stronger position in that proceeding, you or the IRS?

5. Form 900 — *Tax Collection Waiver*

By now the reader should be painfully familiar with the term "waiver." The hit parade continues with Form 900, which is perhaps the most significant waiver a citizen can sign. It is presented for signature by a Revenue Officer, usually with the request that one prepare and submit Form 433. Form 900 is quite simple in terms of its language, but profound in terms of its impact.

Exhibit 4-4 is an example of Form 900. In signing the form, the citizen waives the operation of the statute of limitations on the *collection* of taxes. Just as in the case of assessing taxes, the IRS is limited as to the length of time in which it may legally *collect* a tax.

EXHIBIT 4-4

Form **900** (Rev. January 1988)	Department of the Treasury — Internal Revenue Service **Tax Collection Waiver**				
Name(s) and address of taxpayer(s)					Statutory period extended to
Tax form number	Tax period ended	Assessment date	Taxpayer identification number	Amount Outstanding	

The taxpayer(s) and the District Director of Internal Revenue agree that the above amount outstanding *(plus interest, penalties, and other additions provided by law)* may be collected from the taxpayers by levy or a proceeding in court begun on or before the date to which the statutory period has been extended. Further, they agree that if an offer in compromise is made by the taxpayer(s) on or before the date to which the statutory period has been extended, then the time for making any collection will be further extended beyond that date by the number of days (1) the offer is pending, or (2) any installment remains unpaid, or (3) that provisions of any related collateral agreement are not satisfied, plus 1 year.

Taxpayer's signature	Date	Taxpayer's signature	Date
By (If signed by someone other than the taxpayer)			Date
District Director's name	By Delegated Representative *(signature and title)*		Date

Under Code §6503, the period of limitations upon collection of a tax liability is *six years* from the date the tax is assessed. Beyond that time, unless a suit in court is commenced by the IRS, the tax is uncollectable by reason of time. The debt just simply expires.

As I mentioned above, the IRS does not fancy itself a bank or even a creditor when dealing with delinquent tax accounts. When a bill is due, Revenue Officers demand payment of that money in full—now! Threats are made which involve the seizure of assets and levy of bank accounts and wages which are serious and far-reaching in terms of their consequences. These kinds of threats are then usually tempered with the proviso that if the Form 900 is signed by the citizen, payment arrangements can "possibly" be made and the drastic steps of levy and seizure can be "avoided."

In the hope of buying a reprieve from the harsh effects of enforced collection, citizens regularly extend the period of time in which the tax may be collected *without knowledge* of what they are doing. As you can imagine, a person is likely to sign almost anything to keep the IRS from taking his entire paycheck each and every month, especially when the consequences of signing are not explained. The form extends the collection period for a specified time as determined by the Revenue Officer handling the case.

How it Bites. I said earlier that the Form 900 may be the most significant waiver a citizen can sign. The reason for that should now be apparent but if not, let me paint a clearer picture. After six years have lapsed from the date of assessment, the IRS *cannot* legally collect any more money from the citizen on account of that particular tax year—period. Tax debts expire with the passage of time. That time period is *extended* when a Form 900 waiver is signed.

Executing a Form 900 waiver is a decision which *should not* be made in haste, and most certainly *should not* be made at the time, and under the circumstances, demanded by most Revenue Officers. We normally see the Form 900 presented to the citizen at his first appearance with the Revenue Officer. With it is handed this ultimatum, "If this form is not signed, we may begin levying your paycheck." No explanation is given other than the form is necessary to prevent "enforced" collection action.

A decision to sign the waiver should only be made after one has fully examined the implications of the act, *especially* the length of time remaining until the collection statute expires. It is not uncommon for unwitting citizens, under the terrifying threat of a levy, to sign a waiver extending a statute about to expire in just a few months. Through such act, the citizen heaps upon himself burdens which will linger for years beyond what they would have been had he not signed.

6. Form 1040 — *US Individual Income Tax Return*

Surprised? The Form 1040 is that document which individuals with sufficient gross income are required to file at the close of the calendar year. We all know what type of information the return contains, and the nature of its supporting schedules and forms. What most people do not know however, is . . .

EXHIBIT 4-5

Privacy Act and Paperwork Reduction Act Notice

The Privacy Act of 1974 and Paperwork Reduction Act of 1980 say that when we ask you for information, we must tell you: our legal right to ask for the information; what major purposes we have in asking for it and how it will be used; what could happen if we do not receive it; and whether your response is voluntary, required to obtain a benefit, or mandatory under the law.

For the Internal Revenue Service, this Notice applies to tax returns and any papers filed with them and any questions we need to ask you so we can complete, correct, or process your return; figure your tax; and collect tax, interest, or penalties.

Our legal right to ask for information is Internal Revenue Code sections 6001,

6011, and 6012(a) and their regulations. They say that you must file a return or statement with us for any tax you are liable for. Your response is mandatory under these sections. Code section 6109 and its regulations say that you must show your social security number on what you file. This is so we know who you are, and can process your return and papers. You must fill in all parts of the tax form that apply to you. But you do not have to check the boxes for the Presidential Election Campaign Fund.

We ask for tax return information to carry out the Internal Revenue laws of the United States. We need it to figure and collect the right amount of tax.

We may give the information to the Department of Justice and to other Federal agencies, as provided by law. We may also give it to cities, states, the District of Columbia, and U.S. commonwealths or

possessions to carry out their tax laws. And we may give it to foreign governments because of tax treaties they have with the United States.

If you do not file a return, do not provide the information we ask for, or provide fraudulent information, the law provides that you may be charged penalties and, in certain cases, you may be subject to criminal prosecution. We may also have to disallow the exemptions, exclusions, credits, deductions, or adjustments shown on the tax return. This could make the tax higher or delay any refund. Interest may also be charged.

Please keep this notice with your records. It may help you if we ask you for other information. If you have questions about the rules for filing and giving information, please call or visit any Internal Revenue Service office.

How it Bites. The IRS is required by the Privacy Act of 1974 and the Paperwork Reduction Act of 1980 to inform each citizen of the uses to which any information a citizen provides to the government may be put. The IRS' Privacy Act notice which accompanies the Form 1040 is quite telling. It is reproduced as Exhibit 4-5. The language of concern is found in the second column, beginning with the second paragraph. Read it carefully.

As you can see, the information our government learns from your tax return and its supporting schedules is *not* confidential, nor is it something that cannot be used against you. The IRS coldly observes in the Privacy Act Notice that this information is provided to the Department of Justice which is responsible for prosecuting civil and criminal violations of the tax and other federal statutes. Even beyond that, the information can be, and routinely is, given to other departments of government, both federal, state and local, and *to foreign governments* for use in administering their laws.

The tax laws are replete with penalty provisions, both civil and criminal, for those who file fraudulent or even erroneous returns. So on one hand, the law demands that a person bear his soul, yet punishes him for doing so in a fashion inconsistent with the views of the bureaucracy.

To enforce this directive, the Form 1040, as do most tax forms, contains a perjury clause. On the last line of the 1040, just above the signature space in small print, appears the following language.

> "Under penalties of perjury, I declare that I have examined this return and accompanying schedules and statements, and to the best of my knowledge and belief, they are true, correct and complete.

Income tax perjury violations are prosecuted under numerous federal statutes. Among the prosecution arsenal are two potent statutes, Code §§7206 and 7207. Section 7206(1) makes the filing of a false tax return a felony punishable by a $100,000 fine and three years in prison, while section 7207 makes the same act a misdemeanor punishable by a $100,000 fine and one year in prison. The difference in the statutes is the degree of willfulness or intent which is present in the acts of the defendant charged.

These are just two examples of the criminal statutes available to the IRS. The civil statutes include an addition to the tax of 5% for negligence, up to 25% for delinquency in filing a return, and other penalties based upon the nature of the act or failure to act. In all cases, whether the intended penalty is civil or criminal in nature, the IRS uses as the basis of its charge the information it obtains from the face of your Form 1040. Your own statements are used against you! Therefore, great care must abound when preparing and submitting Form 1040 and its schedules.

7. Form 2261 — *Future Income Collateral Agreement*

There are many forms of Collateral Agreements. The form is used primarily to complete the submission of an offer in compromise (see Chapter Five, Part III). Collateral agreements are also used in other circumstances. In one case Form 2261 was used to complete and memorialize the terms of an agreement reached in a bankruptcy case. Form 2261 and its sisters are the vehicles by which additional consideration, or payment, is transmitted to the IRS in exchange for certain tax liability concessions which the agency may make. An example of Form 2261 is included as Exhibit 4-6.

The Form 2261 is the "Future Income" collateral agreement.

EXHIBIT 4-6 (page one)

Form 2261. (Rev. April 1977)	DEPARTMENT OF THE TREASURY – INTERNAL REVENUE SERVICE **Collateral Agreement** Future Income – Individual

Names and Address of Taxpayers	Social Security and Employer Identification Numbers

To: Commissioner of Internal Revenue

The taxpayers identified above have submitted an offer dated _____ in the amount of $ _____ to compromise unpaid _____ tax liability, plus statutory additions, for the taxable periods _____

The purpose of this collateral agreement (hereinafter referred to as this agreement) is to provide additional consideration for acceptance of the offer in compromise described above. It is understood and agreed:

1. That in addition to the payment of the above amount of $ _____ , the taxpayers will pay out of annual income for the years _____ to _____ , inclusive

    (a) Nothing on the first $ _____ of annual income.

    (b) _____ percent of annual income more than $ _____ and not more than $ _____ .

    (c) _____ percent of annual income more than $ _____ and not more than $ _____ .

    (d) _____ percent of annual income more than $ _____ .

2. That the term annual income, as used in this agreement, means adjusted gross income as defined in section 62 of the Internal Revenue Code (except losses from sales or exchange of property and the deduction allowed by Code section 1202 for long-term capital gains shall not be allowed), plus all nontaxable income and profits or gains from any source whatsoever (including the fair market value of gifts, bequests, devises, and inheritances), minus (a) the Federal income tax paid for the year for which annual income is being computed, and (b) any payment made under the terms of the offer in compromise (Form 656) for the year in which such payment is made. The annual income shall not be reduced by net operating losses incurred before or after the period covered by this agreement. However, a net operating loss for any year during such period may be deducted from annual income of the following year only. It is also agreed that annual income shall include all income and gains or profits of the taxpayers, regardless of whether these amounts are community income under State law.

3. That in the event close corporations are directly or indirectly controlled or owned by the taxpayers during the existence of this agreement, the computation of annual income shall include their proportionate share of the total corporate annual income in excess of $10,000. The term corporate annual income, as used in this agreement, means the taxable income of the corporation before net operating loss deduction and special deductions (except, in computing such income, the losses from sales or exchange of property shall not be allowed), plus all nontaxable income, minus (a) dividends paid, and (b) the Federal income tax paid for the year for which annual income is being computed. For this purpose, the corporate annual income shall not be reduced by any net operating loss incurred before or after the periods covered by this agreement, but a net operating loss for any year during such period may be deducted from the corporate annual income for the following year only.

4. That the annual payments provided for in this agreement (including interest at the annual rate as established under section 6621(a) of the Internal Revenue Code (subject to adjustments as provided by Code section 6621(b)) on delinquent payments computed from the due date of such payment) shall be paid to the Internal Revenue Service, without notice, on or before the 15th day of the 4th month following the close of the calendar or fiscal year, such payments to be accompanied by a sworn statement and a copy of the taxpayers' Federal income tax return. The statement shall refer to this agreement and show the computation of annual income in accordance with items 1, 2, and 3 of this agreement. If the annual income for any year covered by this agreement is insufficient to require a payment under its terms, the taxpayers shall still furnish the Internal Revenue Service a sworn statement of such income and a copy of their Federal income tax return. All books, records, and accounts shall be open at all reasonable times for inspection by the Internal Revenue Service to verify the annual income shown in the statement. Also, the taxpayers hereby expressly consent to the disclosure to each other of the amount of their respective annual income and of all books, records, and accounts necessary to the computation of their annual income for the purpose of administering this agreement. The payments (if any), the sworn statement, and a copy of the Federal income tax return shall be transmitted to:
    Address:

Under its terms, the citizen agrees to provide certain percentages
of his income to the IRS in payment of a tax liability. As can be
seen from the blank spaces in paragraph one of Exhibit 4-6, the

EXHIBIT 4-6 (page 2)

5. That the aggregate amount paid under the terms of the offer in compromise and the additional amounts paid under the terms of this agreement shall not exceed an amount equivalent to the liability covered by the offer plus statutory additions that would have become due in the absence of the compromise.

6. That payments made under the terms of this agreement shall be applied first to tax and penalty, in that order, due for the earliest taxable period, then to tax and penalty, in that order, for each succeeding taxable period with no amount to be allocated to interest until the liabilities for taxes and penalties for all taxable periods sought to be compromised have been satisfied.

7. That upon notice to the taxpayers of the acceptance of the offer in compromise of the liability identified in this agreement, the taxpayers shall have no right, in the event of default in payment of any installment of principal or interest due under the terms of the offer and this agreement or in the event any other provision of this agreement is not carried out in accordance with its terms, to contest in court or otherwise the amount of the liability sought to be compromised; and that in the event of such default or noncompliance or in the event the taxpayers become the subject of any proceeding (except a proceeding under the Bankruptcy Act) whereby their affairs are placed under the control and jurisdiction of a court or other party, the United States, at the option of the Commissioner of Internal Revenue or a delegated official, may (a) proceed immediately by suit to collect the entire unpaid balance of the offer and this agreement, or (b) proceed immediately by suit to collect as liquidated damages an amount equal to the tax liability sought to be compromised, minus any payments already received under the terms of the offer and this agreement, with interest at the annual rate as established under section 6621(a) of the Internal Revenue Code (subject to adjustments as provided by Code section 6621(b)) from the date of default, or (c) disregard the amount of such offer and this agreement, apply all amounts previously paid thereunder against the amount of the liability sought to be compromised and, without further notice of any kind, assess and collect by levy or suit (the restrictions against assessment and collection being waived) the balance of such liability. In the event the taxpayers become the subject of any proceeding under the Bankruptcy Act, the offer in compromise and this agreement may be terminated. Upon such termination, the tax liability sought to be compromised, minus any payments already received under the terms of the offer and this agreement, shall become legally enforceable.

8. That the taxpayers waive the benefit of any statute of limitations applicable to the assessment and collection of the liability sought to be compromised and agree to the suspension of the running of the statutory period of limitations on assessment and collection for the period during which the offer in compromise and this agreement are pending, or the period during which any installment under the offer and this agreement remains unpaid, or any provision of this agreement is not carried out in accordance with its terms, and for 1 year thereafter.

9. That when all sums, including interest, due under the terms of the offer in compromise and this agreement, except those sums which may become due and payable under the provisions of item 1 of this agreement, have been paid in full, then and in that event only, all Federal tax liens at that time securing the tax liabilities which are the subject of the offer shall be immediately released. However, if, at the time consideration is being given to the release of the Federal tax liens, there are any sums due and payable under the terms of item 1, they must also be paid before the release of such liens.

This agreement shall be of no force or effect unless the offer in compromise is accepted.

Taxpayer's Signature	Date
Taxpayer's Signature	Date

I accept the waiver of statutory period of limitations for the Internal Revenue Service.

Signature and Title	Date

amounts and terms of the payments are fully negotiable. An example of how the form may read when figures are placed in the blank spaces is shown below:

> That in addition to the payment of the above amount of $10,000, (such being the amount of cash offered by the citizen), the taxpayers will pay out of annual income for the years 1989 to 1991, inclusive
>
> (a) Nothing on the first $10,000 of annual income.
> (b) 10 percent of annual income more than $10,000 and not more than $20,000.
> (c) 20 percent of annual income more than $20,000 and not more than $25,000.
> (d) 30 percent of annual income more than $25,000.

Under the language of the agreement, the term "annual income" is defined as "adjusted gross income," as set forth in Code §62, (refer to Form 1040, line 30) *minus* the federal income taxes paid during the year in question. To illustrate how much would have to be paid to the IRS under the above hypothetical collateral agreement, consider the following example:

Suppose you had an annual income in 1989 of $32,000. Suppose further that you are married and have two children. Your spouse has no separate income. The personal exemption amount per individual is $2,000 after 1988. The standard deduction amount for a married couple filing a joint return after 1988 is $5,000. Based upon this information, your tax liability would be $2,850.[3] Thus, on the $32,000 wage income, $29,150 will be subject to the collateral agreement (gross income minus tax liability).

Under the collateral agreement, the first $10,000 of income is exempt from any further payments to the government. On the amount between $10,000 and $20,000, the agreed upon rate is 10%. This computes to $1,000. On the amount between $20,000 and $25,000, the agreed upon rate is 20%. This computes to another $1,000. And lastly, on amounts above $25,000, the rate is 30%. In this example, that computes to $1,245. Thus, under our hypothetical colleratal agreement, the citizen is required to pay to the IRS, in addition to his regular income tax liability, the sum of:

---

[3] This is determined by subtracting the four exemptions at $2,000 each and the $5,000 standard deduction from the gross income, and then multiplying this result by the tax rate, which is 15% on incomes under $29,750.

$1,000
$1,000
$1,245
—————
$3,245.

This pattern would continue throughout the term of the agreement, which is three years. At the end of that period, the entire liability covered by the agreement would be fully satisfied.

The "future income" collateral agreement is the most common type of collateral agreement demanded by the IRS when lesser amounts of tax are offered in an effort to settle delinquent liabilities. There are however, other collateral agreements of which the citizen should be aware. They include Form 6621-B, Adjusted Basis of Specific Assets. Under this agreement, the citizen agrees to *reduce* the value of certain specified assets for purposes of depreciation and computing the gain or loss on the sale of the assets. This results in one paying additional taxes during the years covered by the agreement.

Form 2261-C is a Waiver of Net Operating Losses and Capital Losses. Under this agreement, the citizen agrees to *give up* any tax benefits resulting from the loss of money incurred in connection with a business or investments.

How They Bite. Collateral agreements, by their very nature, *bind* the citizen to *future* payments of *additional* taxes. This is accomplished either by cash payments (Form 2261) or concessions of tax benefits which would otherwise have been attributed to certain transactions. The terms of the collateral agreement expressly waive the benefit of the statute of limitations on the collection of tax liabilities (see paragraph 7 of Exhibit 4-6). If the citizen defaults on the agreement, the IRS has the right to immediately proceed to collect the entire tax liability covered by the agreement (see paragraph 6 of Exhibit 4-6).

As I mentioned earlier, collateral agreements are generally submitted with offers in compromise. Consequently, they are usually void if the offer is not accepted by the IRS (see printed statement over the signature line). This proviso acts to *minimize* the citizen's risk in signing the offer, as the benefits to the citizen within the offer itself *should be* such that the detriments of the collateral agreement are outweighed. This is not always the case. Therefore, before an offer is submitted which includes a collateral agreement, the terms of the collateral agreement must be carefully considered in light of the terms of the offer.

8. Form 2751 — *Proposed Assessment of 100% Penalty*

The 100% penalty is assessed under Code §6672. The penalty is assessed against corporate officers who are "responsible for" the withholding of, truthfully accounting for, and paying over to the IRS all employees' federal income taxes which have been withheld from their pay. The penalty is assessed against a "responsible" officer within the corporation when he has acted "willfully" in his failure to see that all corporate withholding responsibilities are correctly carried out.

The 100% penalty is so-called because the amount of the penalty equals (is 100% of) the tax which the corporation was required to pay but did not. The penalty is designed to provide the IRS with recourse for the collection of employment taxes when a corporation is bankrupt and without assets. By assessing the 100% penalty, an *individual* becomes *personally* responsible to pay these taxes. The IRS can collect the taxes from that person's own assets.

Under the procedure established for contesting a 100% penalty, if the IRS assesses the penalty, the smallest portion thereof may be paid by the "responsible officer." He may then file a claim for refund. If the claim is denied, a suit for refund may be prosecuted in the District Court. Under ordinary circumstances, before a suit for refund can be commenced, the *entire* tax must be paid. This is not true with regard to the 100% penalty. The reason is that the penalty has been called a "divisible" tax. The penalty represents the taxes due for several employees over several calendar quarters. When the amount for just one of those employees for one quarter is payed, such payment has been held to be a *complete* payment, triggering the right to file a claim for refund, followed by a suit for refund, if necessary.[4]

In a suit for refund (assuming the claim is denied), the citizen has the right to a *jury trial* on the issue of whether he was: (a) the responsible person, and (b) whether he acted "willfully" in connection with the failure to pay. While the 100% penalty is not subject to the deficiency procedures which gives the citizen the right to go to Tax Court, the "divisible" aspect of the tax virtually guarantees the citizen the right to a *jury trial* without having to pay in full what could be a huge tax liability.

---

[4] Flora v. United States, 362 U.S. 145 (1960); Steele v. United States, 280 F.2d 89 (8th Cir. 1960).

EXHIBIT 4-7

Form **2751** (Rev. May 1985)	Department of the Treasury — Internal Revenue Service **Proposed Assessment of 100 Percent Penalty** (Sec. 6672, Internal Revenue Code of 1954, or corresponding provisions of prior internal revenue laws)
	Report of Corporation's Unpaid Tax Liability

Name and address of corporaton

Tax Return Form No.	Tax Period Ended	Date Return Filed	Date Tax Assessed	Identifying Number	Amount Outstanding	Penalty
941	3-31-80	7-14-80	10-08-87	38-2122167	$ 2432.63	$ 2432.63
941	6-30-80	8-22-86	10-08-87	"	2561.59	2561.59
941	9-30-80	8-22-86	10-08-87	"	1909.71	1909.71
941	12-31-80	8-22-86	10-08-87	"	2002.70	2002.70
941	3-31-81	8-22-86	10-08-87	"	3655.07	3655.07
941	6-30-81	8-22-86	10-08-87	"	4015.75	4015.75
941	9-30-81	8-22-86	10-08-87	"	2974.02	2974.02
941	12-31-81	8-22-86	10-08-87	"	1764.88	1764.88
				Total Penalty	$	continuied page 1 of 2

Agreement to Assessment and Collection of 100 Percent Penalty

Name, address, and social security number of person responsible

I consent to the assessment and collection of the total penalty shown, which is equal either to the amount of Federal employment taxes withheld from employees wages or to the amount of Federal excise taxes collected from patrons or members, and which was not paid over to the Government by the corporation named above; and I waive the privilege of filing a claim for abatement after assessment.

Signature of person responsible	Date

Part 1— This copy to be signed and returned to Internal Revenue Service   Form **2751** (Rev. 5-85)

Form 2751 is prepared by the Collection Division and mailed or presented to the citizen for his signature. Like all waivers, the IRS is lax to say the least in explaining just what is "waived." A demand for signature is all that is clear.

The form does show (see Exhibit 4-7) exactly how much tax is claimed to be owed. The periods in question and the total amount due is broken down into smaller amounts by calendar quarter.

Form 2751 *is not* the assessment of the 100% penalty. It is merely a waiver which if signed, *accepts* the assessment. If the citizen rejects the waiver and provides substantial grounds why the penalty should not be assessed against him, the issue may die. Signing the form however, presents an entirely *different* set of facts.

How it Bites. Just above the signature line on the bottom of the form we find the words, "I consent to the assessment and collection of the *total penalty* shown...and I waive the privilege of filing a claim for abatement after assessment." (Emphasis added.) By signing this waiver, the citizen agrees to become *fully and personally* responsible for the employment tax debts of a corporation which may presently be bankrupt and without assets.

A signature on the form is license to the IRS to collect the full amount of the penalty from the personal assets of the individual who signed. Thus, his home, bank accounts, wages, etc., are subject to seizure by the IRS to satisfy this penalty. *Moreover*, the final clause of the form constitutes a *waiver* of the right to partially pay the tax, and then to file a claim for refund, and if necessary, a suit in court for a refund. A lawsuit is the *only* forum available to the citizen in which to assert and attempt to prove that he was *not* responsible for the corporation's failures. A signed Form 2751 takes away the only hope of contesting the penalty in a judicial theater.

9. Form 2848 — *Power of Attorney*

The power of attorney form is executed by persons who wish to have another represent them in some capacity before the Internal Revenue Service. The form is quite specific in terms of who is authorized to act in behalf of another, the years for which the power is in effect, and the type of tax which is covered by the power of attorney. See Exhibit 4-8.

Because of the one-sided secrecy rules within the IRS, the agency will not disclose any details of one's tax return or related affairs to another person, even if that person has the verbal okay from the citizen. Rather, the IRS demands that a power of attorney be executed which expressly authorizes disclosure of the sensitive material to the party named. With a valid power of attorney duly executed, a person can designate to the IRS who his representative will be in a given case.

How it Bites. Though one will not find this fact written in too many places, the IRS does observe the legal doctrine of "vicarious liability." What that means is that under the law of principal/agent relations, the principal party in a relationship can be legally responsible for the acts of his duly authorized agent.

In a tax case, a representative acting under a power of attorney is the *agent* of the citizen. The citizen is the *principal*. Thus, any statements and representations made by the representative on behalf of the citizen, *whether or not true*, will be held against the citizen by the IRS! This is a critical issue because so many people elect to have return preparers and CPAs represent them before the IRS in audit and appeals cases. The difficulty arises when these professionals, while fully competent in the area of return preparation and accounting, do not usually possess the level of experience or competence necessary to effectively *represent* a citizen before the IRS.

Perhaps unaware of certain doctrines of law, case precedent or statutory guidelines, inexperience may lead to statements or lack

EXHIBIT 4-8

Form **2848** (Rev. October 1983) Department of the Treasury Internal Revenue Service	**Power of Attorney and Declaration of Representative** ▶ See separate Instructions	OMB No. 1545-0150

PART I.— Power of Attorney

Taxpayer(s) name, identifying number, and address including ZIP code (Please type or print)

For IRS Use Only		
File So.		
Level		
Receipt		
Powers		
Blind T.		
Action		
Ret.Ind.		

hereby appoints (name(s), CAF number(s), address(es), including ZIP code(s), and telephone number(s) of individual(s)) *

as attorney(s)-in-fact to represent the taxpayer(s) before any office of the Internal Revenue Service for the following tax matter(s) (specify the type(s) of tax and year(s) or period(s) (date of death if estate tax)):

Type of tax (Individual, corporate, etc.)	Federal tax form number (1040, 1120, etc.)	Year(s) or period(s) (Date of death if estate tax)

The attorney(s)-in-fact (or either of them) are authorized, subject to revocation, to receive confidential information and to perform any and all acts that the principal(s) can perform with respect to the above specified tax matters (excluding the power to receive refund checks, and the power to sign the return (see regulations section 1.6012-1(a)(5), Returns made by agents), unless specifically granted below).

Send copies of notices and other written communications addressed to the taxpayer(s) in proceedings involving the above tax matters to:

1 ☐ the appointee first named above, or

2 ☐ (names of not more than two of the above named appointees) .... ---

----

Initial here ▶ .... if you are granting the power to receive, but not to endorse or cash, refund checks for the above tax matters to :

3 ☐ the appointee first named above, or

4 ☐ (name of one of the above designated appointees) ▶.... ---

This power of attorney revokes all earlier powers of attorney and tax information authorizations on file with the Internal Revenue Service for the same tax matters and years or periods covered by this power of attorney, except the following:

(Specify to whom granted, date, and address including ZIP code, or refer to attached copies of earlier powers and authorizations.)

Signature of or for taxpayer(s)
(If signed by a corporate officer, partner, or fiduciary on behalf of the taxpayer. I certify that I have the authority to execute this power of attorney on behalf of the taxpayer.)

-------------------------------------   .. ..   ----- ----
          (Signature)   (Title, if applicable)   (Date)
(Also type or print your name below if signing for a taxpayer who is not an individual.)

-------------------------------------   ---------------   ----- ----
          (Signature)   (Title, if applicable)   (Date)

* You may authorize an organization, firm, or partnership to receive confidential information, but your representative must be an individual who must complete Part II.

For Privacy Act and Paperwork Reduction Act Notice, see page 1 of the Instructions.   Form **2848** (Rev. 10-83) of statements which are against the citizen's interest. And even though the citizen himself has not made or failed to make the statement, the shortcomings of his representative *will be* held against him.

Consequently, the selection of a representative in a tax matter must be undertaken in a very careful and deliberate manner. Not all expert accountants and return preparers are necessarily expert advocates before the IRS or in Tax Court. Equally true, not all expert attorneys are necessarily expert *tax* attorneys, capable of maneuvering through the labyrinthine bureaucratic structure known as the Internal Revenue Service. Experience in the specific area of tax litigation should be the critical standard by which one judges the competence of his would-be representative.

10. Form 4822 — *Statement of Annual Estimated Personal and Family Living Expenses*

This form has been discussed in Chapter One, Part I(D), but it can *bite*, so here we are again. Furthermore, it is necessary to review a copy of the form so that one can appreciate the full implications of preparing the document. See Exhibit 4-9.

As the reader may recall, Form 4822 is used by Revenue Agents during the course of an audit. The purpose of the form is to have the citizen itemize his living expenses and the manner in which they were paid during the year under audit. This is *supposed* to give the Revenue Agent some measure of the accuracy of the income reported on the tax return.

For example, if the citizen prepares the form claiming that his household expenses for such things as mortgage payments and child care amounted to $20,000 for the year in question, while just $22,000 was reported as income on the return, one can easily see how the IRS agent may infer that unreported income was received during the year in question.

How it Bites. In my estimation, Form 4822 is the world's *worst* way for a person to reconstruct his living expenses for any year. This is particularly true because when one is asked to complete the form, the year for which the reconstruction applies has long since passed. When filling out such a form, it has been my experience that people have a tendency to apply *current* prices as the standard for the amount of money spent in a given category several years *previous*. Obviously, preparing a Form 4822 for, say, 1985 using 1988 price standards will only get a person into trouble.

Furthermore, the nature of the form itself is patently unfair for this reason: the form asks a person to itemize what is spent on

EXHIBIT 4-9

Form **4822** (Rev. 6-83)	Department of the Treasury - Internal Revenue Service **STATEMENT OF ANNUAL ESTIMATED PERSONAL AND FAMILY EXPENSES**				
TAXPAYER'S NAME AND ADDRESS				TAX YEAR ENDED	

	ITEM	BY CASH	BY CHECK	TOTAL	REMARKS
1. PERSONAL EXPENSES	Groceries and outside meals				
	Clothing				
	Laundry and dry cleaning				
	Barber, beauty shop, and cosmetics				
	Education *(tuition, room, board, books, etc.)*				
	Recreation, entertainment, vacations				
	Dues *(clubs, lodge, etc.)*				
	Gifts and allowances				
	Life and accident insurance				
	Federal taxes *(income, FICA, etc.)*				
2. HOUSEHOLD EXPENSES	Rent				
	Mortgage payments *(including interest)*				
	Utilities *(electricity, gas, telephone, water, etc.)*				
	Domestic help				
	Home insurance				
	Repairs and improvements				
	Child care				
3. AUTO EXPENSES	Gasoline, oil, grease, wash				
	Tires, batteries, repairs, tags				
	Insurance				
	Auto payments *(including interest)*				
	Lease of auto				
4. DEDUCTIBLE ITEMS	Contributions				
	Medical Expenses Insurance				
	Drugs				
	Doctors, hospitals, etc.				
	Taxes Real estate *(not included in 2. above)*				
	Personal property				
	Income *(State and local)*				
	Interest *(not included in 2. and 3. above)*				
	Mis-cella-neous Alimony				
	Union dues				
5. PERSONAL ASSETS, ETC.	Stocks and bonds				
	Furniture, appliances, jewelry				
	Loans to others				
	Boat				
	TOTALS ▶				

Form 4822 (Rev. 6-83)

disbursements which are largely non-deductible personal living expenses. As a result, *no records* are kept of these purchases and it thus becomes *impossible* to reconstruct accurately the amounts spent. Who, for example, keeps records of how much is spent on groceries, or on laundry and dry cleaning, or on gifts and allowances, during *any* year? These items cannot be deducted, hence there is no legal reason why such records should be kept.

Yet the IRS oft times demands that the form be prepared, well knowing that the compliant and unsuspecting citizen is quite likely to fall victim to the trap I just described. Believing that Form 4822 is necessary to prove his reported income is correct, the unsuspecting citizen conscientiously prepares it, only to find that the IRS has used it as the basis to do just the opposite: *increase* the citizen's taxable income.

In Chapter Two, I have provided several legally acceptable ways in which a person can verify his income to the IRS, none of which involve the use of Form 4822. I believe that each of those methods is greatly superior to Form 4822 both in terms of its legal credibility and in terms of its pragmatic reliability.

11. Tax Court — *Stipulated Decision Document*

Cases in the Tax Court are settled primarily in one of two ways; either with a trial and decision by a judge, or with a stipulation or agreement between the two parties. The Stipulated Decision Document is the written form of the agreed decision reached by the two parties, the IRS and the citizen/petitioner. See Exhibit 4-10. When this document is executed by the citizen, the terms reflected in the body of the stipulation become a judgment in favor of the prevailing party.

The stipulated decision is a convenient way in which to settle a pending Tax Court case. As a matter of fact, most cases are disposed of in this manner, eliminating the need of a trial. The decision document usually reflects much negotiation between the parties, and memorializes the results of the concessions each has made on the issues in the case.

The beauty of a stipulated decision is that all of the risks of a trial are eliminated. After the decision is final, both parties walk away from the negotiation with a firm settlement in hand. On the other hand, the Tax Court may take months and sometimes years to render a decision in a given case, all the while interest is piling up.

Still, with all of its advantages, to the unknowing or inexperienced Tax Court litigant, the stipulated decision does have its disadvantages.

How it Bites. The decision document is in every way an agreed settlement of all of the issues in the case. It becomes a *judgment* in favor of the prevailing party. As you can see from Exhibit 4-10, the decision document shown there reflects a substantial tax liability decided against the citizen/petitioner.

Furthermore, upon signing the document by both parties, the

EXHIBIT 4-10 (page one)

UNITED STATES TAX COURT

```
                              )
                              )
              Petitioner,     )
                              )
    v.                        )    Docket No. 11932-87
                              )
COMMISSIONER OF INTERNAL REVENUE, )
                              )
              Respondent.     )
```

DECISION

Pursuant to agreement of the parties in this case, it is

ORDERED and DECIDED: That there are deficiencies in income tax and additions to the tax due from the petitioner as follows:

		Deficiencies				
			Additions to the Tax			
Taxable Year	Income Tax	§6651(a)	§6653(a)(1)	§6653(a)(2)	§6654	§6661
1983	$ 5,884.00	$1,471.00	$294.20	*	$360.00	$1,471.00
1984	11,010.00	2,752.50	550.50	*	692.21	2,753.00
1985	3,768.00	734.25	188.40	*	156.40	---

   * It is further decided that there are additions to the taxes due from the petitioner for the taxable years 1983, 1984 and 1985, under the provisions of I.R.C. § 6653(a)(2), equal to 50 percent of the statutory interest due on $5,884.00, $11,010.00 and $2,937.00, respectively, from April 15, 1984, April 15, 1985 and April 15, 1986, respectively, to the date of assessment of tax or, if earlier, the date of payment.

Judge.

Entered:

*   *   *   *   *

tax, interest and penalties shown due in the decision document will become *assessed* against the petitioner, and will be fully collectable by the IRS with all of the enforced collection tools it has available. Ordinarily, a tax cannot be assessed until the Tax Court renders a decision. But the Court does not sign and assent to the stipulated decision until months after the parties have done so. During this interim period, the IRS would be able to collect the

EXHIBIT 4-10 (page two)

Docket No. 11932-87   - 2 -

It is stipulated that the Court may enter the foregoing decision in this case.

It is further stipulated that respondent claims an increased deficiency in income tax for the taxable year 1985 in the amount of $1,462.00, under the provisions of I.R.C. § 6214(a);

It is further stipulated that respondent claims an increase in the addition to the tax under I.R.C. § 6651(a) for taxable year 1985 in the amount of $70.25, under the provisions of I.R.C. § 6214(a).

It is further stipulated that respondent claims an increase in the addition to the tax under I.R.C. § 6653(a)(1) for taxable year 1985 in the amount of $73.40, under the provisions of I.R.C. § 6214(a).

It is further stipulated that respondent claims an increase in the addition to the tax under I.R.C. § 6653(a)(2) for taxable year 1985 in the amount of 50 percent of the statutory interest due on $681.00, under the provisions of I.R.C. § 6214(a).

It is further stipulated that respondent claims an increase in the addition to tax under I.R.C. § 6654 for taxable year 1985 in the amount of $28.40, under the provisions of I.R.C. § 6214(a).

It is further stipulated that there is a prepayment credit for the taxable year ended December 31, 1985 in the amount of $831.00. It is stipulated that the deficiency for the taxable year ended December 31, 1985, is computed without considering the prepayment credit of $831.00.

It is further stipulated that effective upon the entry of this decision by the Court, petitioner waives the restriction contained in I.R.C. § 6213(a) prohibiting assessment of the deficiencies in tax and additions to the tax (plus statutory interest) until the decision of the Tax Court has become final.

WILLIAM F. NELSON
Chief Counsel
Internal Revenue Service

By:

_____   _____
Petitioner   ROBERT F. CUNNINGHAM
                                  Tax Court No. CR0633
                                  District Counsel
                                  Internal Revenue Service
                                  572 Federal Building and
                                      United States Courthouse
                                  316 North Robert Street
                                  St. Paul, Minnesota 55101
                                  Tel. No. (612) 290-3564

assessment.

One further observation on the stipulated settlement is this: the decision is *unappealable*. Because the citizen/petitioner *agrees* to entry of the judgment shown on the document, no Court of Appeals will be much impressed with any argument which attempts to criticize the judgment in some way. So while the stipulated decision is a convenient way in which to dispose of a Tax Court case without the cost and risk of a trial, it shackles the citizen with the terms of its settlement until the tax is paid.

Of course, not every stipulated decision reflects a tax liability. If you have been fully successful in your negotiation with the IRS, the stipulated decision would reflect little or *no tax due*. This type of a settlement cannot hurt you. But where a decision does reflect a tax due, one must be fully aware of the consequences of signing before doing so, and must be satisfied that the decision reflects the true facts because the resultant judgment is *final*.

Conclusion—

This Chapter was an effort to sail the sea of tax forms in the hope of providing the reader with a chart of bad waters. I make no pretenses that this effort has been all-inclusive. It is not. My own opening remarks prove that. But it should be sufficient to give a background to some of the more troublesome forms and their effects.

The brighter side to the tax form blizzard is that the IRS produces a catalog of federal tax forms, form letters and notices. It is Publication 676, and can be ordered by writing to:

> Internal Revenue Service
> TR:FP:F:M: Room 5556
> 1111 Constitution Avenue NW
> Washington, D.C. 20024

This catalog lists thousands of letters and forms and gives a brief description of each. From the same address one can receive sample copies of the various forms listed in the publication. Publication 676 itself is not complete. It does not contain a listing of every IRS form in use. But it is a start. In any event, one can obtain a copy of any form by writing to the above address and making reference to the form number. Good luck!

Chapter Five

4 WAYS TO PAY TAXES ON YOUR TERMS—NOT THEIRS

Introduction

In April of 1942, President Franklin D. Roosevelt made one of his many speeches to the Congress of the United States. In it, he stated that he believed "no American citizen ought to have a net income, after he has paid his taxes, of more than $25,000 a year." This conclusion was based upon Roosevelt's observation that "discrepancies between low personal incomes and very high personal incomes should be lessened."[1]

The era of Roosevelt's "New Dealism" lead to the imposition of personal tax obligations which were theretofore unknown to the American public. Roosevelt claimed in 1942 that "no American" should be allowed to keep that which was earned above $25,000 per year. Just 29 years previous to that, Congress passed the first income tax law. That law *did not even take effect* until one's personal income had *reached* $25,000 per year. Even then, the tax was just *one percent* and was *never* to exceed two percent. With Roosevelt's attitudes on redistributing the wealth of America came Congress' passage of the Victory Tax Act of 1943, a Roosevelt brainchild. For the first time, wage withholding requirements were imposed upon the working class of America. This was the first time most Americans had ever come face-to-face with the nation's income tax laws. Previous to that, gross income thresholds and the absence of withholding laws had left the vast majority of the income of the working class intact.

Since then, tax rate tables have increased steadily while gross income thresholds fell. More and more, Americans by the millions were being caught in the income tax compliance trap. With this explosion of "taxpayers" came an industry designed to "plan" one's affairs in such a fashion as to minimize one's tax bite. Attorneys and accountants specializing in "tax planning" would work night and day, pouring over the thousands of pages of fine print which

---

[1] April 27, 1942, To the Congress: The President Outlines a Seven-Point Economic Stabilization Program. *The Public Papers and Addresses of Franklin D. Roosevelt,* Harper & Brothers, New York, 1942, pages 220-221.

make up our tax laws, looking for ways in which the clever taxpayer willing to take a risk could wriggle free of the law's burdens.

All of the benefits which seemed to accrue from the new "tax planning" industry imparted to the rich. Those who could afford the expensive tax whiz-kids reaped the rewards in terms of many thousands of dollars per year in taxes saved. An individual with a six figure income would gladly pay a lawyer or creative accountant a $15,000 "planning fee" if it saved $50,000 in taxes.

This "industry" flourished in the United States for years. Finally the IRS, with the help of tougher tax laws, has cracked down on the "tax shelter" industry. But the horse is not dead. With each law that is passed comes a new egg-head willing to sit up nights dreaming of ways one can waltz around it. As to the astuteness of citizens in dodging the laws, Rudick writes:

> "Taxes and tax avoidance were probably born twins, and are likely to continue their joint existence until the millenium of a taxless world. Avoidance is hydraheaded and, as the tax gatherers...discover and cut off one escape contrivance, the taxpayer comes up with another."[2]

But to hire the legal talent needed and to make the tax avoidance investment worthwhile in terms of return, one must *have the money*. Without a sufficiently high income, any possible return on the investment is not worth the risk. What this means is that those without sufficient funds to finance the tax avoidance game, bear the brunt of tax collection. In America, the middle class is the hapless lot upon whose shoulders this unshared burden has perennially fallen.

Because those in the world of high finance have always focused upon clever ways in which to *avoid* taxes, the area of determining clever ways in which to *pay* taxes has been overlooked. After all, who can benefit from knowing how to best *pay* taxes? Obviously only those who cannot afford to learn how *not* to pay!

In this Chapter, we will explore several ways in which a person saddled with a tax that has been legitimately assessed, can pay the bill in a manner which best suits his needs. Unless the citizen takes affirmative steps to protect his interests where tax payments are

---

[2] *The Problems of Personal Income Tax*, 7 Law & Contemporary Problems 243 (1940).

concerned, the IRS will collect the taxes in such a way as best suits the treasury. As you might have guessed, that will entail your paying more money to the government than is legally required.

1. The Audit Reconsideration—

The audit reconsideration is the procedure whereby closed tax cases may be re-opened. Knowledge of this procedure could save a citizen thousands of dollars in taxes, not to mention the heartache that accompanies unjust IRS harassment.

There are many circumstances under which the audit reconsideration technique may be used. Illustrating the facts of an actual case would probably be the best way in which to communicate the benefits one might expect to look forward to. Steven, like most Americans, used a tax return preparer to handle his annual tax filing burden. After the return was filed he would forget about taxes for another year.

In April of 1985, Steve received a notice from the IRS that his 1983 return had been selected for audit. He promptly took the notice to the return preparer for the appropriate action. He left his preparer's office with the assurance that she "would handle everything." Confident that she was capable of fulfilling her promises, Steven forgot all about the audit. "There is no need for you to appear," she told him, "since I have a power of attorney, I will take care of everything."

In the months to follow, Steven received a few more letters regarding the audit, and each time he followed the same procedure. The letter was immediately taken to the preparer's office and given over to her care. Each time the two met, additional promises and assurances were given Steven regarding the progress of his case. Based upon the confident and unflinching representation made during each visit, Steven had no reason to believe that all was not "under contorol."

One year later, Steven received a peculiar bill from the IRS for the year 1983. The bill, dated May of 1986, reported that a tax had been assessed and that it remained unpaid. The bill demanded full and immediate payment of $4,915.25! How could this be? The preparer was handling everything. Her repeated assurances indicated that the matter was under control and that there would be no additional taxes due. Obviously, this was not the case.

After confronting the preparer, Steven learned, much to his chagrin, that she had *done nothing* in his case. Each of the notices he received and forwarded to her were duly filed and subsequently ignored. She did not attend the audit conference as she said she would, nor did she mail any letter of explanation to the IRS.

After having learned of the incompetence of his preparer, Steven sought other help. After discussing the problem with me, we began the process of determining from where the additonal $4,900 in taxes and interest came. Steven had a copy of the original letter he had received from the IRS establishing the audit date for the 1983 return. The audit notice contained, as most do, a description of the items which the IRS was questioning and which it intended to review at the audit. The fact that nobody attended the audit or explained the failure led to the IRS simply disallowing those particular items and sending Steven a bill. Hence, the original letter allowed us to determine how the tax was computed.

Next, a letter to the local Chief of the Examination Divison was drafted. The letter asked for an *audit reconsideration.* Under the language of Revenue Regulation §601.105(j), the Chief of the Examination Division has the authority to "approve" any request to re-open a case. The audit reconsideration allows a citizen to re-adjust an assessment *after* all appeal rights have been waived.

As you may have recognized from this account, Steven did not avail himself of any of his appeal rights with respect to the assessment for 1983. The reason was that he was unaware that any assessment had been made in his case. The return preparer who was "supposed" to handle all of the technical aspects of the case had ignored all IRS paperwork.

The procedures for invoking a request for audit reconsideration apply in limited circumstances. Under the terms of established IRS procedures,[3] the remedy applies to all cases in which:

> "the prior audit and conference action, if any, *did not* extend beyond the jurisdiction of the office of the District Director. It *does not* apply to cases previously closed after consideration by Appeals Offices or District Counsels." (Emphasis added.)

The "jurisdiction of the District Director," in the context of our discussion, is limited to that of the power to audit. What this means is simple. If one is audited, as was Steven, but does not appeal in

---

[3] Rev. Proc. 85-13, 1985-1 C.B. 514.

any way the decision of the auditor, the remedy of reconsideration is available. On the other hand, if the audit decision was taken to the Appeals Division or beyond, say to Tax Court (District Counsel jurisdiction), the remedy of reconsideration is *not* available. The theory of the reconsideration is that one always has the right to have the decision of the original auditor reviewed before it becomes final.

A letter to the Chief of the Examination Division seeking the reconsideration must set forth the facts of the case as completely as possible. It must enable the appropriate IRS authorities to make the decision that the case should be re-opened. Your letter should be *clear* on the following facts:

(a) The decision of the auditor became final without your taking *any appeal* of that decision;

(b) A clear and concise statement as to why no appeal was taken from the decision of the auditor, with the explanation that the failure was due to "no fault of the taxpayer;"

(c) You are in possession of all records and documents necessary to demonstrate that the decision of the auditor was erroneous, and that you are prepared to present such evidence to the IRS. The evidence which you have should be described as completely as possible to the IRS; and

(d) As with all IRS communications, you should make a specific *demand* that the case be re-opened and your evidence considered. Without a reconsideration, you should charge that you are deprived of your right to a face-to-face meeting with the IRS before your tax return is changed. This right is provided for in IRS regulations.[4]

In another audit reconsideration case, Mike submitted a demand which contained the points outlined above. Mike was assessed several thousand dollars in taxes and penalties after an audit. He was unable to appeal the decision because he had moved prior to being notified of the results. While the IRS mailed the notice of deficiency to Mike's last known address, it did not reach him in time to permit an appeal to the Tax Court. After the tax had been assessed for several years, and after moving back to the original city in which he lived, the IRS began levying his paycheck. This naturally alerted Mike to the presence of the assessment.

---

[4] Revenue Regulation §601.105.

After much correspondence with the IRS at both the Audit and Collection levels, a reconsideration was ordered. A conference was held pursuant to the reconsideration at which Mike presented the new auditor with all of the information he had in his possession. This same information would have been presented had he been afforded the opportunity to appeal this case.

The audit reconsideration led the IRS to substantially alter its stance in Mike's case. Mike was eventually given credit for most of the deductions which had previously been *disallowed.* With the decision came an abatement of that portion of the tax, penalties and *interest* as was represented by the newly allowed deductions.

In the final analysis, Mike ended up paying only the amount of tax that he would have paid had he taken advantage of his appeal rights in the first place. In this respect, the audit reconsideration, is a negotiation technique which allows a person to re-open a closed case provided the requisite conditions are met. By doing so, he will pay only the *correct* tax, if any at all, not that which has been assessed arbitrarily. This is truly an effective way in which to pay taxes on your terms, not theirs.

2. The Extension of Time to Pay Tax—

The most common mistake made by persons unfamiliar with IRS procedures, and this *includes* many accountants and return preparers, is to file an income tax return *without paying the tax.* Too often, people have their tax returns prepared before April 15th only to discover, to their horror, that they have a huge tax bill and no way in which it can quickly be paid.

In an effort to keep his client in "compliance" with the law, the accountant will instruct the client to file the tax return without making the payment. "The fact that you do not have the money does not excuse you from the obligation to file the return," you will be told. "Besides," they continue, "you can always make payments."

This reasoning may sound perfectly plausible to the uninformed citizen. But while it is "technically" correct, it is just *not* that simple. It is a lot like saying that *you* can earn a million dollars a year playing baseball. All *you* have to do is hit the ball four out of every 10 times it is pitched to you during the course of the season. That does not sound difficult, does it? Anybody who knows anything about baseball knows it is quite difficult!

The reality is that most collection problems I have seen over the years have been *caused* by the citizen himself, *not* the IRS. In this respect, probably 90% of these conditions were brought about by persons filing their returns without paying the tax. What happens when this occurs? A tax return which shows a tax due *constitutes* an assessment. This assessment is recorded as a *judgment* against the citizen. Hence, the only remaining step which the IRS must take to legally collect the tax is to mail, via certified mail, a 30-day notice and demand for payment. After the 30 days have expired, the IRS may lien, levy and seize anything the citizen owns, *without further notice.*

Citizens faced with such hardships routinely ask, "Can I get an extension of time in which to file my return?" The answer is "yes," but the extension of time to file the return *does not* extend the time to pay the tax.[5]

In the age of Automated Collection Sites and computerized collection practices, one is taking a serious risk by filing the return, or even seeking an extension do do so, without making payment. Under these circumstances, what can one do to protect himself when faced with difficult financial conditions? I believe the answer lies within a tax form which receives very little attention from the accounting and tax preparation community— not to mention the IRS.

The form is IRS Form 1127, *Application for Extension of Time for Payment of Tax.* See Exhibit 5-1. While hundreds of thousands of *tax return* filing extensions (Form 4868) are submitted each year, how many citizens and tax experts know that the heartache, hassle and possible financial ruin caused by an unpaid tax assessment can be avoided by filing Form 1127? Based upon experience, I submit that not many know of the benefits inherent in this negotiation tactic.

The first rule of filing Form 1127 is simple. The application must be filed "on or before the date prescribed for payment" of the tax. It must be filed with the office of the district director covering the district where the citizen resides. Acceptance of the application is *not* automatic, however. Form 1127 must contain a statement of facts which demonstrates that "payment on the due date of the amount with respect to which the extension is desired will result in undue hardship."[6]

In seeking the extension, it is important that "undue hardship" be fully demonstrated with specific facts, and *not* in general or

---

[5] Rev. Reg. §55.6161-1(a)(3).
[6] IRM Part 5700 §57(14)8. 1(1).

EXHIBIT 5-1 (page one)

Form **1127** (Rev. May 1986) Department of the Treasury Internal Revenue Service	APPLICATION FOR EXTENSION OF TIME FOR PAYMENT OF TAX *(Please read conditions on back before completing this form)*

District Director of Internal Revenue at _____
(Enter City and State where IRS Office is located)

I request an extension of time from _____, 19 ____, to _____, 19 ____,
(Enter Due Date of Return)

in which to pay tax of $ _____ for the year ended _____, 19 ____,

This extension is necessary because *(If more space is needed, please attach a separate sheet):* _____

_____

_____

_____

I am unable to borrow money to pay the tax because: _____

_____

_____

As evidence of the need for the extension, I am attaching: (1) a statement of assets and liabilities as of the last day of the preceding month (showing book and market values of assets and whether any securities are listed or unlisted); and (2) an itemized list of receipts and disbursements for the 3 months before the date the tax is due.

I propose to secure the liability covered by this extension as follows:

_____

_____

Under penalties of perjury, I declare that I have examined this application, including any accompanying schedules and statements, and to the best of my knowledge and belief it is true, correct, and complete.

_____	_____
(SIGNATURE OF APPLICANT)	*(DATE)*
_____	_____
(ADDRESS OF APPLICANT)	*(EMPLOYER IDENTIFICATION OR SOCIAL SECURITY NUMBER)*

The District Director will let you know whether the extension is granted or denied and will give you the form of bond, if necessary. However, he or she cannot consider an application if it is filed after the due date of the return. A list of approved surety companies will be sent to you upon request.

(The following will be filled in by the IRS.)

This application is   ☐ approved   for the following reasons:
                    ☐ disapproved

_____

_____

Interest _____ Date of assessment _____ Identifying no. _____

Penalty _____   _____   _____

(SIGNATURE)   *(DATE)*

(over)   Form **1127** (Rev. 5-86)

EXHIBIT 5-2 (page two)

CONDITIONS UNDER WHICH EXTENSIONS OF TIME FOR PAYMENTS MAY BE GRANTED UNDER SECTION 6161 OF THE INTERNAL REVENUE CODE

The District Director may grant an extension of time for payment of your tax if you can show that it will cause you undue hardship to pay it on the date it is due. To receive consideration, your application must be filed with the District Director on or before the date prescribed for payment of the tax.

1. **Undue hardship.**—This means more than mere inconvenience. You must show that you will have substantial financial loss if you pay your tax on the date it is due. (Such a loss could be caused by having to sell property at a sacrifice price.) You must show that you do not have enough cash, above necessary working capital, to pay the tax. In determining cash available, include anything you can convert into cash, and use current market prices. Also show that you are unable to borrow money to pay the tax, except under terms that will cause you severe loss and hardship.

2. **Limitations.**—As a general rule, an extension of time to pay any part of income or gift tax shown on a return is limited to 6 months from the date fixed for payment. An extension may be granted for more than 6 months if you are abroad.

An extension of time to pay any part of a deficiency (an amount determined to be due after an examination of your return) in income or gift tax is limited to 18 months from the date fixed for payment and, in exceptional cases, for an additional period of not more than 12 months.

No extension is granted to pay a deficiency that is due to negligence, intentional disregard of rules and regulations, or fraud with intent to evade tax.

3. **Interest.**—Interest is charged at the annual rate established under Code section 6621(a) (subject to adjustments as provided in Code section 6621(b)).

4. **Security.**—Security satisfactory to the District Director is required as a condition for granting an extension. This is to assure that the risk of loss to the Government will be no greater at the end of the extension period than it was at the beginning. The determination of the kind of security, such as bond, filing of notice of lien, mortgage, pledge, deed of trust of specific property or general assets, personal surety, or other, will depend on the circumstances in each case. Ordinarily, when you receive notice of approval of your application, you should deposit with the District Director any collateral that was agreed upon for security purposes. No collateral is required if you have no assets.

5. **Due date of payment for which extension is granted.**—On or before the end of the extension period, pay the tax for which the extension is granted (without notice and demand from the District Director).

6. **Filing requirements.**—If you need an extension of time to pay tax, submit an application with supporting documents on or before the date the tax is due. File the application with the District Director where you maintain your legal residence or principal place of business. If, however, the tax is to be paid to the Director, Foreign Operations District, file the application with that office. If you need an extension to pay estate tax, file Form 4768, Application for Extension of Time to File U.S. Estate Tax Return and/or Pay Estate Tax.

Form 1127 (Rev. 5-86)
☀ U.S.G.P.O: 1986- 491-481/54266

conclusory fashion. The IRS manual [7] defines the phrase "undue hardship" in the following manner:

> "The term 'undue hardship' means more than an inconvenience to the taxpayer. It must appear that substantial financial loss, for example, loss due to the sale of property at a sacrifice price, will result from making payment on the due date of the amount with respect to which the extension is desired."

The definition given is not intended to be exhaustive on the issue of "undue hardship." For example, a person who has been out-of-work for an extended period of time, or who has suffered losses due to medical or other uncontrollable factors may be faced with "undue hardship." When definitions by example are given, readers have a tendency to assume that only those circumstances which mirror the examples meet the criteria in question. Be careful that this self-imposed limitation does not occur in this very important area.

When the extension of time in which to pay the tax is granted, the citizen will be given *six months* to come up with the money to satisfy the debt. Without applying for the extension, the IRS begins enforced collection action almost immediately. This action will invariably lead to severe financial repercussions. Not only will the IRS levy paychecks and bank accounts to collect the unpaid balance "right now," they will *add* to the tax a *penalty* for failure to pay in a timely manner.[8] But that too can be avoided. The key is found in Revenue Regulation §301.6651-1(c). That regulation reads in part as follows:

> "* * * A failure to pay will be considered to be due to reasonable cause to the extent that the taxpayer has made a satisfactory showing that he exercised ordinary business care and prudence in providing for payment of his tax liability and was nevertheless either unable to pay the tax or would suffer an undue hardship (as defined above) if he paid on the due date. In determining whether the taxpayer was unable to pay the tax in spite of the exercise of ordinary business care and prudence in providing for payment of his tax liability, consideration will be given to all the facts and circumstances of the taxpayer's

---

[7] See previous footnote.
[8] Code §6651, and Rev. Reg. §301.6651-1(a)(2).

financial situation, including the amount and nature of the taxpayer's expenditures in light of the income (or other amounts) he could, at the time of such expenditures, reasonably expect to receive prior to the date prescribed for the payment of the tax.* * * A taxpayer *will be considered* to have exercised ordinary business care and prudence if he made reasonable efforts to conserve sufficient assets in marketable form to satisfy his tax liability and nevertheless was unable to pay all or a portion of the tax when it became due." (Emphasis added.)

Taken together, the language of the manual as well as the regulation gives us the formula for obtaining an extension of time to pay the tax. The cumbersome dissertation can be distilled into the following synopsis:

(a) File Form 1127 *on or before* the date the tax is required to be paid. Simply submitting the Application for Extension to File (Form 4868) is *not* good enough. A Form 4868 *does not* extend the time for *paying* the tax. It extends only the time for filing a return.

(b) Demonstrate with facts and circumstances how payment of the tax at the time it is due would impose "undue hardship" upon you. In order to carry this out, one must submit with Form 1127 a "statement of the assets and liabilities of the taxpayer and an itemized statement showing all receipts and disbursements for each of the 3 months immediately preceding the due date" of the tax in question.[9] This can be accomplished on IRS Form 433, but be careful! You may recall that Form 433 can bite! See Chapter Four, part 1.

(c) Make an argument that you observed "reasonable care and business prudence" in order to assure that you had sufficient funds in liquid form to pay the tax at the time it was due, but nevertheless, were unable to do so. This statement must also be specific and based upon the actual facts and circumstances of your case. Care should be taken to avoid generalities or vague remarks or references to events which to the uninformed reader, seem irrelevent. Facts should be offered in a sequential presentation, with a "cause and effect" relationship shown between the facts stated and your inability to pay the tax in full.

The little known Form 1127 is a useful and significant way in which the average person can pay taxes on *his* terms, *not* theirs.

---

[9] IRM §57(14)8. 1(2).

3. The Offer in Compromise—

Internal Revenue Code §7122 provices that the IRS "may compromise any" civil or criminal case involving the tax laws. In the context of a civil case, the term "compromise" is not defined but is widely accepted, both inside and outside of the IRS, to mean that the government will accept a *lesser* amount of tax than has been assessed. The regulation[10] overseeing this question recognizes just *two* grounds upon which a compromise may be accepted by the IRS.

(a) Where there exists proven doubt as to one's actual "liability" for the tax assessed; or

(b) Where there exists proven doubt as to the government's ability to "collect" the tax assessed.

The regulation goes on to state that "No such liability will be compromised if the liability has been established by a valid judgment or is certain, and there is no doubt as to the ability of the Government to collect the amounts owing with respect to such liability."

By submitting an offer in compromise, the citizen makes a *proposal* to the Internal Revenue Service. The proposal is that the citizen will agree to pay the IRS a *lesser* amount of tax than has been assessed. In making this offer, the citizen bears the burden to prove that either or both of the recognized conditions for accepting a compromise exist in the case. This is done on the face of the forms which are submitted to the IRS in support of the offer. If the IRS agrees to accept the offer, the difference between what was assessed and what was agreed upon as the lesser amount is abated and "all questions of such liability are conclusively settled thereby."[11]

The offer in compromise is submitted on Form 656. See Exhibit 5-2. If the offer is based upon doubt as to *collectability*, then a completed Form 433, *Financial Statement*, must accompany the offer (see Chapter Four, part 1). The IRS *will not* consider a "collectability" offer without the financial statement attached.

An offer which is based upon doubt as to *liability* does not require a financial statement, but the citizen must be willing to undergo an audit-type examination conducted either by the Examination Division or the Appeals Division, before the offer will be accepted.

---

[10] Rev. Reg. §7122-1(a).
[11] See previous footnote.

EXHIBIT 5-2

Form 656 (Rev. March 1985)	Department of the Treasury · Internal Revenue Service ## Offer in Compromise	▶ File in Duplicate ▶ See Instructions Page 4

Names and Address of Taxpayers		For Official Use Only	
		Offer is *(Check applicable box)*	Serial Number
		☐ Cash *(Paid in full)*	*(Cashier's stamp)*
Social Security Number	Employer Identification Number	☐ Deferred payment	
To: **Commissioner of Internal Revenue Service**	Date	Amount Paid $	

1. This offer is submitted by the undersigned proponents (persons making this offer) to compromise a liability resulting from alleged violations of law or failure

to pay an Internal Revenue liability as follows: _____
(State specifically the alleged violation involved, the kind of unpaid tax liability, and each period involved)

_____

_____

_____

2. The total sum of $ _____ paid in full or payable on a deferred payment basis as follows: _____

_____

_____

with interest at the annual rate as established under Section 6621(a) of the Internal Revenue Code (subject to adjustments as provided by Code Section 6621(b) and compounded under Code section 6622(a)) on the deferred payments, if any, from the date the offer is accepted until it is paid in full, is voluntarily tendered with this offer with the request that it be accepted to compromise the liability described above, and any statutory additions to this liability.

3. In making this offer, and as a part of the consideration, it is agreed (a) that the United States shall keep all payments and other credits made to the accounts for the periods covered by this offer, and (b) that the United States shall keep any and all amounts to which the taxpayer-proponents may be entitled under the Internal Revenue laws, due through overpayments of any tax or other liability, including interest and penalties, for periods ending before or within or as of the end of the calendar year in which this offer is accepted (and which are not in excess of the difference between the liability sought to be compromised and the amount offered). Any such refund received after this offer is filed will be returned immediately.

4. It is also agreed that payments made under the terms of this offer shall be applied first to tax and penalty, in that order, due for the earliest taxable period, then to tax and penalty, in that order, for each succeeding taxable period with no amount to be allocated to interest until the liabilities for taxes and penalties for all taxable periods sought to be compromised have been satisfied.

5. It is further agreed that upon notice to the taxpayers of the acceptance of this offer, the taxpayers shall have no right to contest in court or otherwise the amount of the liability sought to be compromised; and that if this is a deferred payment offer and there is a default in payment of any installment of principal or interest due under its terms, the United States, at the option of the Commissioner of Internal Revneue or a delegated official, may (a) proceed immediately by suit to collect the entire unpaid balance of the offer; or (b) proceed immediately by suit to collect as liquidated damages an amount equal to the liability sought to be compromised, minus any deposits already received under the terms of the offer, with interest on the unpaid balance at the annual rate as established under section 6621(a) of the Internal Revenue Code (subject to adjustments as provided by Code section 6621(b) and compounded under Code section 6622(a)) from the date of default; or (c) disregard the amount of the offer and apply all amounts previously deposited under the offer against the amount of the liability sought to be compromised and, without further notice of any kind, assess and collect by levy or suit the balance of the liabilty, the right of appeal to the United States Tax Court and the restrictions against assessment and collection being waived upon acceptance of this offer.

6. The taxpayer-proponents waive the benefit of any statute of limitations applicable to the assessment and collection of the liability sought to be compromised, and agree to the suspension of the running of the statutory period of limitations on assessment and collection for the period during which this offer is pending, or the period during which any installment remains unpaid, and for 1 year thereafter. For these purposes, the offer shall be deemed pending from the date of acceptance of the waiver of the statutory period of limitations by an authorized Internal Revenue Service official, until the date on which the offer is formally accepted, rejected, or withdrawn in writing.

7. The following facts and reasons are submitted as grounds for acceptance of this offer: _____

_____

(If space is insufficient, please attach a supporting statement)

8. It is understood that this offer will be considered and acted upon in due course and that it does not relieve the taxpayers from the liability sought to be compromised unless and until the offer is accepted in writing by the Commissioner or a delegated official, and there has been full compliance with the terms of the offer.

I accept the waiver of statutory period of limitations for the Internal Revenue Service.	Under penalties of perjury, I declare that I have examined this offer, including accompanying schedules and statements, and to the best of my knowledge and belief it is true, correct and complete.
Signature of authorized Internal Revenue Service Official	Signature of Taxpayer-proponent
Title	Date	Signature of Taxpayer-proponent

Form **656** (Rev. 3-85)

As a further condition of making the offer, the citizen must agree to waive (and in fact does so by signing the Form 656) the statutes of limitations both with respect to *assessment and collection* of the tax liability at issue. The waiver extends those statutes for the period in which the offer is pending, or the period during which installment payments are to be made under the offer if accepted, *and* for one year thereafter.[12] Whether or not the offer is accepted, the waiver is effective for the entire period that the offer is pending before the IRS. See Form 656, Exhibit 5-2.

The "waiver" conditions in Form 656 are profound. For this reason, care should be taken to determine the expiration dates of all appropriate statutes of limitations, in particular, the limitation period on *collection*. For example, if the limitation period on collection of a tax liability is to expire in one year, the wisdom of filing an offer in compromise at such a late date may be questioned. The reason is that during the period the offer is pending before the IRS, which itself may be as long as one year, the statute of limitations *ceases to run.* Moreover, under this example, an *additional year* is added to the statute if the offer is rejected by the IRS.

Under these facts, one could expect the following result: Suppose one files an offer in compromise just one year prior to the expiration of the collection period. Let us further suppose that the offer is pending before the IRS for one year before it is *rejected.* Upon being rejected, the citizen will be notified and informed that the interest and penalty *continued to accrue* while the offer was being considered.[13] So not only must the full tax liability be paid, but an additional year's worth of interest and "failure-to-pay" penalties are added to the bill. And as if that is not enough, the IRS now has *two more years* in which to collect the tax (the year the offer was pending *plus* one year). If no offer had been submitted, the IRS would have had just *one year* in which to collect the tax, without the accrued interest and penalty.

A. How is an Offer in Compromise Helpful?

There can be no question that the "down side" to filing an offer in compromise is significant. Still, there are positive and measurable benefits to an offer which should not be overlooked.

---

[12] Ibid, at subsection (f).
[13] IRM Part 5700 §57(10)(13).1(3).

1. *Questioning Liability*—

The first of two available grounds for compromising an assessment is when there is proven doubt as to one's *liability* for the tax. One specific example comes to mind where an offer questioning the assessed *liability* was successful. It involved a man who had filed a petition in the United States Tax Court and due to certain procedural failures on his part, as well as having submitted untenable legal positions to the court, lost his case.

Not only did the court assess a sizable tax liability against Gerry, but it imposed the $5,000 penalty for maintaining frivolous litigation before the Tax Court. Gerry petitioned the Tax Court jointly with his wife Judy. After the case went into Collection, we began negotiation with the Revenue Officer assigned to collect the outstanding bill. Efforts were being made by us to pay the tax in a fashion that was manageable by Gerry given his financial condition.

In the early stges of the negotiations, Gerry and Judy *both* were presented with *separate* bills. These bills, each for $5,000 over and above the tax assessment, purported to cover the penalty imposed by the Tax Court. The Revenue Officer insisted that the penalty had been assessed against each person, and further insisted that each person was separately liable for the $5,000 penalty.

We objected to the imposition of the *second* $5,000 penalty. I maintained that the Tax Court had assessed *one* penalty against *both* persons and not one penalty against *each* person. The Revenue Officer disagreed, as they routinely do, and pointed only to the certificate of assessments and credits as her proof. The certificate of assessments and credits is the computer-maintained statement of account which the IRS compiles for each citizen. The certificate is prepared by the IRS, usually at the Service Center. It is based upon data entered into the computer by IRS personnel. Hence, the information reflected in the assessment could only be as accurate as the person who placed it there.

I challenged the assessment on these grounds, and argued that the statute in question, §6673, authorized the assessment of *one* penalty per case in the maximum amount of $5,000. As the IRS viewed the case, *two* penalties had been assessed, one against each of the petitioners for a total of $10,000. Despite my presentation, the Revenue Officer would not budge from her position, holding tightly to the information contained in the certificate.

To remedy the problem, we filed an offer in compromise. the offer challenged the validity of the second $5,000 assessment.

Consequently, the offer was based upon the question of *liability* as opposed to the *collectability* of the tax. As proof that the second $5,000 penalty was improperly assessed, we submitted with the offer a full and complete copy of the Tax Court's Opinion and Judgment. The language of the Opinion and Judgment clearly stated that based upon the facts of the case, *one* $5,000 penalty was to be assessed against both citizens. Under the plain language of the Opinion, Gerry and Judy would be separately responsible to pay a maximum of *$2,500* each.

Furthermore, a copy of the statute itself was attached to the Form 656 as supporting documentation. Under the language of the statute, a *maximum* of $5,000 can be assessed in a given case. There is no authority in the statute to assess separate petitioners, in a joint case, $5,000 *each*. Based upon these facts, the offer proposed was that the IRS abate the second $5,000 penalty.

As a result of this presentation, the IRS did indeed abate the second $5,000 penalty within a short period of time. The offer in compromise procedure saved Gerry and Judy not only $5,000 but the interest and *additional* failure-to-pay penalties that would have been attached to that amount. When projected over a period of time, the savings were significant.

Other circumstances where an offer based upon *liability* may be beneficial are:

(a) Where an assessment has been made but never appealed;

(b) Where an assessment was made without consideration of important evidence or documentation necessary to fully understand the circumstances; or

(c) Where penalties have been added to the bill but never challenged in court for whatever reason.

The IRS defines its purpose of the offer based upon doubt as to "liability" thusly:[14]

> "Where there is a 'bona fide' dispute about a question or fact of law with respect to the merits of a tax liability, including interest and fraud or negligence penalties, *there is room for mutual concession.* The adequacy of the concession or consideration sufficient to justify accepting an offer in compromise is determined by an evaluation of the supporting evidence and circumstances." (Emphasis added.)

---

[14] IRM Part 5700 §57(10)7.42.

Based upon the above explanation, one can easily see that the sweep of an offer grounded in doubt as to "liability" is broad. Moreover, at least as a policy matter, the IRS approaches the offer with an open mind and in a spirit of negotiation. Whether the particular agents working *your* offer reflects that spirit is, of course, another matter!

The IRS Manual is also instructive as to what must be shown in order to prevail on an offer questioning the legality of an assessment. It provides[15] the following insight:

> "* * *The degree or quality of doubt necessary to afford a basis for compromise is not specific (in the statute). However, it has not been the practice of the Service to compromise a tax liability on the *mere suspicion* of doubt as to the amount legally due. A compromise is an adjustment or settlement of the tax liability by *mutual concessions* and, therefore, there must be room for 'give and take.' The amount acceptable will depend upon the degree of doubt found in the particular case. It is not the practice of the Service to use the compromise procedure in any case where a *definite determination* of the tax liability may be made through regular channels." (Emphasis added.)

In order to increase the "degree of doubt" present in your case, all definitive information available at the time the offer is made should be used to document your claim that the assessed liability is incorrect." The IRS generally will not accept vague or undefined claims of error in connection with an offer. As I demonstrated in the earlier example involving Gerry and Judy, the IRS will almost always perceive their assessment to be absolutely correct unless the case agent can be taken by the hand and shown otherwise. This is *your* responsibility when an offer is submitted.

Furthermore, offers based upon doubt as to "liability" will generally be rejected where the question of that liability has already been ruled upon by a court.[16] Under the language of the Manual, any liability determined by a court is "conclusively determined" as far as offer in compromise procedures are considered.

---

[15] IRM Part 5700, §57(10)7.41.
[16] IRM Part 5700, §57(10)7.431 and .432.

2. *Questioning Collectability*—

The second and only remaining ground for compromising a tax assessment is based upon doubt as to the *collectability* of the tax. Offers based upon this ground are *rarely* granted. The reason is that wide discretion is placed in the hands of the evaluating agents and officers. It is their responsibility to determine the amount of money which a given person is capable of paying against an assessment. The Manual[17] tells us that to be:

> "adequate, an offer to compromise a legally due tax liability must reflect the taxpayer's maximum capacity to pay, i.e. *all that can be collected* from the taxpayer's equity in assets and income, present and prospective." (Emphasis added.)

As you can see, the IRS expects a person to liquidate *everything* to pay his taxes. All assets, present and *future* are to be committed to the payment of the tax before the liability will be compromised. It does not take much experience to know that very few persons are willing to submit *every dime* to the IRS to pay a tax. Furthermore, what one person considers the value of an asset is not necessarily the value that will be ascribed to that same asset by the IRS. Indeed, when the IRS is to sell a seized asset at auction or by sealed bid, the value placed upon such an asset is *criminally low*. Yet when the IRS considers the same asset in the context of an offer in compromise, the value has a way of sailing like a balloon filled with helium.

The inequity of this inconsistency operates against the citizen in this manner. Suppose your car is worth $10,000. If the IRS were to seize the vehicle, it could be expected to sell it at auction for a fraction of its value, say $2,500. Yet when you make an offer in compromise, the IRS will claim the vehicle is worth the full $10,000, and will demand that amount in payment of the tax.

Consequently, the citizen is caught in the pincer movement by the IRS. When an offer is proposed, the IRS considers a person's ability to pay to be much greater than does the citizen. The difference is always due to the way in which the IRS perceives the value of your assets. As a result, the offer is rejected. In the same breath, the IRS will then seize your assets and present them for sale at *half the price* they would have realized had they accepted

---

[17] IRM Part 5700, §57(10)7.51.

your offer.

If all one has available to him as a negotiation maneuver is the offer based upon the *collectability* of the tax, conditions are bleak indeed. Still, for the creative negotiator and one unwilling to take "No" for an answer, there is room to move in connection with an apparently unacceptable offer.

Finesse in connection with a "collection" offer begins with an understanding of how the IRS values assets in the context of an offer. I will introduce you to three terms during this discussion. The terms refer to the value ascribed to assets. They are: (1) "forced sale value," which is the amount the IRS could obtain from a distraint sale of the asset; (2) "market value," which is the amount arrived at between a willing buyer and a willing seller; and (3) "Quick sale value," which is a compromise between "forced sale value" and "market sale value."

Each of these property values plays a role in determining what the IRS will accept as a final figure when passing upon the merits of a "collection" offer. Note however, that it is the "quick sale value" which shapes the IRS' thinking on the issue. Consider with me the following language from the Manual:[18]

> "For offer in compromise purposes, the taxpayer's equity in assets is defined as the *quick sale value* less any encumbrances against the asset which have priority over the Federal tax lien. *Quick sale value* is a valuation unique to the offer process. It is employed because of the nature of the offer investigation and the fact that the taxpayer and the Service are in a position to *negotiate, to make mutual concessions.* The two values normally considered in the collection of accounts are *forced sale value* and *fair market value.* The former represents the amount the Service can collect from a distraint sale of the taxpayer's assets; therefore, this value *does not* represent any concession on the taxpayer's part. The latter represents the value arrived at between a willing buyer and a willing seller and normally indicates the *maximum* valuation for the taxpayer's assets. *Between these two values there exists a wide range of possible asset valuations* (i.e. *quick sale value*) and any asset valuation in this range *can be acceptable* if negotiated and agreed upon by the taxpayer and the offer examiner. If the Service is in a

---

[18] IRM Part 5700, §57(10)7.51(3).

position to gain more revenue at less cost than can be secured through the enforced collection of all the taxpayer's assets, then the offer is a valuable collection tool. *The negotiation process should be open* and asset valuations (including determination of forced sale and market sale value) should be the result of *mutual agreement.* * * *" (Emphasis added.)

This Manual language is very, very significant and quite telling to those willing to listen. Even the published authorities on IRS procedure tend to overlook the importance of what is said here. Let us put it into perspective. The largest percentage of offers in compromise are submitted on the basis of inability to pay. And, the vast majority of these offers in compromise are *rejected* by the IRS. The reason for rejection is almost always that the IRS believes it can obtain more money from the citizen than is offered, either through "forced sale" of his assets or through future earnings. "Future earnings" are an important aspect of what the IRS considers when presented with such an offer.

In my experience, rejected offers are *rarely* negotiated despite the fact that IRS officers are instructed by *their manual* to negotiate the specific question of *asset value.* See Manual quotation cited previously. "There exists a wide range of possible asset valuations," say the manual. Within this wide range, any valuation "can be acceptable if negotiated and agreed upon by the taxpayer and the offer examiner." (Ibid.)

How then does one capitalize on this bit of information? First, avoid making the mistake most commonly made with offers which are based upon collectability. The mistake occurs when the value of assets is fixed by the citizen at the "forced sale value" under the theory that if the IRS were to sell the property itself, that amount is all it would realize. The IRS will not accept "forced sale value" in compromise negotiations. The reason is, forced sale value represents *no compromise* by the citizen. The IRS could obtain that amount *anyway.* Why should it compromise a tax in favor of an amount they could receive *without* a compromise? As the manual itself states, such a value "does not represent any concesson on the taxpayer's part."

Next, we must recognize what is plainly written between the lines within the manual. While the IRS does not say so in the same simple language with which it addresses the issue of accepting the "forced sale value" of assets, it nevertheless plainly suggests that "market sale value" is *equally negotiable.* You will recall that the "market sale value" is that which can be realized from the sale of property to a willing buyer from a willing seller. That is the "maximum valuation" of one's assets.

While IRS offer examiners will often insist that "market sale value" is that which must form the basis of the offer, *the manual clearly states otherwise. "Beween these two valuations,"* proclaims the manual, is where the common ground is found upon which the compromise is based. It requires negotiaton. More importantly, it requires *knowledge* of the issues which are negotiable.

Asset value is not the only issue which is considered by the IRS in connection with a collection offer. The IRS will also carefully consider the "taxpayer's earning capacity."[19] In this respect, information about one's age, education, profession or trade, experience, health, past and present income and *future* prospects will be evaluated. It is within these intangible areas that offers often times become bogged down. The reason is that no clear guidelines exist with respect to evaluating these aspects of the case.

It is important to restate the fact that any offer based upon "collectability" which *does not* present a financial statement will be rejected summarily. The reason for this is that the IRS will consider *all assets* which the citizen owns when deliberating the offer. These assets, as shown in Form 433, *Statement of Financial Condition* (Chapter Four, Exhibit 4-1), include cash, securities, life insurance, pension and profit sharing plans, furniture, fixtures and pesonal effects, machinery and equipment, trucks and automobiles, inventory, receivables, business licenses, the value of an ongoing business, and real estate.

These assets will be evaluated by Collection personnel to determine whether the offer presented is acceptable under the circumstances. Generally, the citizen is offered an opportunity to meet with Collection personnel after the offer is submitted in order to discuss the various aspects of the offer. Of particular interest in this meeting is the value of assets shown on Form 433, and one's ability to pay.

This is where the citizen must be prepared to negotiate what may very well be a hard line position espoused by the Revenue Officer *vis-a-vis* the value of assets.

---

[19] IRM Part 5700, §57(10)7.51(6).

3. How much do I offer?—

This is a very difficult question to answer because offers in compromise are rarely accepted, even when they are reasonable and well-documented in all respects. The manual states[20] that the objective of the offer in compromise is to "effect maximum collection with the least possible loss or costs to the Government." Within this very broad framework, we can begin to identify some guideposts to which one can look to find an answer to this question.

First of all, as we just discussed at length, one must determine the existing equity in the assets he owes. Remember that for purposes of the offer, the "equity" is defined as the "quick sale value." Any offer which represents *at least* one's "quick sale" equity *should* be acceptable. Let me illustrate. Suppose the citizen has an unpaid income tax liability, with interest and penalties, in the amount of $45,000. Further suppose that the citizen's only asset is the family homestead, worth $120,00. The home has a mortgage at First Bank in the amount of $70,000. The mortgage pre-dates the tax assessment. Therefore, the bank's mortgage has "priority" over the IRS' claim. The citizen's maximum equity in the property is $50,000.

Before IRS Revenue Officers will consider a seizure and forced sale of the property, they will consider the fact that First Bank *must* receive the value of their mortgage ($70,000) *before* any other creditor, including the IRS, will be paid. Hence, in order for a forced sale to be of any benefit to the IRS, the property must be offered for *more than* $70,000. Still, IRS sale habits being what they are, it would be unusual for a Revenue Officer to sell such a parcel for much more than the mortgage value of the asset. It is not unheard of for the IRS to sell such a parcel of property for just 25% *or less* of the owner's equity. What that means is the $120,000 home would be sold for $82,500. Since $70,000 must be paid to the bank, just $12,500 is left to be applied against the tax liability.

These events leave the citizen not only homeless, but with a remaining tax liability in excess of $32,000. Obviously, the Government's purposes of collecting tax revenues are not served, as only 27% of the liability has been collected and the citizen has no further assets from which the liability could be satisfied. But clearly the most significant damage is done to the citizen. One would think that the IRS would endeavor to sell a citizen's only

---

[20] IRM Part 5700, §57(10)1.4.

asset for the *maximum amount* possible in order to satisfy the greatest possible amount of the liability. Not so. I have come to believe that the IRS sells property just for the sake of the sale, without regard to the amount of money which is either owed to the government or can be realized from a legitimate sale.

Based upon this knowledge however, it can be said that an offer in compromise which presents an amount that is *more* than the "forced sale value," but *less* than the full market value of one's equity, would be acceptable. Following our earlier example, the citizen could have offered the IRS a full 50% ($25,000) of his maximum equity in the property. If accepted, the IRS would have realized *twice* as much money than if they had proceeded to a forced sale of the property under ordinary conditions. This would have saved the citizen not only $20,000 in taxes (the difference between the total owed to the IRS and the amount offered), but most importantly, it would have *saved his home!*

An important question to consider when structuring an offer is, how much money does the citizen earn each year? Obviously, the higher the "disposable" income (income after taxes), the more cash the IRS can expect to receive through wage levies. The difficulty with this aspect of the negotiation is that the IRS, if it chooses, could levy *all* but $150 per pay period of a person's paycheck. This reality sometimes leaves Revenue Officers cold to the idea of a compromise. Still, there is a time value to money. Money paid now is worth more than money paid over a lengthy period of time. This must be considered too.

A third consideration is the age of the citizen, his health and capacity to earn income in the future. An elderly citizen with poor prospects for future income sufficient to fully pay the liability weigh in favor of a low offer. In addition, a young citizen with little or no skills, or one employed in a highly capricious industry such as construction, may stand a better chance of selling a low offer than would a corporate executive only temporarily out of work.

A fourth, very important consideration is this: It is important to communicate to the Revenue Officer your good faith and a sincere desire to *resolve* the situation. If the Revenue Officer believes you are stalling or otherwise not attempting to negotiate in good faith, your offer could be summarily rejected.[21] On the other hand, if the Revenue Officer takes you seriously and works with you to

---

[21] Rev. Reg. §301.7122-1(d)(4).

prepare an acceptable offer, two very important goals are achieved. First, enforced collection action will be *stayed* if the interests of the IRS are not jeopardized by the stay.[22] Secondly, the Revenue Officer assigned to the case becomes somewhat of an ally working with you to have the offer accepted by his managers. Without the support of the Revenue Officer in this respect, chances are *de minimus* that your offer will be accepted against the judgment or recommendation of the Revenue Officer. For these reasons, the offer must be sufficiently high as to avoid being perceived as "frivolous" and summarily rejected.

Through all of this, the question remains, "How much should I offer?" A clear answer continues to elude us because it is a question which has no clear answer. The answer is entirely dependent upon all of the facts and circumstances of each case. I *can* say this: My experience has taught me that one is in a much better position if he is *responding* to an offer of settlement, rather than *making* an offer of settlement.

Let me explain. I once *tried* to sell a used car. My classified newspaper ad explained that my asking price was $4,200. A man arrived with his daughter to see the car. After a ride, a description of the car's features and some conversation, we worked around to the issue of money. "I would like to get $4,200," I said.

"Will you take less than that?" he asked.

Right away I responded by saying "I suppose if I had to, I'd take $3,800."

At the very moment I made that statement, my hope of ever getting $4,200 from this prospect had completely evaporated. Why should he pay full price when I already agreed to take *at least* $400 less? And that was just the beginning!

Whether negotiating with the IRS or trying (futilely in my case) to sell a used car, the principles are the same. When *you* state a position with respect to price (assuming price is the point of negotiation), your adversary is in an ideal posture to *move you off that position.* Therefore, the best possible way to fix a starting point for price (or in this case, payment) purposes, is to let your adversary do the fixing!

But where the offer in compromise is concerned, *you* are the one making the offer. How then can you put the *IRS* into the position of fixing the starting point? It is sometimes difficult, but it can be

---

[22] Ibid, at §(d)(2).

done. It happens this way:

I stated earlier that it is important to enlist the support of the Revenue Officer to the extent possible. It is accomplished through discussions with the Revenue Officer, in general terms, about the prospects of making an offer. Remember, the recommendation of the officer will no doubt be carefully considered when higher-ups are deciding whether to accept or reject the offer. The Revenue Officer will probably never suggest to you the precise terms which your offer should present, but may offer guidance on what is *unacceptable.*

To illustrate, in a recent negotiation with tax collection officials, an attorney and I were attempting to settle the question of Darryl's $75,000 tax liability. Rather than ask the question "Will you take $45,000 (the amount Darryl was capable of paying) to settle this case?," I presented the question this way: "What will the government be willing to consider as a reasonable offer to settle this case?"

After some careful deliberation, we got an answer. The response was that officials would probably be willing to cut "half the interest off the bill to settle the matter completely." Half the interest amounted to about $17,000. That would make the total due $58,000, still well above the amount Darryl had in mind. However, the affirmative response *fixed a starting point.* More importantly, *they* fixed it—we did not!

After this initial conference, we structured a written offer of $25,000! With the offer, we presented detailed reasons why the offer was not frivolous, though it was well below the amount "mentioned" by the government in negotiations. Of course the offer was rejected, but with the rejection came a clear signal of what we would have to do in order to settle the case. With the rejection we were told that Darryl would have to, "Pay all the tax."

"All the tax" amounted to $44,000 plus change, almost exactly what Darryl was willing to spend. An agreement was reached and the paperwork was set in motion to seal the deal.

The success of this negotiation hinged upon one thing. We subtly maneuvered the agent into a position of fixing a figure. Once this had been done, we took advantage to assure that our predetermined payment amount, if not less, would be accepted.

It is not always possible to put a Revenue Officer into a position of fixing an amount. Some Revenue Officers will not even discuss amounts. "Make an offer," they bark. "Then we'll see what happens." Surely under these circumstances one must simply proceed accordingly.

4. *Collateral Agreements—*
IRS Form 2261 is the collateral agreement. In some cases, a collateral agreement is demanded by the IRS before an offer will be accepted. The IRS describes the purpose of the collateral agreement as follows:

> "By accepting an offer in compromise, the Government releases the taxpayer who is unable to pay the account in full from the payment of assessed liabilities and/or any proposed assessment. The assessment is abated once the taxpayer satisfies all terms of the offer. In return for this abatement, it is reasonable to expect that the taxpayer will agree to pay additional sums from future income (contingent on financial success) or be willing to give up potential tax benefits as additional consideration for acceptance of the offer." IRM Part 5700 §57(10) (11).21.

Collateral agreements are not always required. They are sought only when "there is a reasonable possibility of recovering more than a nominal amount."[23]

The most common collateral agreement is the "future income" collateral agreement. An example of this form is found in Chapter Four, Exhibit 4-6, along with a description of other collateral agreements. With this agreement the IRS obtains from the citizen an agreement to pay additional sums of money, either in cash or through waived tax benefits, as consideration for the abatement granted by the offer. When an offer proposes to pay amounts in installment payments, the "future income" collateral agreement will be used to secure those installments.

5. *Deposits submitted with the Offer—*
While it is not *formally* required, the recognized practice with respect to offers in compromise is to submit with the offer a deposit against the amount offered. For example, an offer to pay $10,000 in installments over three years may be accompanied by a $1,000 or ten percent deposit, as a demonstration of good faith and sincerity.

---

[23] Ibid. §.31.

If the offer is rejected, the IRS is *required* to refund the deposit in the absence of specific authorization from the citizen to apply it to the tax bill. However, care should be taken when considering whether and what amount to provide as a deposit with the offer. The reason is that if the offer is rejected, it is not unusual for the IRS to *keep* the deposit, regardless of its rules to the contrary!

6. *When the answer is "NO."—*
An offer in compromise which is not summarily rejected as frivolous but is rejected nevertheless, may be appealed to the Appeals Division. The procedure for doing so is virtually identical to that followed in appealing an adverse audit decision. When an offer is rejected, IRS pattern letter 931(DO) will be mailed to the citizen with the bad news.

Where the amount in controversy is less than $2,500, the citizen need only respond to letter 931(DO) within the time specified. Your response would request an appeal of the decision to reject the offer. Where the amount in controversy is in excess of $2,500, the citizen must submit a written protest in order to receive Appeals Division consideration of the case.[24]

The Appeals conference affords the citizen the right to present to a fresh face, all of the facts and circumstances of the case. As we already know, the Appeals Division has a much more reasonable approach to most matters than do other divisions, especially the Collection Division.

If properly prepared and negotiated, the Offer in Compromise can be a most effective way in which to pay taxes on your terms, not theirs.

4. Designating Payments of Taxes

Designating payments to the IRS could well be the least understood procedure created by the government for the administration of taxes. Designating payments of taxes is indeed a "science." Properly done, it can save a citizen thousands of dollars.

We begin the study of "designology" with this basic premise: Not all remittances of money to the IRS are considered by the IRS as "payments of tax." Why is this important? It is important because under certain circumstances, "payment of tax" to the IRS *eliminates* one's right to contest the assessment of additional taxes.

---

[24] IRM Part 5700, §57(10)(16).3(2).

At the same time, a "payment of tax" may be ignored by the IRS and treated in some other fashion. When this happens, a citizen shockingly discovers that his "tax payments" were not "tax payments" at all. Rather, they were applied only to interest and penalties.

Unless a remittance to the IRS is designated in some fashion, the IRS will usually, but not always, consider that remittance to be a "payment of tax." This can become a problem if, after an audit, the IRS agent convinces the citizen that "pre-paying" the tax will afford some degree of relief from interest. It is true that "pre-paying" will provide some relief, but it is equally true (and unexplained) that pre-paying will *deprive* one of his right to appeal the adverse decision through conventional channels.

After the IRS has issued an examination report, but *before* it has issued a notice of deficiency, the examiner will encourage the citizen to pay the tax even though he may disagree with the amounts proposed. The theory is that "pre-payment" will prevent additional interest from accumulating on the amount due, interest which can amount to thousands of dollars. If one does pre-pay the tax, the IRS will *not* send a notice of deficiency to the citizen.

It is important at this juncture to understand that receipt of a notice of deficiency is the one and only condition upon which a person may gain access to the Tax Court. Without a notice of deficiency, the only remedy available to contest the tax is to file a claim for refund. If the claim is denied, a suit for refund can be filed in the United States *District Court*. These procedures are generally considered more complex than the Tax Court route, and are almost *never* explained to the citizen.[25]

Undesignated remittances are perhaps the most common forms of payment received by the IRS. The reason is that never, in my experience, does the IRS explain the significance of designating remittances.

The IRS classifies *undesignated* remittances in one of two ways. Payments are received either *before* the IRS has proposed any additional tax increases, or *after* an examination report suggesting the changes has been mailed.[26] Persons often make payments to the IRS before it has recommended changes as a result of being convinced by the agent that (1) there is likely to be a tax due at the completion of the audit, and (2) pre-payment will

---

[25] See *The Naked Truth*, pages 87-90.
[26] Rev. Proc. 84-58, 1984-2 CB 501, effective with respect to remittances made on or after October 1, 1984.

stop interest from accumulating. Undesignated remittances received *before* any tax increases are proposed are treated in the following manner:

(a) These funds are considered deposits against any future liability;

(b) They *are not* subject to claims for refund or credit as they are not considered overpayments;

(c) They *will not* earn interest even though they may exceed the amount of the liability ultimately determined by the IRS;

(d) They *will be* returned at the citizen's request unless a jeopardy assessment is made or a liability for other years is outstanding; and

(e) Since they are treated as deposits, the interest on any liability ultimately determined, *will cease* running as of the date the remittance was received.

Undesignated remittances received by the IRS *after* any tax increases are proposed will be treated much differently. They will be applied as follows:

(a) They will be considered a remittance in "payment of tax" and will *prevent* a notice of deficiency from being issued;

(b) They will be applied first to tax, then to penalty and interest beginning with the earliest year at issue and proceeding in the same order through the remaining years.

As is easy to see, merely sending the IRS money without designating it in some way, very seldom works to the benefit of the individual. For this reason, one should be aware of the various ways in which to designate remittances to the IRS, and under the circumstances, to designate such payments in a manner which will best suit your needs. In Revenue Procedure 84-58,[27] the IRS has established procedures whereby a person can make remittances of money in order to *both* stop the running of interest *and* preserve one's option of petitioning the Tax Court for a review of the deficiency. Let us review those procedures.

A. *Deposit in the nature of a cash bond—*

Remittances of money will be considered deposits in the nature of a cash bond if:

1. They are made *before* a notice of deficiency is mailed; and

2. They are designated *in writing* as a "deposit in the nature of a cash bond."

---

[27] See previous footnote.

When this type of payment is made, interest on the additional tax will stop accumulating on the date the deposit is received, even if the liability is not actually assessed at that time. The significance of the "deposit in the nature of a bond" is that the citizen *will be* mailed a notice of deficiency even though he has made the deposit. This fact leaves open the alternative of petitioning the Tax Court for a redetermination of the deficiency.

If one actually decides not to petition the Tax Court, at the expiration of the 90-day period the tax will be assessed and the deposit posted as payment of the tax. Since the interest ceased accumulating at the time of the deposit, no further interest would be due on the liability. The matter would be closed.

A deposit will be returned to the citizen upon request at any time *before* the tax is assessed. Therefore, in the event the Tax Court were to rule in favor of the citizen, he need only request his money back in order to receive a refund of all or part of the deposit.

B. *Post-statutory notice remittances—*

As I have explained, payments made before a notice of deficiency is mailed to a citizen could well eliminate as a review option the right of a Tax Court trial. On the other hand, payments made *after* the notice of deficiency was mailed will *not* deprive the Tax Court of jurisdiction to hear your case should you opt that avenue of review.

Any payment in complete or partial satisfaction of the deficiency that is made *after* a notice of deficiency has been mailed is considered a "payment of the tax." It will be posted to one's account. If a payment is designated as a "deposit in the nature of a cash bond," the IRS will treat it as such. Both the post-statutory notice payment and the "deposit in the nature of a cash bond" will result in a termination of the accumulation of additional interest at the time the remittance is received.

C. *Payments of Tax—*

"Payments of tax" are the third way in which remittances to the IRS may be designated. Remittances will be considered "payments of tax" if so designated, or if the payment:

(a) is *not* designated as a deposit;

(b) is made in response to a proposed liability, such as a Revenue Agent's report; and

(c) fully satisfies the liability.

When a "payment of tax" is made, the IRS will post the

amount to one's account. No notice of deficiency will be mailed and hence, no Tax Court review will be afforded. The interest will stop running, and any excess will be returned to the citizen. These procedures are followed when the payment equals or exceeds the amount of the tax claimed. "Payments of tax" are treated as assessed amounts and in the event the tax has been *overpaid*, interest and compound interest will apply.

You may have noticed that in my discussion of designating payments I have concentrated on those payments which are made *before* the tax liability actually becomes assessed. It is very important to designate payments under these circumstances for the reasons expressed, the most notable being the possibility of eliminating Tax Court as a viable avenue of review.

Where remittances are made *after* the tax has been assessed, i.e., after a notice of deficiency has expired or a waiver consenting to assessment has been signed or one has lost his case in the Tax Court, other factors must be considered. For example, payments against an assessment such as that just described is supposed to be applied first to tax, then to penalty and lastly to interest, beginning with the earliest year in question. This same order will be followed for each subsequent year if more than one is in question. I say, "supposed to," because it is all too common for the IRS to apply payments contrary to this.

For example, a small construction corporation got behind on its employees' withholding payments. The debt was $17,000 and covered three calendar quarters. It was less than one year old when the IRS contacted Ken, the corporation's officer. Ken began making immediate payments to the IRS and within eight months, had paid $17,000. After the final payment was made, the Revenue Officer phoned Ken and stated that his payments satisfied only the "interest and penalties" and that he still owed $16,000 to the IRS. This type of act is a regular occurrence.

Since interest rates have seen much fluctuation over the years, it may be desirable to pay taxes assessed for one year before the payment of taxes in an earlier or later year. To accomplish this, payments of tax may be designated to any year by so stating in writing. Provided the tax has already been assessed, one may also designate partial payments between interest and taxes.

Before sending any money to the IRS, it behooves a person to first determine whether any assessment has been made. If the answer is no, great care should be taken to designate one's payment in such a manner as to preserve the greatest degree of flexibility in the review process. Then, any remittance should be mailed to the IRS with a letter plainly designating the manner in which the remittance is to be treated.

If an assessment has been made, then one should consider which year (if more than one is concerned) should be paid first. One factor to consider here is the rate of interest which is charged at the time the assessment is due. It is my opinion that any partial payments of an assessed liability should be designed to the "tax" for a given year. This will prevent the kind of treatment afforded Ken and his corporation.

Another factor will be discussed later and involves the question of bankrupting tax liabilities.

Next, one must consider whether it is desirable to apply payments to interest as well as to taxes. As we all know by now, the itemized deduction available for interest paid on personal indebtedness is disappearing quickly. It may be desirable to designate payments to interest while the deduction still exists, at least in part.

Conclusion—

If I have learned anything dealing with the IRS over the years, it is that *nothing* can be taken at face value. Even something so simple and honest as a person's desire to pay a tax to avoid additional interest can come back to haunt him if not properly carried out. It is my desire that the procedures discussed in this chapter will provide hope to one convinced that his tax assessment is a hopeless situation. Negotiation by its very definition means the employment of *alternatives* to achieve a solution. When tax collection is the problem, these alternatives have provided significant relief to many citizens.

Chapter Six

3 IRS TOOLS OF COLLECTION AND HOW TO NEUTRALIZE THEM

Introduction

"The physical power to get the money does not seem to me a test of the right to tax. Might does not make right even in taxation."
—Supreme Court Justice Robert H. Jackson in
International Harvester Company v. Wisconsin Department of Taxation, 322 US. 435 (1944)

The IRS is a federal agency unique in the degree of its power, the sweep of its reach, and the dimension of its authority. The IRS asserts, and federal courts too often agree, that there is no citizen beyond the grasp of its ability to assess and collect taxes. One court described the powers as "herculean muscularity of Goliathlike reach. . ."[1] While this description may be an example of poetic overindulgence, it is nevertheless true.

Since the beginning of income taxation in the United States, the federal courts have taken the paternal view that tax collection is an "overriding governmental concern." This exaltation of tax collection has allowed Congress and the IRS to take liberties with individual rights which the courts have by and large refused to sanction. The result has been the promulgation of statutes, regulations and court decisions which have seriously eroded, and in some cases even eliminated one's rights under the Constitution.[2]

Even beyond this, the IRS has been wildly aggressive with respect to tax collection, so much so that it has created an *adversarial* environment in this area. The "us-against-them" attitude has caused IRS personnel to become insensitive to the financial problems faced by many Americans. Consequently, rather than finding ways to help a financially troubled person get into compliance with the law, the IRS goes on the "attack," too often without regard to the reasons why a person may be delinquent.

---

[1] **Carson v. United States,** 560 F.2d 693 (5th Cir. 1977).
[2] *The Naked Truth,* Chapter Six.

The underlying belief that individual IRS agents can do anything to "get the money," has lead to unlawful acts by government agents which would never be tolerated by the courts had they been performed in any other area of law enforcement. But because of the idea that tax collection is paramount, often individual rights are made to suffer. In simpler terms, the IRS indeed believes that "might *does* make right."

The IRS' power to lien, levy and seize property is the "might" which is thrown around in a most reckless manner. As I have already pointed out in Chapter One, the incidents of levies and seizures by the IRS between 1981 and 1986 have increased by 154% and 119% respectively. What makes these figures troubling is that such dramatic increases occurred at a time when delinquent tax accounts rose by only 35%. The worst part is that the levy and seizure power of the IRS is probably the most devastating power which the IRS, or for that matter, any federal agency, possesses. The power to levy a person's paycheck seizing all but $150 per pay period is a very sobering notion.

While most citizens may not personally have had such telling experiences with the tax collector, they know or have heard of someone who has. Reports abound of how this or that person was treated unfairly, or in fact illegally, by the IRS. The result is that the people of this country are terrified of the IRS. And the question resounds, "What can be done about it?"

For years, the suggested answer to this question has been a Taxpayers' Bill of Rights Act. This legislation, in one form or another, is said by its proponents, both within and without government, to be the only way in which a "run-away" IRS train can be brought under control. This type of legislation is nothing new. It dates back to the time of Henry Bellmon. In 1969, Senator Bellmon called upon the Congress to shackle the IRS' abusive tendencies. But reform was not to be.

Since that time, some version or another of the Taxpayers' Bill of Rights Act has bounced around Congress. In October of 1988, a Taxpayers' Bill of Rights Act was finally passed. Whether this act, S. 1774, will accomplish what its proponents say it will, remains to be seen.

Some time ago, I did a radio interview on a popular Cincinnati talk show. The subject was the Taxpayers' Bill of Rights Act which was working its way through Congress at the time. As the Bill was receiving much attention from tax activist groups, the show's controversial host wanted to discuss the issue with me. I had made no secret of the fact that I had studied the Bill and had some definite reservations regarding its various provisions.

"The Bill is legislative window dressing," I told the host and his many listeners over the airwaves. "I do not believe that Congress is considering legislation which will have a major, favorable impact on the rights of the individual. As a matter of fact, this Bill is more in the nature of 'election year' legislation. I wouldn't be surprised if this kind of thing doesn't pass for another year."

Shortly after this radio broadcast was completed, the Taxpayers' Bill of Rights Act as proposed in the spring of 1987, was defeated in Congress. It was introduced in April of 1987 by Senator David Pryor as S.604. After conducting many hearings and listening to much testimony from countless witnesses, Congress chose to reject the proposal.

On September 25 of 1988 (an election year) Pryor re-introduced the Bill as S.1774. After conducting almost no hearings and taking virtually no testimony, the Bill *passed* both the House and the Senate just about two weeks after it was introduced. Now why do you suppose I am not surprised that the Bill of Rights Act passed Congress with little or no opposition in 1988, when in all the previous years that similiar legislation had been proposed, it was killed and never even given a decent burial? You guessed it! It is an election year!

Legislative window dressing now graces the halls of Congress, enabling those who supported the Bill (almost everybody this time around) to go back to his constituency bragging, "I helped pass the Taxpayers' Bill of Rights Act. I deserve to be re-elected." Just days after the Act passed, both 1988 presidential candidates announced his support for the legislation, while previous to that, not a word was uttered.

I have been an outspoken critic of the Taxpayers' Bill of Rights Act as proposed and passed, but not because I am against the idea of taxpayers' rights. On the contrary, my writings over the years have demonstrated that my work is dedicated in the most basic of ways to the *enforcement* and *enhancement* of taxpayers' rights. Rather, I have opposed the recently enacted legislation because I did not believe, and still don't, that the Bill provides the kind of taxpayer-relief from IRS abuse which the citizens of this country so desperately need and deserve.

David Pryor is the Chairman of the Subcommittee on Private Retirement Plans and Oversight of the Internal Revenue Service. This Subcommittee is part of the Senate Committee on Finance, of which Lloyd Bentson of Texas, is Chairman.

Among those in Congress supporting Pryor were Senators
Charles Grassley of Iowa and Carl Levin of Michigan. In 1980,
Senator Levin, as Chairman of the Senate Subcommittee on
Oversight and Government Operation, held hearings on the
"impact of IRS collection practices upon small businesses."[3] In his
prepared statement which was made part of the record of the
hearings on June 22, 1987, Senator Levin claimed that the Tax
Equity and Fiscal Responsibility Act (TEFRA) of 1982,
represents "some progress" in the area of improving "taxpayers'
rights."[4]

With my knowledge of TEFRA and the adverse affects that it
created, not only on "revenue enhancement," but upon IRS
collection practices, I find it nothing short of astonishing that
Senator Levin would refer to TEFRA as manifesting "some
progress" in the area of "taxpayers' rights."

Not only did TEFRA represent the largest single tax increase in
the history of the United States,[5] but the law added countless new
penalty provisions to the Code. Ironically, many of the penalty
provisions were structured to *bypass* the taxpayer-protection
apparatus within the Code. This renders the new penalties
immediately collectable *without any right* of appeal.

After adding so-called "assessable penalties,"[6] TEFRA added a
total of 5223 IRS employees for the *express purpose* of achieving
"better compliance with the Internal Revenue laws," many of
which were just then created.[7]

Of the 5000 plus new employees, 3000 are Revenue Officers
whose sole function is to collect assessed taxes. Revenue Officers
are the IRS employees who are empowered to use the seizure, lien
and levy. These are the collection tools which have received the
most criticism by Senator Pryor and others in hearings on the Bill
of Rights.

For example, Senator Levin pointed out the startling statistics
to which I referred earlier. He claimed that, "In fiscal year 1981,
there were 8848 seizures by the IRS nationwide. In fiscal year
1986, there were 22,450, over two and a half times as many (a 154

---

[3] Transcript of S. 604 Hearings held June 22, 1987, pages 15-16, and prepared statement of Senator Levin,
page 1.
[4] Statement of Levin, page 3.
[5] The July 12, 1982, Senate Finance Committee Report announced that the "budget effects" of the law would
raise a total of $288.3 billion over the six-year period from 1982-1987.
[6] Defined as those which may be collected without any taxpayer right of appeal.
[7] Finance Committee Report on TEFRA, page 310.

percent increase). The number of levies has also more than doubled, going from 740,103 in fiscal year 1981 to 1,617,982 in fiscal year 1986 (a 119 percent increase)."

"During this same period," Levin continued, "the number of tax delinquent accounts rose by only about a third, going from 1,436,000 in fiscal year 1981 to 1,938,000 in fiscal year 1986 (a 35 percent increase."[8]

Levin's apparent dismay over these dramatic increases defies understanding. It was Congress in 1982, which provided the IRS the tools and intitiative to "collect additional tax revenues of at least $1 billion in fiscal year 1984 and $2 billion in fiscal year 1985"[9] It was Congress who handed the IRS more laws designed specifically to utilize the seizures, liens and levies which only IRS Revenue Officers command. Congress handed the IRS over 5000 employees—60 percent of which were hired solely to wield these formidable collection weapons. Congress also handed the IRS additional funding to carry these directives to the people.[10]

Should Levin, or any other senator[11] be confused as to why the IRS has so dramatically increased its enforced collection actions when there has been no corresponding increase in delinquent tax accounts? I think not, since the Senate Report on TEFRA discloses that these enforcement personnel were *projected* to collect a total of $10.1 billion in the six years from 1982-1987.[12] The facts seem to indicate that these 5000 plus tax collectors are doing their jobs quite efficiently.

The issue now is whether the very same senators who gave the IRS their awesome and arbitrary power and the means to exercise it, have through the Taxpayers' Bill of Rights, earnestly and sincerely attempted to emasculate the Frankenstein monster they have created. As to this question, history alone will be the judge. In the meantime, citizens need help. How to neutralize the ravaging effects of the tax lien, levy and seizure is of paramount importance and is the focus of this Chapter.

1. The Tax Lien—

An unpaid tax liability creates a lien in favor of the IRS A tax lien is much more potent than the typical lien because unlike any

---

[8] Levin's prepared statement, page 2.
[9] Finance Committee Report on TEFRA, page 310.
[10] Ibid, page 311.
[11] It should be noted that Senator Grassley was a member of the Senate Finance Committee in 1982, and had a hand in the TEFRA legislation.
[12] TEFRA Report, page 415.

other lien, the tax lien attaches to "all property and rights to property, whether real or personal" which belongs to the citizen.[13] Tax liens are generally filed with the Register of Deeds for the county in which the citizen resides. This constitutes "public notice" of the existence of the tax liability and the fact that the IRS has taken steps to protect its interest.

The presence of a lien will geneally prevent and real property from being sold and often times discourages any bank or other creditor from making new or additional loans to the citizen. Left unattended, tax liens can wreak havoc on a citizen for these and many other reasons. Their effects can be neutralized in the following ways:

A. *The Bond.* Tom owned a condominium in a fashionable Minneapolis suburb. He also had an unpaid tax liability in the amount of $50,000. The liability came as a result of a failing business which eventually led Tom into personal bankruptcy, but not before the IRS had filed its tax lien. Tom was attempting to sell his condominium to use the equity to pay creditors and the IRS. The real estate agency had located a buyer who had come to terms with Tom and his wife and was approved for credit. The only hitch was that the final title search revealed the presence of the lien. The closing company made it clear that unless the lien was satisfied and removed, the sale would not close.

Tom took his case to the Revenue Officer who had filed the lien. Tom logically suggested that if the IRS would just release the lien and permit the sale to close, it would receive full payment of the tax due from the profit he would realize from the sale. "After all," said Tom, "that is exactly why I am selling it."

But the Revenue Officer would hear none of it. He insisted that the lien could not be removed without full payment. Equity or no equity, the IRS would not release the lien and allow the sale to close. What too often happens under these circumstances is that after killing the sale of the property, the IRS will seize it. It will then be sold for fraction of what would have been realized had the IRS kept its hands off. The result is that the owner loses all of his equity in the house and ironically, the IRS generally receives only a fraction of the tax bill in payment.

Given the fact that Tom had a significant amount of equity in his home, I recommended that he provide the IRS with a bond. If

---

[13] Code §6321.

accepted, the bond would lead to a release of the lien. This is how it works:

The law authorizes the IRS to release a tax lien within 30 days after it has been provided with a bond for the tax, "together with all interest" on the tax.[14] We contacted a local bonding company. After paying the fee, which is typically 10% of the amount underwritten, the company issued a bond which met IRS requirements. To be valid, the bond must provide for the payment of the tax assessed, with interest, within six months of the date the statute of limitations on collection is due to expire. Included as Exhibit 6-1 is a copy of the bond form which the IRS uses. Unlike most IRS forms, it does not have a number. This form would be prepared by the citizen or his bonding company, and signed by both.

When the bond was created, the bonding company, or "Surety," agreed to be responsible for Tom's tax liability. The bond was written proof of that. In exchange for this promise, the bonding company was assured that if it had to pay the liability, Tom had sufficient assets which it could attach to cover the loss. As we already know, Tom had sufficient assets in the form of equity in his home. In addition, the bonding company wanted its fee to perform the service.

Once the bonding company was satisfied that Tom had sufficient assets to back the bond, it generated the paperwork and we picked up the completed documents. We then hand-carried the bond to the IRS Revenue Officer. We had a pre-arranged agreement to exchange the bond for a certificate of release of the lien. The certificate of release is the document on which the IRS notifies the public that the assessment has been satisfied or that their claim is otherwise no longer valid. We then hand-carried the certificate to the closing company. Upon reviewing it, they were satisfied that the lien was removed and that the sale could be finalized. Next, we filed the certificate of release with the County Recorder.

After the sale had been consummated and Tom received his money, we made another trip to see the Revenue Officer. This time we brought money which Tom had realized from the sale of his home. Pursuant to the terms of the bond, we paid the tax with interest, well within six months before the statute of limitations on

---

[14] Code §6325(a)(2).

EXHIBIT 6-1

Eh. 6-1

BOND FOR RELEASE OF FEDERAL TAX LIEN

(Section 6325(a)(2) of the Internal Revenue Code)

THIS BOND IS GIVEN BY_____OF _____
_____, AS PRINCIPAL, AND,_____
_____AS SURETY, TO THE UNITED STATES OF AMERICA.
THE PRINCIPAL AND SURETY ARE OBLIGATED TO THE UNITED STATES OF
AMERICA IN THE SUM OF_____DOLLARS!
($_____), LAWFUL MONEY OF THE UNITED STATES , PLUS ANY ADDITIONAL
ACCRUED INTEREST AND PENALTY AFTER_____UNTIL PAYMENT IS MADE
TO THE DISTRICT DIRECTOR, FOR WHICH WE JOINTLY AND SEVERALLY OBLIGATE
OURSELVES, OUR HEIRS, ADMINISTRATORS, SUCCESSORS, AND ASSIGNS.

IN VIEW OF THE FACT THAT --
          THE PRINCIPAL IS INDEBTED TO THE UNITED STATES IN THE SUM OF
_____ DOLLARS ($_____),
          ON ACCOUNT OF AN ASSESSMENT OF FEDERAL_____TAX;
          A NOTICE OF LIEN UPON ALL THE PROPERTY AND RIGHTS TO PROPERTY OF
          OF THE PRINCIPAL ON ACCOUNT OF THE ABOVE TAX INDEBEDNESS HAS BEEN
          FILED IN ACCORDANCE WITH SECTION 6323 OF THE INTERNAL REVENUE CODE
          OF 1954 OR CORRESPONDING PROVISIONS OF PRIOR LAW;

          SECTION 6325(a)(2) OF THE INTERNAL REVENUE CODE PROVIDES THAT THE
          DISTRICT DIRECTOR OF INTERNAL REVENUE MAY ISSUE A CERTIFICATE OF
          RELEASE OF THE LIEN FOR TAXES OF THE UNITED STATES IF HE IS FURNISHED
          AND ACCEPTS *** A BOND THAT IS CONDITIONED UPON THE PAYMENT OF THE
          AMOUNT ASSESSED, TOGETHER WITH ALL INTEREST AND PENALTY IN RESPECT
          THEREOF, WITHIN THE TIME PRESCRIBED BY LAW (INCLUDING ANY EXTENSION OF
          TIME), AND THAT IS ACCORDANCE WITH SUCH REQUIREMENTS RELATING TO
          TERMS,CONDITIONS, AND FORM OF THE BOND AND SURETIES THEREON, AS MAY BE
          SPECIFIED BY SUCH REGULATIONS,AND

          THE AMOUNT OF THIS BOND IS SUFFICIENT TO COVER THE INDEBETEDNESS
          DUE TO THE UNITED STATES BY REASON OF THE ABOVE TAX, TOGETHER
          WITH ANY RELATED INTEREST AND PENALTY:

THE PRINCIPAL DESIRES TO OBTAIN FROM THE DISTRICT DIRECTOR OF INTERNAL
REVENUE FOR THE_____DISTRICT A RELEASE OF THE ABOVE TAX LIEN
UPON THE PROPERTY AND RIGHTS TO PROPERTY COVERED BY THE LIEN, BY
FURNISHING THE DISTRICT DIRECTOR OF INTERNAL REVENUE THIS BOND AS
PROVIDED IN SECTION 6325(a) OF THE INTERNAL REVENUE CODE.

IN ADDITION, THE CONDITIONS OF THIS OBLIGATION ARE SUCH THAT IF THE
ABOVE TAX LIEN IS RELEASED BY THE DISTRICT DIRECTOR OF INTERNAL
REVENUE AND IF THE PRINCIPAL SHALL PAY TO THE DISTRICT DIRECTOR
ON OR BEFORE THE_____DAY OF_____,
FOR AND ON BEHALF OF THE UNITED STATES, THE FULL AMOUNT OF THE ABOVE
FEDERAL_____TAX TOGETHER WITH ANY RELATED INTEREST
OR PENALTY, THEN THIS OBLIGATION IS TO BE VOID. OTHERWISE, THIS
OBLIGATION IS TO REMAIN IN FULL FORCE AND EFFECT IRRESPECTIVE OF ANY
STATUTE OF LIMITATIONS AGAINST THE A COLLECTION OF THE ABOVE TAX.

WITNESS OUR SIGNATURES AND SEALS THIS   PRINCIPAL _____
                                         PRINCIPAL _____
      DAY OF_____19
SIGNED IN THE PRESENCE OF-
BOND APPROVED THIS   SURETY   _____
DAY OF_____19   SURETY   _____
                                         DISTRICT DIRECTOR

collection was to expire. Again, we had a pre-arranged agreement with the Revenue Officer to exchange cash for the bond which we had submitted several weeks earlier.

Now that we had the bond back in our possession, we marched into the office of the bonding company and had it canceled. Of course Tom did not receive a refund of the fee he had to pay before the bond was issued, but by canceling the bond, he was assured that he would never be called upon to make good on its promise. Before it would be canceled, we had to certify to the satisfaction of the bonding company that *it* would not be called upon by the IRS to fulfill the bond's promise. To accomplish this, we provided a receipt from the Revenue Officer which verified that the tax was paid in full.

The bond enabled Tom to guarantee that the sale of his home would not be killed by the tax lien. At the same time, it took his home out of the grasp of the IRS. The bond gave Tom the time he needed to raise the cash necessary to pay his taxes with the least amount of financial harm.

B. *Property double the amount of the liability.* Because of the "all-inclusive" nature of the tax lien, the IRS can and regularly does tie up property significantly greater in value than the amount of the liability. The tax lien need not identify a particular parcel of property in order to be operative against that parcel. The tax lien is a "general" lien; it attaches to all property owned by the citizen. This factor causes a problem which, if not properly addressed, can lead to a seizure of most, if not all of this property.

Suppose for example you own three homes. The first is your principle residence and the other two are rental properties. Let us further assume that your homestead is also worth $75,000, but the bank has a first mortgage on each unit in the amount of $25,000. Based upon all of this, your net worth (assuming no other assets or liabilities) is $175,000.[15]

Now let us assume that you owe the IRS $25,000. The government has filed a lien and because of it, the bank will not make a loan to you in order to pay the taxes. Banks will usually shy away from lending money under these circumstances for one major reason; they do not want to be a lender under conditions which make their security interest *secondary* to that of the IRS'. If

---

[15] Net worth is determined by adding the value of all assets, then subtracting the amount of all liabilities.

the bank were to lend money against the homestead (worth
$75,000), the mortgage created by that loan would be secondary to
the IRS' lien, since the lien was created prior to the mortgage.

The negotiation goal is to induce the IRS to release its lien from
the homestead. This will allow the bank to make a loan of $25,000
which can be used to pay the tax. Full payment will release the
remaining parcels from the lien as the liability will be satisfied.

Under a little-understood IRS Code section,[16] the IRS may
discharge a *portion* of property from a tax lien when the "fair
market value of that part of the property *remaining subject* to the
lien is *at least double* the sum of the amount of the unsatisfied
liability secured by the lien and of the amount of all other liens
upon the property which have priority over the lien."[17] (Emphasis
added.)

Let me explain how this arrangement works: We already know
that, under our example, we have three parcels of property. The
combined fair market value[18] is $225,000. The prior liens upon the
property, i.e., money owed to the bank for its mortgage, equal
$50,000 (two at $25,000 each). We must now add the value of the
unsatisfied tax liability ($25,000) to the amount of the prior liens
($50,000). The sum of these amounts is $75,000.

Before the IRS will release the lien on the homestead allowing
us to obtain a mortgage to pay the tax, we would have to
demonstrate that the fair market value of the remaining
properties (the two rental homes) is at least *twice* the amount of
$75,000 (the sum of the liability and the prior liens). In this case,
the combined fair market value of the rental properties is
$150,000 ($75,000 each), which is "at least double" the value of all
liens in question.

After presenting the IRS with the accounting necessary to
demonstrate these calculations, one can persuade the IRS, under
the authority of the law, to release a particular piece of property
from the lien. This move allows a person to obtain financing to pay
the tax. This will prevent the IRS from selling *all* property at a
fraction of what the property is worth.

Revenue Officers cannot be expected to inform citizens
burdened with a tax lien that these procedures are available. In
fact, while the IRS has a printed form to cover virtually every tax

---

[16] Code § 6325 (b)(1).
[17] Rev. Reg. §301.6325-1(b)(1).
[18] The term "fair market value" is defined the regulation as "that amount which one ready and willing but not
compelled to buy would pay to another ready and willing but not compelled to sell the property."

collection eventuality, there *is no form* applicable to the procedure I just described. The IRS leaves the matter entirely to the citizen to learn of this procedure and to submit his request to carry it out.

C. *The Subordination.* Another extremely effective method of negotiating around federal tax liens is the "subordination." Under this technique, the IRS agrees to make its lien "subordinate" to that of another creditor. Like the other methods, it can prevent the IRS from selling your property for pennies on the dollar.

Jim was a brilliant psychiatrist with a successful practice. After being "watched" by the IRS for a period of time, Jim's business and personal tax returns were audited by the IRS with a vengeance. After all was said and done, the IRS claimed that Jim owed $550,000 in taxes. Later however, it was proven that the IRS made at least $500,000 in "mistakes" and that the most Jim could have owed was "$23,000." Still, after all the arguing, the IRS was holding fast on its claim to $53,000 in taxes and penalties.

Despite the mistreatment that Jim received, he was doing his best to comply with the demands of the Revenue Officer assigned to the case. Jim owned a home on three acres of land in a highly publicized, nationally-known vacation area. The home was worth about $250,000, against which the bank held a $100,000 mortgage. The $150,000 equity in the home was more than adequate to pay the $53,000 tax bill. Jim had made arrangements with his banker to borrow the money. The sole proviso was that the IRS must agree to lift its lien, allowing the bank to rest in the first position as a security holder in the property.

Hopeful that the matter could be put behind him, Jim presented to the Revenue Officer the idea that the IRS could be paid in full "within three days" if he would simply lift the lien. The answer was as unreasonable as it was short, "No." Jim was eventually pushed into bankruptcy by a combination of IRS incompetence and unwillingness to permit him to work out of the difficulties they themselves had created.

What the Revenue Officer failed to inform Jim was that under the law,[19] the IRS has full authority to lift, or "subordinate" its lien under either of the following circumstances:

1. The IRS is paid an amount equal to its lien; or

---

[19] Code §6325(d).

2. The IRS would ultimately collect more money by subordinating the lien, and collection of the tax liability "will be facilitated by subordinating the lien."

The very purpose of the lien subordination procedure is to "facilitate tax collection." That is, to allow the IRS to do its job. Yet it is repugnant that Revenue Officers will not inform citizens of their ability to follow these procedures to obtain a lien subordination. Just as with the procedures mentioned earlier, there is *no IRS form* on which to submit an application for subordination. IRS Publication 784 does describe "How to Prepare" the application, but as one IRS official explained to me, "it makes the procedure seem far more complicated than it actually is." Despite this, I have included Publication 784 as Exhibit 6-2.

In a case such as Jim's, an IRS regulation[20] speaks directly to the matter. It states as follows:

> "* * *For example, if a notice of Federal tax lien is filed and a delinquent taxpayer secures a mortgage loan on a part of the property subject to the tax lien and pays over the proceeds of the loan to a district director after an application for a certificate of subordination is approved, the district director will issue a certificate of subordination. This certificate will have the effect of subordinating the tax lien to the mortgage."

Jim had "secured the mortgage" and fully intended to pay the proceeds to the IRS. This would have fully satisfied his tax liability. What Jim did not do, because he did not realize he was required to, was make an "application for a certificate of subordination" before the IRS would release the lien. All the Revenue Officer had to do was *inform* Jim that such was the case, but he refused.

The application for certificate of subordination must be "in writing."[21] According to IRS procedures,[22] it must be made in triplicate and must contain the following information:

1. Your name and address.

2. Whether the subordination is made under the first criterion (relating to "paymet of the amount subordinated" or the

---

[20] Rev. Reg. §301.6325-1(d)(1).
[21] Rev. Reg. §301.6325-1(d)(3).
[22] Rev. Proc. 68-8, 1968-1 CB 754.

EXHIBIT 6-2 (page one)

 Department of the Treasury
Internal Revenue Service
Publication 784 (Rev. 2-85)

How to Prepare

Application for Certificate of Subordination of Federal Tax Lien

(Submit your typewritten application and all accompanying documents in triplicate. Please read additional information on back.)

Address application to: District Director of Internal Revenue
(Address to District in which the property is located.)

Attention of: Chief, Special Procedures Staff

Give date of application:

Please give the name and address of the person applying, under section 6325(d)(1) or section 6325(d)(2) of the Internal Revenue Code, for a certificate of subordination. Give name and address of the taxpayer, and describe property as follows:

1. Give a detailed description, including the location, of the property for which you are requesting the certificate of subordination. If real property is involved, give the description contained in the title or deed to the property, and the complete address (street, city, State).

2. Attach a copy of each notice of Federal tax lien, or furnish the following information as it appears on each filed notice of Federal tax lien:

   a. The name of the Internal Revenue District;
   b. The name and address of the taxpayer against whom the notice was filed;
   c. The date and place the notice was filed.

3. Describe the encumbrance to which the Federal tax lien is to be subordinated, including:

   a. The present amount of the encumbrance;
   b. The nature of the encumbrance (such as mortgage, assignment, etc.);
   c. The date the transaction is to be completed.

4. List the encumbrances (or attach a copy of the instrument that created each encumbrance) on the property which you believe have priority over the Federal tax lien. For each encumbrance show:

   a. The name and address of the holder;
   b. A description of the encumbrance;
   c. The date of the agreement;
   d. The date and place of recording, if any;
   e. The original principal amount and the interest rate;

   f. The amount due as of the date of the application for certificate of subordination, if known (show costs and accrued interest separately);
   g. Your family relationship, if any, to the taxpayer and to the holders of any other encumbrances on the property.

5. Furnish an estimate of the fair market value of the property for which you would like a certificate of subordination.

6. If you are submitting the application under the provisions of section 6325(d)(1), show the amount to be paid to the United States.

7. If you are submitting the application under section 6325(d)(2), attach a complete statement showing how the amount the United States may realize will ultimately increase and how collection of the tax liability will be made easier.

8. Furnish any other information that might help the District Director decide whether to issue a certificate of subordination.

9. Furnish any other specific information the District Director requests.

10. Give a daytime telephone number where you may be reached.

11. Give the name, address and telephone number of your attorney or other representative, if any.

12. Make the following declaration over your signature and title: "Under penalties of perjury, I declare that I have examined this application (including any accompanying schedules, exhibits, affidavits, and statements) and to the best of my knowledge and belief it is true, correct, and complete."

EXHIBIT 6-2 (page two)

Additional information regarding

Application for Certificate of Subordination of Federal Tax Lien

Please follow the instructions in this publication when applying for a Certificate of Subordination of Federal Tax Lien.

The District Director has the authority to issue a certificate of subordination of a lien that is filed on any part of a taxpayer's property subject to the lien. The following sections and provisions of the Internal Revenue Code apply:

Section 6325(d)(1), if you pay an amount equal to the lien or interest to which the certificate subordinates the lien of the United States.

Section 6325(d)(2), if the District Director believes that issuance of the certificate will increase the amount the United States may realize, or the collection of the tax liability will then be easier. This applies to the property that the certificate is for, or any other property subject to the lien.

1. No payment is required for the issuance of a certificate under section 6325(d)(2) of the Code. Payment is required for certificates issued under section 6325(d)(1). Do not send the payment with your application, however. The District Director will notify you after determining the amount due.

2. The District Director will have your application investigated to determine whether to issue the certificate, and will let you know the outcome.

3. A certificate of subordination under section 6325(d)(1) will be issued after approval and upon receipt of the amount determined to be the interest of the United States in the property under the Federal tax lien. Make remittances in cash, or by a certified, cashier's, or treasurer's check drawn on any bank or trust company incorporated under the laws of the United States or of any State or possession of the United States, or by United States postal, bank, express, or telegraph money order. (If you pay by uncertified personal check, issuance of the certificate of subordination will be delayed until the bank honors the check.)

4. Instead of the description required in item (3) on the other side of this publication, you may submit a copy of each instrument under which you believe an encumbrance exists.

5. In certain cases the District Director may require additional information such as written appraisals by disinterested third parties, a list of all the taxpayer's property, or other information needed to make a determination.

Publication 784 (Rev. 2-85)

☆U.S. Government Printing Office: 1985—461-505/32287

second criterion (relating to "facilitating the collection of tax");[23]

3. A detailed description of the property for which the subordination is sought, including the street address and legal description as shown in the deed;

4. A copy of any Notice of Federal Tax Lien (IRS Form 668) must be attached, including a statement revealing the IRS district shown on each lien, the name and address of the "taxpayer" shown on each lien, and date and place of filing each lien;

5. A copy of the proposed documents which will create the liability to which the tax lien will be subordinate. An example of this would be a mortgage for any loan which a bank intends to make. You must also submit a description of the transaction, such as "mortgage to pay tax," and the date the transaction is to be completed;

6. If any other encumbrances exist upon the property, they must be disclosed, including the name of the holder of the

---

[23] These criteria are expressed in Code §§6325(d)(1) and (2).

encumbrance, the date it was created, the principle amount due, and a description of the encumbrance;

7. You must give an estimate of the fair market value of the property in question;

8. When seeking the subordination in order to obtain a mortgage, you must state the amount of money which will be paid to the IRS if the subordination is granted;

9. When seeking the subordination in order to "facilitate the collection of taxes," you must make a statement showing why you feel this will be accomplished if the subordination is granted;

10. Any other information which in your opinion might have a bearing upon the decision to subordinate;

11. The name and address of your attorney or representative if any; and lastly,

12. Your signature over a statement which declares that, "under penalty or perjury, all facts contained in the application are true and correct," and which *specifically requests* that the application be granted.

The most important of these steps are those described in paragraphs 5, 6, 8, 9 and 10. I mentioned earlier that Publication 784 makes the subordination procedure seem overly complex. The complexity may be avoided by focusing on the key paragraphs which I just identified.

Under the circumstances of Jim's case, there was no legal or other justifiable reason why the application should not have been granted. Jim's only downfall was that he *did not know* what you have just learned. His ignorance cost him his home. That need not happen to you.

D. *The Quiet Title Action.* A "quiet title" action is a suit in the district court which seeks to settle the question of property ownership. A quiet title action is usually brought when one party disputes another party's claim of ownership interest in real property. When a tax lien is filed and encumbers a parcel of property, the IRS is claiming, for all practical purposes, an ownership interest in that property to the extent of its lien. A quiet title action can sometimes clear a title clouded with a tax lien.

Doug was an airplane pilot who, like most pilots, deducted certain education expenses every year. The IRS disallowed these deductions on a nationwide basis. Doug's union sponsored a case to the United States Tax Court in which many pilots, including Doug, had joined. The Tax Court suit challenged the IRS' actions and sought a judgment permitting the pilots to deduct the expenses.

Doug claimed the deductions in question on his 1978 income tax return. They were disallowed in 1980, and unfortunately, the Tax Court ruled against the pilots in 1982. In the summer of 1982, Doug paid his tax bill, which amounted to $2,500. As far as Doug was concerned, the matter was closed.

In 1984, just over two years after paying the tax, Doug began receiving notices from Automated Collection. The bills stated that the tax liability has not been paid and that Doug owed $2,500. The notices also pointed out that if the tax was not paid immediately, "enforced collection action would be taken."

Knowing that the tax had been paid and confident that someone had merely overlooked this fact, Doug simply sent a pleasant letter to the IRS pointing this out. For convenience, he enclosed his copies of the canceled checks to prove he had fulfilled his responsibility, along with the letter. A few months later, he received another letter from ACS. Like the first letter, it stated that taxes for 1978 were due and owing, and that they had better be paid. This time, Doug got on the phone. Using the toll free number, he called the ACS office shown on the letter.

While on the phone with IRS personnel, he was unable to persuade someone to recognize that, yes, an error had been made. If he would just send another coy of his canceled checks (apparently the first copies had been lost), the discrepancy could be rectified. Faithfully, Doug re-mailed copies of the canceled checks with a cover letter reciting the details of the conversation. About a month later he received *another* threatening notice and then, much to his bewilderment, a tax lien was filed encumbering all of his property. The lien came at a most inopportune time as he was just then attempting to sell his house.

After recovering from the shock of the lien, he re-mailed to ACS copies of the checks a third time, and sent a second copy of the cover letter. He received no response. In the meantime, the lien prevented the sale of his house, which in turn prevented Doug and his wife from closing on a second home which the two were about to purchase.

Frustrated in his efforts to settle the matter, Doug turned to the federal courts for help. A little-known federal law[24] authorizes one

---

[24] 28 U.S.C. §2410.

to sue the United States if the purpose of the suit is to "quiet title to
. . . real estate or personal property on which the United States has
or claims a mortgage *or other lien.*" (Emphasis added.)[25] When
circumstances are ripe, the quiet title statute is a most effective
way to force the IRS to the table to settle the issue of a tax lien.

Once Doug's lawsuit was filed, an attorney was assigned to
represent the government in the case. The attorney made contact
with Doug and discussions began. Doug provided proof that his
tax liability had been paid in full. By the time all discussions had
been completed, the attorney agreed to lift the lien if Doug would
drop his suit. Since the only purpose of the suit was to remove the
lien, Doug saw nothing standing in the way of complying with this
request.

When the final paperwork changed hands, Doug obtained a
certificate of release of federal tax lien, which he carried to the
courthouse and filed. With the death of the lien, Doug's house sold,
allowing him and his wife to purchase their new home.

E. *Expiration.* I have talked much about the statute of
limitations on collection of taxes. I have stated repeatedly that a
tax may be collected for just six years beyond the date on which it
is assessed. Once that period of time has expired, the tax becomes
uncollectable by reason of age. Regulations[26] provide that the IRS
must release a tax lien when "the entire tax liability listed in such
notice of Federal tax lien has been fully satisfied. . .*or has become
legally unenforceable.*" (Emphasis added.)

One of the major failings with which the IRS has been charged
during Taxpayers' Bill of Rights hearings, was the failure to
release tax liens when taxes have been paid or when the period for
collection has expired. While I will never suggest that the IRS
should *not* take responsibility for its improper liens, I can say that
the *solution* to the problem is simple. It lies within the regulation
referred to in the previous paragraph.[27] The regulation provides
that citizens requesting a release of federal tax liens *may apply* for
such action by following several *simple* procedures. They are:

1. The request must be made in writing to the district
director for the district in which the lien was filed;

2. It must state the name and address of the person making

---

[25] Other factors come into play when suing the IRS. These are discussed in detail in Part 3(B) of this Chapter.
[26] Rev. Reg. $401.6325-1(a).
[27] Rev. Reg. §401.6325-1(f).

the request;

    3. It must include a copy of the lien which is the subject of the request; and

    4. It must state "the grounds upon which the issuance of a release is sought."

Just as with the subordination, there *is no form* on which a citizen can make this application. IRS Publication 783, entitled, "Instructions on How to Apply For" a certificate of discharge is, like its sister Publication 784 (Exhibit 6-2) *overly complex.* Nevertheless, I have included Publication 783 as Exhibit 6-3.

This *is not* a complex procedure, but it does put the responsibility on *your* shoulders. The citizen must make application for release of the lien. That application must conform to the requirements I have set out above. If the application is not made, there is nothing to suggest that the IRS will voluntarily release the lien. The Taxpayers' Bill of Rights Act does not change this fact, though much was made of this issue during the Bill of Rights hearings.

Section 22 of the Bill of Rights created a new IRS Code section which speaks to this issue. The new Code section is §7432. This new section allows a citizen to sue the United States when any "officer or employee of the United States knowingly, or by reason of negligence, fails to release a lien under section 6235..." The statute allows the citizen to recover the actual damages he sustained as a result of the IRS' failures, or $100 per day, whichever is greater.

As the statute is brand new, there are no judicial interpretations with respect to it. However, I do not believe that the statute necessarily places the burden on the IRS to take affirmative action with regard to a lien. I say this because the new law refers to the clear language of the existing lien statute §6325. Under §6325, the IRS will release the lien *only* when the citizen makes a showing that the lien should be released either because the tax has been paid or because the tax is uncollectable by reason of age.[28] I have already described what this showing must be. The new law *may,* however, give us a hammer with which to ensure that legally justified applications for release of the lien may be acted on quickly and properly. We shall see.

---

[28] Code §6325(a)(1).

EXHIBIT 6-3 (page one)

Instructions on how to apply for

Certificate of Discharge of
Property From Federal Tax Lien

Department of the Treasury | **Internal Revenue Service**

Publication 783 (Rev. 1-84)

Submit your typewritten application and all accompanying documents in triplicate to:

District Director of Internal Revenue
(Address to District in which the property is located)

Attention of: Chief, Special Procedures Staff

Give Date of Application

Information required on application

Please give the name and address of the person applying, under section 6325 ( )( )( ) of the Internal Revenue Code, for a certificate of discharge. Give the name and address of the taxpayer, and describe the property as follows:

1. Give a detailed description, including the location of the property for which you are requesting the certificate of discharge. If real property is involved, give the description as contained in the title or deed to the property, and the complete address (street, city, State). If the certificate is requested under section 6325(b)(1), also give a description of all the taxpayer's property remaining subject to the lien.

2. Show how and when the taxpayer has been, or will be, divested of all rights, title and interest in and to the property for which a certificate of discharge is requested.

3. Attach a copy of each notice of Federal tax lien, or furnish the following information as it appears on each filed notice of Federal tax lien:

- The name of the Internal Revenue District;
- The name and address of the taxpayer against whom the notice was filed;
- The date and place the notice was filed.

4. List the encumbrances (or attach a copy of the instrument that created each encumbrance) on the property which you believe have priority over the Federal tax lien. For each encumbrance show:

- The name and address of the holder;
- A description of the encumbrance;
- The date of the agreement;
- The date and place of the recording, if any;
- The original principal amount and the interest rate;
- The amount due as of the date of the application, if known (show costs and accrued interest separately);
- Your family relationship, if any, to the taxpayer and to the holders of any other encumbrances on the property.

5. Itemize all proposed or actual costs, commissions and expenses of any transfer or sale of the property.

6. Furnish information to establish the value of the property for which you are applying for a certificate of discharge. In every case furnish an estimate of the fair market value of the property which will remain subject to the lien. In addition,

- If private sale—Submit written appraisals by two disinterested people qualified to appraise the property, and a brief statement of each appraiser's qualifications.
- If public sale (auction) already held—Give the date and place the sale was held, and the amount for which the property was sold.
- If public sale (auction) to be held—Give the proposed date and place of the sale, and include a statement that the United States will be paid in its proper priority from the proceeds of the sale.

7. Give any other information that might, in your opinion, have bearing upon the application.

8. Furnish any other specific information the District Director requests.

9. If you are submitting the application under the provisions of section 6325(b)(3), dealing with the substitution of proceeds of sale, attach a copy of the proposed agreement containing the following:

- Name and address of proposed escrow agent;
- Caption, type of account, name and address of depositary for the account;
- Conditions under which the escrow fund is to be held;
- Conditions under which payment will be made from escrow, including the limitation for negotiated settlement of claims against the fund;
- Estimated costs of escrow;
- Name and address of any other party you and the District Director determine to be a party to the escrow agreement;
- Your signature, and those of the escrow agent, District Director and any other party to the escrow agreement;
- Any other specific information the District Director requests.

10. Give a daytime telephone number where you may be reached.

11. Give the name, address and telephone number of your attorney or other representative, if any.

12. Make the following declaration over your signature and title: "Under penalties of perjury, I declare that I have examined this application, including any accompanying schedules, exhibits, affidavits, and statements, and to the best of my knowledge and belief it is true, correct, and complete."

EXHIBIT 6-3 (page one)

Additional Information

Please follow the instructions in this publication when applying for a Certificate of Discharge of Property From Federal Tax Lien.

The District Director has the authority to issue a certificate of discharge of a lien that is filed on any part of a taxpayer's property subject to the lien. The following sections and provisions of the Internal Revenue Code apply:

Section 6325(b)(1), if it is determined that the property remaining subject to the lien has a fair market value of at least *double* the sum of the amount of the unsatisfied tax liability and the amount of all other liens and encumbrances having priority over the Government's lien.

Section 6325(b)(2)(A), if there is paid in partial satisfaction of the liability secured by the lien an amount determined to be not less than the value of the interest of the United States in the property to be discharged.

Section 6325(b)(2)(B), if it is determined that the interest of the United States in the property to be discharged has no value.

Section 6325(b)(3), if the property subject to the lien is sold and, under an agreement with the Internal Revenue Service, the proceeds from the sale are to be held as a fund subject to the liens and claims of the United States in the same manner, and with the same priority, as the liens and claims on the discharged property.

1. No payment is required for the issuance of a certificate under section 6325(b)(1) or section 6325(b)(2)(B) of the Code. Payment is required for certificates issued under section 6325(b)(2)(A). Do not send the payment with your application, however. The District Director will notify you after determining the amount due.

2. The District Director will have your application investigated to determine whether to issue the certificate, and will let you know the outcome.

3. A certificate of discharge under section 6325(b)(2)(A) will be issued upon receipt of the amount determined to be the interest of the United States in the subject property under the Federal tax lien. Make remittances in cash, or by a certified, cashier's, or treasurer's check drawn on any bank or trust company incorporated under the laws of the United States or of any State, or possession of the United States, or by United States postal, bank, express, or telegraph money order. (If you pay by uncertified personal check, issuance of the certificate of discharge will be delayed until the bank honors the check.)

4. If application is made under section 6325(b)(2)(A) or 6325(b)(2)(B) because a mortgage foreclosure is contemplated, there will be a determination of the amount required for discharge or a determination that the Federal tax lien interest in the property is valueless.

Within 30 days from the date of the application, the applicant will receive a written conditional commitment for a certificate of discharge. When the foreclosure proceeding has been concluded, a certificate of discharge will be issued in accordance with the terms of the commitment letter.

5. If application is made under the provisions of section 6325(b)(3), the District Director has the authority to approve an escrow agent selected by the applicant. Any reasonable expenses incurred in connection with the sale of the property, the holding of the fund, or the distribution of the fund shall be paid by the applicant or from the proceeds of the sale before satisfaction of any claims and liens. Submit a copy of the proposed escrow agreement as part of the application.

F. *The Appeal.* Another new section created by the Bill of Rights Act is Code §6326. This new law authorizes a person to appeal "the imposition of a lien. . .on the property or the rights to property of such person." We now have the right to appeal administratively the filing of a tax lien.

The problem, however, is this: seldom does the *filing* of a tax lien cause legal difficulties. It is the IRS' *failure* to *remove* a lien which causes the problems faced by persons such as those discussed here. The statute does not state that a person has the right to appeal the IRS' decision to *deny* a request for subordination, or a request for release of the lien, or an application for a bond. These are the important issues which must be addressed if the citizens of this country are to be handed rights which actually mean something.

Even worse, the statute does not state when and how this appeal is to be taken. It places in the hands of the IRS the *sole authority* to dictate the time and the manner in which the appeal is to be taken.

This is much like placing the fox in charge of the chickenhouse. We must keep an eye on the regulations which the IRS promulgates in this regard. They will determine exactly how this "right" is to be carried out.

2. The Levy—

The levy is an extremely potent enforced collection tool. It is the means whereby the IRS attaches a person's wages, his bank account or other money which the citizen owns or which is owed to him by another. Under the law, [29] the IRS may take enforced collection action, which includes the use of the levy, if a citizen refuses to pay the assessed tax in full within 30 days[30] of mailing a "notice and demand" for payment.

A. *Wage Levy Exemptions*. Wages are not exempt from levy by the IRS. In fact, the IRS can expect in most cases to collect the lion's share of an outstanding tax bill through the wage levy. Code §6334 provides a little "relief" from the wage levy. Nevertheless, one must be aware of certain limitations on the wage levy in order to preserve as much of his wages as possible under the circumstances.

When a levy is executed against the wages of a citizen, the citizen bears the responsibility to claim the exemptions allowed under §6334(d)(1). The exemptions are claimed on IRS Form 668-W, Claim for Dependent Exemption. See Chapter Three, Exhibit 3-6. The Claim for Dependent Exemption gives the citizen under levy an exemption for himself and each dependent disclosed on the form. The exemptions are valued at $150 per pay period for the citizen himself, and $50 per pay period for each dependent.[31] The Claim for Dependent Exemption must be filed within three days of levy in order to be effective.

B. *Exempt Property*. While there is no particular *class* of property which is completely exempt from the IRS levy, certain *amounts* of property are exempt. The IRS has a "shoot-first-and-ask-questions-later" attitude with regard to most levies. It will often leave it to the citizen to assert any right with respect to exempt property which he believes may apply. For this reason,

---

[29] Code §6631.

[30] This time period was increased from 10 days by §13(a) of the Bill of Rights Act.

[31] These amounts were increased from $75 and $25 respectively by §13(c)(3) of the Bill of Rights Act.

one must know what amounts of property are exempt from levy and be prepared to demand that the IRS "back-off" any act to levy such property.

Section 6334(a) of the Code exempts from levy the following property in these amounts:

1. Wearing apparel and school books: no limit on value;

2. Fuel, provisions, furniture, and personal effects in one's household, including livestock and poultry: $10,00 limit;

3. Books and tools of a trade, business, or profession necessary for the citizen's trade or business: $10,000 limit;

4. Unemployment compensation: no limit;

5. All undelivered mail;

6. Pensions or annuities under the Railroad Retirement Act, Railroad Unemployment Insurance Act, and certain military retirement benefits paid to a person on the Medal of Honor roll.

7. Workman's Compensation: no limit;

8. All amounts necessary to pay child support judgments;

9. Dependent exemptions as discussed in Part 2(A) above;

10. All amounts payable to a person as a Service-connected disability payment; and

11. When placed in a bank or credit union account, funds exempt under paragraph 9 cannot be levied for a period of 30 days after being deposited.

The Taxpayers' Bill of Rights Act created additional exemptions which warrant discussion, although fine print within the law does not make these exemptions as firm as those just mentioned. Under §13(c)(4) of the Act, the following additional property is exempt unless "a district director or assistant district director of the Internal Revenue Service personally approves (in writing) the levy of such property, or the Secretary finds that the collection of tax is in jeopardy:"

1. The citizen's principle residence: no limit;

2. The citizen's motor vehicle used as the primary means of transportation to his place of business: no limit; and

3. Any tangible personal property used in carrying on a trade or business, but only if levy on such property would prevent the citizen from carrying on his trade or business: no limit.

My experience has been that most people, especially Revenue Officers, do not understand that certain property is exempt from levy by the IRS. Therefore, the unfortunate citizen under levy must be prepared to assert his entitlement to any exemption.

C. *Neutralizing ACS.* Automated Collection is your worst nightmare personified. The major difficulties created by ACS have already been addressed in Chapter Three, Part 8, but it bears restating that ACS will automatically issue liens and wage levies with indiscriminate abandon. When in receipt of a bill from ACS, one must take immediate action. That action is comprised of a two-pronged counter-attack.

The first step is to make every reasonable effort to have control of the case transferred from ACS to the local Collection office. This procedure has been covered in detail in Chapter Three, Part 8. To review, one must make a written request that the case be transferred. The request for transfer must be specific and set forth facts which will allow ACS personnel to draw the conclusion that the case should be transferred.

The next step of the process involves persuading ACS that enforced collection action through the use of liens and levies is not warranted. In this respect, a letter should be written to ACS which explains your financial situation and points out that full and immediate payment cannot be made. In order for ACS to accept anything less than full payment, several points have to be established. They are:

1. That you do not have sufficient funds readily available to pay in a lump sum;

2. That you do not have sufficient assets which can be liquidated in order to pay in full;

3. That you have no creditors to whom payments can be forestalled, enabling you to pay in full within a very short period of time; and

4. That monthly expenses necessary to meet your personal "health and welfare needs," such as food, clothing and shelter, and the support of dependents, make large monthly payments impossible.

The conclusion of your letter should be a request that ACS accept monthly payments in an amount determined by *you.* You should also include your first payment with the letter. Your letter should be carefully written to designate how the payment should be applied. See Chapter Five, Part 4.

If you are successful, enforced collection action will be averted and the case will be transferred to the district. This will allow you to meet with a Revenue Officer and work out the terms of payment in a manner which is least likely to lead to dire financial consequences.

D. *Installment Agreements.* Prior to the enactment of the Taxpayers' Bill of Rights Act, there was no legal authority for the IRS to accept installment payments from citizens. The IRS *did* enter into installment agreements, but the matter was entirely discretionary. Although Bill of Rights advocates suggest differently, the Act *does not* change this fact. The Act does include a section which "authorizes" the IRS to accept installment payments of overdue tax bills, but the ability to make installments is still not a "right" enjoyed by the citizen. In fact, under the language of the act, the option to enter into installment agreements remains within the sole discretion of the IRS, "if the Secretary determines that such agreement will facilitate collection of such liability."[32]

Still, an installment agreement, if one can persuade the IRS to accept it, will do a number of things. First, it will cause the IRS to release any levy on wages or salary. Next, one can expect the IRS to release from seizure any property, such as an automobile or home. Properly negotiated, the installment payment will be in such an amount as to not financially cripple the citizen. And lastly, the fixed monthly payment allows the citizen to budget around what he knows the IRS must receive each month.

Installment payment negotiations break down to the disadvantage of the citizen for one principle reason. In most cases, the IRS will not accept the amount of payment offered by the citizen. It wants more, much more than most people are either capable of, or willing to pay to the government each month.

Before an installment agreement will be accepted, the IRS will demand that a completed Form 433 be submitted. You will recall from Chapter Four (see Exhibit 4-1) that Form 433 is the *Statement of Financial Condition and other Information.* The last page of the financial statement contains a statement of monthly living expenses. It is from this information that the IRS will determine the amount of payment it will accept from a citizen. Here is where the problem is created:

The statement of monthly expenses is completed, but when called upon; the citizen is *unable* to verify that some or all of the amounts declared are in fact *incurred* each month. Without some type of expense verification, such as a canceled check or monthly invoice, the Revenue Officer working the case will "disallow" the

---

[32] Bill of Rights Act, §12(a), creating new Code §6159.

EXHIBIT 6-4

Form **433-D** (Rev. December 1985)	Department of the Treasury – Internal Revenue Service **Installment Agreement**	
Name and address of taxpayer(s)	Social security or employer identification number	Agreement locator number
	Kinds of taxes *(Form numbers)*	
	Tax periods	
	Amount of tax owed	Agreement review date

The undersigned agrees that the Federal taxes shown above, plus any interest and penalties provided by law, will be paid as follows:

$_____ to be paid on _____ and $_____ to be paid

on the _____ of each _____ thereafter until the liability is paid in full, and also agrees that the above tax

installments will be increased as follows:

Date of increase					
Amount of increase	$				
New installment amount	$				

Conditions:

- This agreement is based on your current financial circumstances and is subject to revision or cancellation if subsequent financial information required by IRS reflects a change in your ability to pay.
- If this agreement is still in effect after 36 months, your financial circumstances will be re evaluated. The agreement may be changed or canceled at that time.
- All Federal taxes that become due during the term of this agreement will be paid on time.
- All Federal tax returns that become due during the term of this agreement will be filed on time.
- Any Federal or State refunds that might otherwise be due will be applied to this liability until it is satisfied.
- Permission to make installment payments may be withdrawn, and the entire tax liability may be collected by levy on income or by seizure of property if the conditions of this agreement are not met, or if it is determined that collection of these taxes is endangered.
- This agreement may require managerial approval. If it is not approved, you will be so notified.

Additional conditions:	Originator's name and IDRS assignment number:

Your signature	Title *(if corporate officer or partner)*	Date	For assistance call:
Spouse's signature *(if joint income tax return)*		Date	or write:
Agreement examined and approved by *(signature)*		Date	

General Information

Employer *(Name and address)*	Taxpayer's Telephone Number(s) ▶	*(Home)*
		(Business)

Banks *(Names and addresses)*

Notice of Federal tax lien filing determination *(check one)*

☐ Notice of tax lien filed   ☐ Notice of tax lien not required

☐ Notice of tax lien to be filed--taxpayer notified   ☐ Notice of tax lien not filed *(Form 3991 attached)*

Part 1 – IRS Office Copy   Form **433-D** (Rev. 12 85)

expense for installment payment purposes. This has the effect of *increasing* the amount of money which the IRS will demand each month.

Bob had his paycheck under levy by the IRS. The Revenue Officer refused to lift the levy, so Bob was, for all practical purposes, out of work. To resolve the situation, we completed Form 433-A[33] and submitted it to the IRS. Before the form was completed, I instructed Bob and his wife to gather all documentation which would verify each of their monthly living expenses, including such things as mortgage payments and utility bills. With these documents in hand, we comleted the final page of Form 433-A. We carefully listed all monthly expenses Bob and his wife incurred.

When me met with the Revenue Officer, we were prepared to prove that each of the monthly expenses was necessary to maintain the "health and welfare" of Bob and his family. We were also prepared to present documents which demonstrated that each expense was legitimate and not contrived. Before the meeting was completed, we had reached an agreement that Bob would make $300 per month installments, and this was memorialized in Form 433-D, *Installment Agreement* (see Exhibit 6-4). With Form 433-D signed and sealed, the levy was lifted and Bob's paycheck was returned to him.

3. The Seizure—

The seizure of property can be the most destructive of all IRS collection techniques. Property seizures have included homes, automobiles, businesses, and personal property of every description. When one is delinquent in his tax payments, any property which he either owns outright or in which he has an ownership interest, may be seized and sold by the IRS to satisfy that debt. Surely one can imagine the impact that such power would have on the average citizen when used to its fullest potential.

The Taxpayers' Bill of Rights Act was supposed to reduce, or ideally, eliminate the IRS' power to destroy the average man financially. The Bill of Rights did add some new exemptions to the law which I have already examined. Yet, as is the case with nearly all of the Act's provisions, fine print within the Act itself either

---

[33] This form is a much shorter version of Form 433 and is often used with individual, non-business citizens.

waters down or completely vitiates any potential benefit of these provisions.

A perfect example of this is the provision which states that the principle home or automobile of the citizen may not be seized by the IRS. I firmly believe that it is about time federal law addresses the problem of allowing the government to seize a family homestead and in the name of tax collection, turn that family into the street. Sadly, the law is not sufficiently strong to prevent this atrocity from recurring. The law itself permits the IRS to continue this type of heartless collection action when the act is "approved" by a district director of the IRS.

Taking the power of such an act out of the hands of low-level Revenue Officers is a step in the right direction, but citizens are still not safe. The problem with the law is that no *objective standards* are written into it which allows us to determine the circumstances under which such action will or will not be permitted. The major problem with all tax collection statutes remains in this new addition; too much discretion is placed in the hands of the IRS. With such broad discretion inevitably comes abuse of that discretion and that is what has led to the wholesale destruction of the American family by the IRS.

What this means is that we must understand how the impact of an IRS seizure may be neutralized. To this end, I offer the following discussion.

A. *The Minimum Bid Worksheet.* The minimum bid worksheet is submitted to the citizen after his property has been seized, but before it has been sold. The purpose of the form is to transmit to the citizen the figures used to calculate the *minimum* amount the IRS will accept when selling the property. An example of the minimum bid worksheet is shown in Chapter Three, Exhibit 3-9. A citizen whose property is under levy has five days in which to object to the minimum bid price established by the form. A proper response could save the property from sale altogether.

Don's house was under seizure by the IRS. It was about to be sold but before doing so, the Revenue Officer mailed Don a minimum bid worksheet. Though the market value of Don's house was about $85,000, the IRS initially planned to sell the property for just $2,000 plus change. It is not difficult to imagine that the IRS would have been successful in selling an $85,000 home for just $2,000.

Within the 5-day period, we responded to the minimum bid worksheet prepared by the Revenue Officer. We pointed out in specific terms how the minimum bid was (1) grossly understated, and (2) that raising the minimum bid would only serve to "facilitate tax collection." Obviously the IRS' case is better served by demanding *more*, not less, for a parcel of property about to be sold. Our objections were well-taken by the Revenue Officer.

The letter caused him to go back to the drawing board with respect to the sale. He was forced to recompute the minimum bid, raising it substantially. This fact benefited Don in a number of ways. First of all, with the substantially higher minimum bid price, chances that the IRS would actually sell the home had greatly diminished. The higher the price of an item, the fewer buyers there are available to purchase that item.

More importantly, the Revenue Officer was forced to postpone the sale date which he had originally set. This allowed Don the time he needed to take steps which would eventually prevent the IRS from selling his home altogether (see Chapter Seven). Hence, objections to the minimum bid worksheet can be most beneficial.

B. *The Lawsuit for Injunction.* What would you do if the IRS mailed you a tax bill for $25,000? What would you say if they told you the tax was on $33,000 you never received? How would you act if they showed up at your doorstep threatening to seize your home if the money were not paid?

Curtis and Rachel were faced with these very questions. This is what happened:

In 1982 the couple earned combined wages of just over $50,000, and they prepared a tax return reporting the figure as their income. Next, they brought the return to a tax preparer to have their figures checked and the return filed. The liability shown on the return came to just about $10,000, which was almost entirely paid through wage withholding.

On August 26, 1983, the two received a letter from the IRS stating that their tax liability had been adjusted, and that they owed an additional $1,906.49 in tax for 1982. The notice did not give any clear reason for the increase. On January 27, 1984, another horrifying letter was received from the IRS. It stated that the couple's *income* had been adjusted—*upward*—to $83,229.94! This figure was over $33,000 more than they earned during the year!

Next, a Notice of Deficiency was mailed. It too stated that their income had been increased by over $33,000. With interest and penalties added, the IRS demanded payment of $25,149.54. What was even more bizarre was the reason for the increased tax. The IRS stated that "the amount reported as gross receipts on Schedule C has been moved to Line 7, form 1040."

"Schedule C? What Schedule C?" As far as they knew, no Schedule C had been filed. They filed a joint income tax return with Forms W-2. There had to be a mistake somewhere! Instead of petitioning the Tax Court, Curtis sent a letter demanding that the matter be cleared up without further delay.

The letter brought results—or so Curtis thought. In June of 1984, prior to the expiration of the time to petition the Tax Court, the IRS notified Curtis that their account showed a "credit balance of $9,892." Had the IRS corrected its records? Apparently it had.

Believing the problem was solved, the Notice of Deficiency was discarded and no Tax Court petition was filed. That is when the trouble really started. By letter dated August 27, 1984, one month after the expiration of the 90-day grace period, the IRS again reversed itself and demanded payment of $25,000. Several more notices were sent and by April 30, 1985, the amount demanded had risen to $26,629.38. The couple was also informed that "enforced collection" would be taken if the amount was not paid "within 10 days."

In late May of 1985, a lien was filed and on July 9, 1985, the IRS arrived at the offices of Curtis' employer with a wage levy in hand. The liability had now escalated to over $27,500. Curtis was told by his employer that if he did not "obtain a Release by 5:00 p.m., August 2, 1985," the money would be taken from his check.

The problem seemed insurmountable. The IRS wanted over $27,500. The couple had given up their right to petition the Tax Court by allowing the 90-day grace period to lapse. True enough, the IRS had misled them by stating that there was a credit on their account, but nevertheless, the time to petition the Tax Court had passed. The other option—to pay the tax and sue for a refund—was unfeasible by virtue of economics. They simply did not have $27,500 to pay the IRS even if they wanted to.

The only viable solution to the dilemma was to sue the IRS. This route posed a new set of hardships due to federal legislation preventing many suits against the IRS. The legislation is known as "The Anti-Injunction Act."[34] But the couple invoked one little known, and even less understood exception to that rule based upon the Supreme Court case of **Commissioner v. Shapiro.**[35]

Under **Shapiro,** when an assessment is arbitrary and erroneous, *and* the citizen can demonstrate that (1) collection of the tax will cause irreparable harm, and (2) no adequate remedy exists to prevent the harm, a court can enjoin collection of the tax without regard to the Anti-Injunction Act.[36]

When it can be shown that a tax is both arbitrary *and* erroneous, we are no longer talking about "tax collection." We are talking about "exactions in the guise of a tax."[37] If the IRS cannot support its assessment with facts sufficient to create the substantial likelihood that you in fact owe the tax, then a court would be entitled to decree that the tax is "arbitrary and erroneous."

Next, you must demonstrate that you do not possess the financial wherewithall to withstand collection of the amount at issue. If it can be shown that you will suffer irreparable harm— financial constraints which will result in irreversable hardship— then you have met this prong of the test.

Lastly, you must prove that any administrative avenues available are not adequate to prevent the impending deleterious financial hardship which is about to ensue. Having made such a showing to a court, it would be permitted to prevent the IRS from taking its threatened collection action, regardless of the apparently inflexible nature of the Anti-Injunction Act.

Supporting documents consistent with the **Shapiro** rules were filed with Curtis' lawsuit. Then, on July 29, 1985, just five days before the levy was to take effect, a federal judge signed a Temporary Restraining Order preventing the levy from going forward.

At that point, Curtis asked me to work with the IRS and the government lawyer to solve the problem. I contacted the Justice Department lawyer and after lengthy conversation, persuaded him not to take any action until after we had worked the matter out with the local IRS Collection Office.

I discussed the case with the Collection Officer, pointing out how the IRS had made a serious error in computing Curtis' income. By

---

[34] Code §7421.
[35] 424 U.S. 614 (1976).
[36] Other cases which support this proposition are **Miller v. Standard Nut Margarine Co.**, 248 U.S. 498 (1932) and **Enochs v. Williams Packing Co.**, 370 U.S. 1 (1962).
[37] See **Miller v. Standard Nut Margarine Co.**, previous footnote.

February, 1986, I had documents in my hands evidencing the fact that the IRS had abated the excessive tax. I sent the documents to the IRS attorney, along with a stipulation, or formal agreement memorializing the abatement. Throughout all this time, not one penny of Curtis' wages had been levied and no action was taken to seize the family home.

The success of this case is attributable to one thing: understanding the limits of the IRS' ability to collect an assessment. Over the years, the Anti-Injunction Act has proven to be a most formidable adversary to those wishing to contest an assessment. The IRS takes the invariable position that the Act is etched in stone and knows no exceptions. But the Supreme Court and other federal courts have taken a different view. Exceptions to the Act have been carved out.

An overview of these exceptions will help anybody facing the same or similar circumstances. Case and statute law give us this hope: Where the IRS, (1) has not followed proper administrative procedures in making an assessment, or (2) has assessed an arbitrary and erroneous tax, even if done correctly, or (3) intends to execute their levy upon property not belonging to the person against whom the tax is assessed, the Act will afford no comfort to the IRS. Collection may be enjoined.

The efficacy of efforts to stop the IRS depends on precise presentation of the applicable exceptions to the Act. The courts are quick to side with the government in these debates, and government attorneys do not like to agree that the exceptions exist. It is your burden to show just how the exceptions apply. That requires a thorough understanding of the rules. This knowledge saved Curtis and Rachel from financial ruin.

C. *The Separate Interest.* Very often property is owned jointly by a husband and wife. It is also common for the husband, but not the wife, to have a tax liability. Despite the fact that the wife may not owe taxes, the Supreme Court has ruled that the IRS may sell the couple's joint property in order to liquidate the debtor's (the husband's) interest in that property.[38] Even though the property may be sold, the court has also ruled that the non-debtor (the wife) must be compensated by the IRS after the sale. What this means simply, is that while the IRS may sell joint

---

[38] See **United States v. Rogers**, 461 U.S. 677 (19830.

property when just one owner owes taxes, it may not retain 100% of
the proceeds. The non-debtor must be compensated to the extent of
her ownership interest. If she owns the property "jointly," she
would be entitled to 50% of the proceeds as compensation.

True to form, the IRS will inevitably overlook this "minor"
detail in the law. When it seizes and sells joint property, it often
makes no provision to compensate the non-debtor. We can learn of
its intentions in this regard by reviewing the minimum bid
worksheet. If the IRS proposes to sell any more than a one-half
interest in the property, it can be assumed that it does not intend to
consider the ownership interest of the non-debtor spouse.

A little-known federal statute provides a remedy when one is
faced with this problem. The statute is known as the "Wrongful
Levy Statute."[39] This statute allows a person to enjoin an IRS levy
or sale if the government proposes to *overlook* the ownership
intersets of a non-debtor.

Margaret filed such a suit in the district court in Chicago. Her
husband owed thousands of dollars in taxes and the IRS had seized
the couple's jointly-owned rental property with the intention of
selling it.

In her suit, Margaret established her ownership interest in the
property by presenting the court with copies of the deed of title. In
its order, the court instructed the IRS to restructure its sale of the
property in order to protect Margaret's interest. She was entitled
to be compensated from the proceeds of the sale and the IRS was
ordered to see that she was. Without the suit having been filed, the
IRS would have sold the property and completely ignored
Margaret's ownership interest. Her share of the property would
have been lost along with her husband's.

Another important way in which the "Wrongful Levy Statute"
can be employed is where the IRS intends to sell the homestead
residence of the citizen. In **United States v. Rogers**,[40] the
Supreme Court ruled that district courts do possess the power to
prevent the sale of one's principle residence under certain
circumstances. The court held that the statute under which the
IRS seeks to sell property, §7403, does not "require" that the
property be sold. Rather, the court pointed out that when the non-
debtor spouse could not be adequately compensated with money, a
court should prevent the sale. As the Supreme Court observed,

---

[39] Code §7426.
[40] See note 38.

"money is not always adequate compensation for a roof over one's head."

When it can be demonstrated that the non-debtor will be irreparably harmed if the home is sold, and that "money's worth compensation" will not be adequate to rectify this damage, sale of the home can be prevented. This comes as important news, even in the face of the Bill of Rights. The reason, as I have already stated, is that the fine print within the Bill of Rights enables the IRS to sell a person's homestead residence. However, by asserting the separate interest claim under the "Wrongful Levy Statute," a non-debtor spouse can be spared the misery of this loss.

D. *The Premature Assessment.* Under Code §6213(a), the IRS may *not* assess a tax unless it has first issued a notice of deficiency to the citizen. Once the notice has been mailed, the IRS may *not* make the assessment until after the 90-day time period has expired. If the citizen files a petition in the Tax Court within the 90-day period, the IRS may *not* make the assessment until the Tax Court has made a final decision on the case, and only then may assess the amount deemed owing by the court.

However these rules do not always stop the IRS from making assessments and taking action to collect the taxes. Despite the fact that these acts are completely improper, the IRS does it all the time! Unfortunately, when it happens the citizen is often at a loss as to what can be done to remedy the problem. In the one provision of the Bill of Rights which is not replete with negative fine print, Congress has provided a solution to this problem. Section 16 of the Bill of Rights adds language to Code §6213(a). The new language provides that if a timely petition for redetermination is filed with the Tax Court, the court has "exclusive jurisdiction to enjoin" any premature assessment.

By motion before the Tax Court, a citizen may now prevent his property from being seized pursuant to a premature assessment if his case is pending in the Tax Court. The truth be told, this is a breath of fresh air!

Conclusion—

As long as the Automated Collection Service is alive and well in the United States, we all have cause to be concerned about liens, levies and seizures. Even with the Bill of Rights Act, I cannot say that the incredible power of the IRS to seize property has been effectively curtailed. Indeed, the Bill of Rights is silent on many important issues of concern. In particular, the Act has failed to provide objective guidelines which would bind Revenue Officers in their use of awesome collection powers.

Bill of Rights or no Bill of Rights, Revenue Officers remain the least regulated of all IRS employees. This broad and often unchecked discretion can however, be neutralized if one is cognizant of the appropriate procedures. These techniques have helped others. They can help you.

Chapter Seven

2 WAYS TO ELIMINATE TAXES YOU CANNOT PAY

Introduction

Would you like to know a secret? Federal income taxes *are* dischargeable in bankruptcy! That's right! This fact is perhaps the best kept legal secret in the United States. Would you like to know another secret? Federal income taxes *have been* dischargeable in bankruptcy for over 22 years! That's right! The Bankruptcy Reform Act of 1966 passed the Senate on June 21, 1966, and became law shortly thereafter.[1]

In case you may yet be skeptical, permit me to recite the introductory language of Senate Report No. 1158:[2]

"The purpose of the bill (H.R. 3438) is *to make dischargeable* in bankruptcy debts for taxes. . ." (Emphasis added.)

Because we have all been told that federal income taxes are not dischargeable in bankruptcy, you may still be questioning the validity of these startling revelations; justifiably so, because there was a time when this was true. However, after a Congressional investigation in 1966, the law was changed. The Senate Report to which I have just referred, points out that Congress discovered two specific problems that were created by the fact that taxes were once nondischargeable. The first problem, the Senate observed, was that:

"Frequently, the (nondischargeability) prevents an honest but financially unfortunate debtor from making a fresh start unburdened by what may be an overwhelming liability for accumulated taxes. The large proportion of individual and commercial income now consumed by various taxes makes the problem especially acute. Furthermore, the non-dischargeability feature of the law operates in a manner which is unfairly discriminatory against the private individual or the

---

[1] Public Law 89-496, U.S. Code Congressional and Administrative News, 1966, Vol. 2, page 2468.
[2] May 12, 1966, report to accompany H.R. 3438.

unincorporated small businessman. Although a corporate bankrupt is theoretically not discharged, the corporation normally ceases to exist upon bankruptcy and unsatisfied taxes, as well as all other unsatisfied claims, are without further recourse even though the enterprise may continue in a new corporate form." (U.S. Code Cong. & Adm. News, 1966, Vol. 2, pg. 2471).

In addition to the fact that taxes under the previous law were nondischargeable, federal taxes were given a "priority" over other debts. That is to say, taxes were always the *first* items to be paid with the assets obtained from a bankruptcy estate. Many times, this left precious little or no funds which could be paid to other creditors. The Senate addressed this problem as well, stating:

"The result has frequently been that tax collectors, assured of a prior claim on the assets of a failing debtor and assured of the nondischargeability of uncollectable tax claims, *have allowed taxes to accumulate and remain unpaid for long periods of time.* With the proliferation of new taxes and the increased rates of old taxes, often nothing is left for distribution to general creditors who provided goods and services to the bankrupt." (Ibid.) (Emphasis added.)

The actions of arrogant tax collectors would ensure that no other creditor would receive any distribution from the assets obtained from a failed business, though creditors other than the government often had an actual investment in the unfortunate business. The Senate observed that it was fundamentally unfair to allow the tax collector's claim to remain a priority over other creditors indefinitely. Moreover, the very nature and purpose of the bankruptcy laws are to provide a financially overburdened citizen with a fresh start and a clean slate; to provide a second chance in life. As taxes are often the largest debt which an insolvent person has incurred, the underlying purpose of the bankruptcy law is defeated if taxes were to remain nondischargeable. The Senate's conclusion was logical and just: taxes must be made dischargeable in bankruptcy. Hence, the passage of the Bankruptcy Reform Act over 22 years ago.

What has not changed in 22 years, however, is the public's perception of federal income taxes and their relationship to the bankruptcy laws. I have spoken with hundreds of people all over the United States, including lawyers, accountants, IRS personnel and even bankruptcy experts. With precious few exceptions, no one realizes that taxes can be discharged in bankruptcy. A glaring example of this is found in a feature on bankruptcy which appeared in the *St. Paul Pioneer Press and Dispatch*.[3] In an article entitled, *How Do You Spell Relief?*, *B-A-N-K-R-U-P-T-C-Y*, the writer states that a Chapter 7 bankruptcy "Doesn't allow the following debts to be discharged: income taxes. . ." The amazing aspect of this statement is that the journalist responsible for the article interviewed several of the area's leading bankruptcy experts. Apparently all had imparted to her incorrect information regarding tax liabilities. Similar articles appear regularly in responsible newspapers across the nation.

Perhaps the reason for this ignorance is that bankruptcy experts do not have much occasion to concern themselves with tax matters, or that tax experts generally do not get involved with bankruptcies. A more likely explanation is that the IRS has published false information about the ability to bankrupt federal income tax liabilities.

Whatever the reason, this gross negligence (or maliciousness) has caused many thousands of persons to be harassed needlessly by the IRS for years beyond which is legally required.

The results are tragic. One Texas couple committed suicide on the front lawn of their home in the presence of IRS personnel, the media and prospective bidders, just as their home was about to be auctioned by the IRS for back taxes. In another case, a 15-year-old Florida youth committed suicide with a .357 magnum because of severe depression created by IRS harassment of his parents which dragged on for over five years. In northern Arizona, nearly 20 horses were starved to death, and another 20 suffered serious malnutrition at the hands of the IRS when it seized their owner's ranch. The IRS refused to allow the owner to set foot on the property in order to feed the animals. When questioned by Humane Society officials about the deplorable neglect of the horses, an Arizona IRS spokesman coldly stated, "We are not in the horse business. We are in the tax collection business."

IRS Publication 908, Bankruptcy—

The Internal Revenue Service has a publication for distribution

---

[3] April 26, 1988.

to the public which discusses virtually every subject. Bankruptcy is no exception. This publication is however, woefully deficient in its explanation of the bankruptcy laws and the rules under which one may discharge his federal income tax debts. On page two of the two page publication, under the heading *Discharge of Unpaid Taxes*, we find this most "helpful" language:

> "As a general rule, there is no discharge for an individual debtor at the termination of the bankruptcy case for any pre-petition (petition in bankruptcy) taxes, or for taxes for which no return, a late return. . .or a fraudulent return was filed."

This "explanation" leaves the reader with the impression that tax liabilities are simply not subject to the bankruptcy laws. Moreover, questioning any IRS employee on the subject will usually lead one to the same conclusion. The deliberate falsity of Publication 908 led me to "blast" the document in the May, 1988, issue of my monthly newsletter, *Pilla Talks Taxes*.[4] In that article, written by Donald W. MacPherson,[5] Publication 908 was criticized as being "as obscure as the proverbial 'polar bear in a snowstorm'."

Just *one month* after the May, 1988 issue of *Pilla Talks Taxes* hit the streets, the IRS issued an internal memorandum regarding the inaccurate publication. The memo, dated June 15, 1988 (see Exhibit 7-1) in effect *recalled all existing copies of Publication 908!*[6] The reason given for the recall was that revisions to the law since the publication was issued in 1982 have "made it out-of-date and *could be misleading to taxpayers."* (Emphasis mine.)

Misleading indeed! The publication is outright deceptive! But in light of the 1966 Bankrupty Act, it begs the question, why did the IRS wait until June of 1988, 22 years after the law was changed, but just one month after *Pilla Talks Taxes* printed the *truth* about Publication 908, in which to decide that the information "could be misleading to taxpayers?" The reader can answer that question for himself.

The IRS is expected to issue its revised Publication 908 around January 1, 1989. I will be most anxious to review it! In the meantime, the cat is out of the bag. Since I began my research on

---

[4] WINNING Publications, $107/2 years; $57/1 year; $37/6 months.
[5] MacPherson is a practicing attorney specializing in the areas of tax and criminal law. MacPherson is a regular contributor to *Pilla Talks Taxes.*
[6] I obtained the memo from the IRS in mid September, 1988.

EXHIBIT 7-1 (IRS MEMO)

MSG # 88-00967, SENT 13:17:05 CDT, 88/06/15.- RCVD 08:43:06 CDT, 88/06/16.

***** PUBLIC MESSAGE *****

    TO: MID WEST
          IRS/RG3   *ARc (DP)*
                                                          D + s c
    FROM: INVENTORY GROUP
          NATIONAL OFFICE

SUBJECT: PUB 908

MESSAGE NUMBER (150)   6/15/88   (JEAN GARRETT)

TO/CHIEF, PUBLISHING SERVICES
   ALL REGIONS

CHIEF, PUBLISHING SERVICES
FM/CHIEF, PUBLISHING SERVICES
   NATIONAL OFFICE

SB/PUB 908, "BANKRUPTCY"

THIS IS A REMINDER . THE 11/82 REVISION OF PUB 908 SHOULD NOT BE
ISSUED TO THE PUBLIC. LEGISLATION ENACTED SINCE THIS REVISION WAS
PRINTED HAS MADE IT OUT-OF-DATE AND COULD MISLEAD TAXPAOYERS. A
NEW REVISION OF PUB 908 SHOULD BE AVAILABLE AFTER JANUARY 1, 1989.
ANY TAXPAYER REQUESTING PUB 908 SHOULD BE SENT AN INFORMATION NOTICE
STATING, " THE REVISED ITEM YOU ORDERED HAS NOT BEEN APPROVED
FOR PRINT. PLEASE RE-ORDER AFTER JANUARY 1, ~~1988~~." ANY EXISTING *1989*
SSTOCK OF PUB 908 (11/82) SHOULD BE DISPOSED OF.

IF THERE ARE ANY QUESTIONS. PLEASE CONTACT ~~JUDY PHILLIPS~~ ON ~~566-3125~~.
                                          REX BELL   *8FC-5260*

---

the question nearly two years ago, I have seen almost $2 million in
taxes, interest and penalties discharged in bankruptcy. Most of
these people were desperate, facing crippling liens, had almost no
income on which to live because of crushing wage levies, and worst
of all, were given no hope of ever extricating themselves from such
grave financial circumstances.

We now know that there is hope. We know that there is no such
thing as an unsolvable IRS collection problem. No longer will
Americans have to commit suicide because they have been driven
to financial ruin by their own government. The law provides the
hope and the remedy. The IRS, with its half-truths and deceptions
would have that hope dashed on the rocks of ignorance. However,
it is not to be! Pay close attention!

Who Can Bankrupt Taxes—

The United States Bankruptcy Code[7] governs the subject of which debts are and are not dischargeable in bankruptcy. Sections 507(a)(7) and 523(a)(2) and (3) of the Code discuss taxes and set out the rules which make income tax assessments dischargeable. The rules are summarized as follows:

Rule 1. The tax must be for a year which pre-dates the bankruptcy petition by at least three years. For example, a tax assessed for the year 1984, due April 15, 1985, would be three years old on April 15, 1988. A bankruptcy petition filed *after* the latter date would cover the taxes assessed for the year 1984.

Rule 2. The tax must have been officially *assessed* by the IRS for at least 240 days. An assessment occurs at the time of either filing the return, or, when the IRS mails a notice of deficiency and no appeal is taken to the Tax Court, or, the Tax Court renders a decision in favor of the IRS. The date of the assessment is recorded by the IRS in a computer file maintained for each citizen.

Rule 3. The tax must not be capable of being assessed after the petition in bankruptcy has been filed. In essence, if one meets both the three year rule *and* the 240-day rule, he will necessarily fall under this rule.

Rule 4. The return for the year in question must have been filed in a *timely* manner. If it was filed late, that filing must pre-date the filing of the bankruptcy petition by at least two years.

Rule 5. The tax must not be the result of a fraudulent return or a willful attempt in any manner on the citizen's part to evade or defeat the tax.

When all five of the above conditions are met, (which is the situation in the lion's share of all tax cases), the liability is considered "non-priority" and is completely dischargeable in bankruptcy.

This is How it Works—

Bankruptcy is nothing more or less than the process by which a debtor clears the slate with his creditors and begins life anew. This is accomplished in either of two ways. The first is through a liquidation of all his assets under Chapter 7 of the Code. The second is through a "wage-earners plan" under Chapter 13 of the

---

[7] Title 11, United States Code. This title is commonly referred to as the Bankruptcy Code.

Code. Let me explain the difference:

1. *Chapter 7, Liquidation.* When a proceeding is commenced under Chapter 7 of the Bankruptcy Code, the debtor is asking the court to "liquidate" his assets and to use the proceeds to pay his creditors. To the extent that his assets are insufficient to meet the obligations he has incurred, (he is bankrupt) the difference will be discharged.

In any bankruptcy proceeding, there are three general classes of debts. These must be defined before we go any further. The three classes are "priority debts," "secured debts," and "unsecured, non-priority debts." The nature of the debt determines the class into which it falls.

Some examples of priority debts include: unpaid wages an employer owes to an employee up to $2,000 per person; contributions to an employee benefit plan up to $2,000 per person; and taxes which are less than three years old or which have not been assessed for at least 240 days.[8] *Priority* debts *are not* discharged in a Chapter 7 bankruptcy.

Some examples of secured debts are the mortgage on your home and automobile, contracts for deed, valid liens filed by creditors, and other debts which are memorialized by mortgage documents or security agreements. A secured debt is discharged only to the extent that the debt exceeds the value of the property against which the security is held.

Some examples of unsecured, non-priority debts are debts owed to credit card companies, debts for goods and services purchased in the ordinary course of business which are not secured by some type of documentation, and money owed to any other person. Unsecured, non-priority debts are fully discharged in a Chapter 7 bankruptcy. Taxes which meet all five of the rules discussed earlier fall into this category.

When a petition under Chapter 7 is filed, a legal entity known as the bankruptcy "estate" is created. The estate, upon filing the petition, becomes the owner of all assets of the debtor, both real and personal, which he had at the time the petition was filed. It also becomes responsible for all the secured and non-priority debts. As I mentioned, priority debts are never discharged in a Chapter 7 bankruptcy.

A trustee is placed in control of all the assets of the estate. He is

---

[8] A complete list of priority debts is provided in Bankruptcy Code §507(a).

responsible to sell those assets and to distribute the proceeds to the creditors in the correct order of priority. Secured creditors are, after a period of time, generally entitled to take possession of the secured asset before it is sold by the trustee. For example, if at the time of filing in Chapter 7 your only secured creditor was the ABC Leasing Company which owned your office copy machine, that company would be entitled at some point to take its copy machine. The difference between the value of the machine at the time it is repossessed and the balance of the lease would then revert to the classification of a non-priority debt.

To illustrate, suppose you leased the machine for three years and the payment was $100 per month. You filed in Chapter 7 after one year of making payments. Hence, the balance due on the lease agreement would be $2,400 (24 months x $100/month). Suppose further that due to the wear and tear on the machine, it is worth only $1,000 when it is repossessed by the lease company. The difference of $1,400 ($2,400 owed minus $1,000 present value) would then be considered non-priority debt and would be dischargeable.

A Chapter 7 bankruptcy is enormously effective in solving tax problems, particularly when the debtor owns no property. Since he owns no property, there can be no secured creditors. After filing the petition, the trustee will hold a meeting of the creditors. This meeting is for the purpose of questioning the debtor regarding his assets. Any creditor has the right to attend, but it is unusual for any representative of the IRS to appear at the meeting. Shortly after the meeting of the creditors is held, a discharge is issued by the court and the case is closed. It is that simple.

Chapter 7 filings which involve property can be more complex. In these cases, the trustee is called upon to sell the property and to distribute the proceeds on a *pro rata* basis to the creditors. Moreover, if you have any equity in property, such as your home, the presence of this equity creates a security interest in favor of the IRS if it has filed a tax lien.

Suppose your home is worth $100,000 and you have a $50,000 mortgage balance. Suppose further that you owe the IRS $150,000 in non-priority taxes. The IRS has filed a lien against you. Because you have $50,000 equity in your home, the IRS would have a *secured* claim to that equity. Even though the taxes are classified as non-priority, the security created by the lien guarantees that the IRS would obtain $50,000 when the asset is sold. Still, $100,000 of the tax bill would be completely discharged.

The beauty of a Chapter 7 is that one need not sell his home in order to satisfy the IRS' claim. Unlike the sometimes impossible circumstances with which one is presented when dealing with IRS Collection personnel, many negotiation avenues are available in a Chapter 7 bankruptcy. For example, a most successful technique is to use the trustee as a go-between with the IRS. In this respect, you may be able to "purchase" your home from the estate by paying $50,000 to the trustee. While it might well be impossible outside of bankruptcy to persuade the IRS to take $50,000 in satisfaction of a $150,000 tax bill, the trustee will readily recognize that the equity in the home is the *limit* to which the IRS is entitled to recover. Hence, the trustee could require the IRS to release its lien on the property allowing you to obtain a second mortgage in the amount of $50,000. The result is that the IRS is paid, its lien is released and you retain possession of your home for one third what it would have cost to do business directly with the IRS.

A recent case history involving Chapter 7 illustrates just how helpful Chapter 7 can be. Faced with nearly one million dollars in federal income tax assessments and no way to pay them, Bill and Jeanette stood at the threshold of financial ruin. The IRS, circling like hungry vultures, prepared to seize all of the couple's assets, including their home and family business.

Unfortunately, seizure of all their assets would not have come close to settling the outstanding tax debt. The IRS, true to form, was prepared to sell three separate parcels of commercial rental property, including their home and business—total market value $852,000—for the whopping sum of $251,134.10. This would have left the couple with no home, no business, no rental property and no way to pay what would have been a $603,096.24 remaining balance.

With interest and penalties compounded daily on that balance, it would have been quite impossible to ever relieve themselves of the impending devastation. It would have been equally impossible to ever extricate themselves from the resulting poverty. In the meantime, the IRS was cleaning out their bank accounts at regular intervals, leaving their day-to-day business operations in shambles.

In desperation, they turned to their attorney and accountant for help. Two years and several thousand dollars in legal fees later, they were told that nothing could be done. They were told they would lose everything. The attorney went so far as to tell Jeanette that she would not even be allowed to keep her dishes! "Prepare to lose the business," he said, "the house, all your furniture, everything! There is nothing you can do!" All this "advice" despite the fact that he billed himself as a "tax attorney."

By the time I met Bill and Jeanette in late January, 1987, the IRS had already served notice of its intent to sell all the property. The sale was set for the end of February, just one month later. I quickly made contact with the Revenue Officer assigned to the case in an effort to work out a settlement.

He told me that the word had come down from "upstairs" that no settlement would be accepted. He had to go through with the seizure and sale of the property in order to "close the file." I bought some time. The agent agreed not to take any action until the end of March. After that, all the property would be seized and sold to satisfy the liability. A Chapter 7 petition was filed in mid-March, just weeks before the deadline set by the agent would expire.

Once the petition was filed, the provisions of the "automatic stay" came into effect.[9] The so-called "automatic stay" prevents *any* creditor, including the IRS, from taking any further action of any kind to collect the debt they claim is due. This is just one magical provision of the Bankruptcy Code and is discussed further in this Chapter. The stay will not only prevent further liens and seizures, it will *immediately* stop all wage levies. By filing the petition, we outflanked the IRS' move to seize the property.

What happened next was that the Bankruptcy trustee, not the IRS, sold the property which was owned by Bill and Jeanette when they filed their petition. The proceeds were distributed to the IRS. Their home was another story, however. The trustee made the offer to sell the home back to Bill and Jeanette, just as I explained above. This would enable them to re-purchase the home free of the tax lien and avoid the trauma of an IRS-induced forced sale.

So, while Bill and Jeanette did lose much of their property, the majority of their tax liability was completely erased. Had they followed the advice of their attorney and done nothing, the IRS would have sold everything, including their home and business, for barely over $200,000. This would have left them with a tax bill in excess of $600,000 and no way to pay it. Not only penniless, they

---

[9] Bankruptcy Code §362.

would have still been hounded by federal tax collectors. Had any money or property ever been accumulated by them, the IRS would have been right there to relieve them of it.

Relief under Chapter Seven of the Bankruptcy Code, in the case of Bill and Jeanette meant the difference between financial ruin and the chance to begin life with a clear slate.

2. *Chapter 13, Wage-Earner's Plan.* Chapter 13 is called a "wage earner's plan." It is a form of reorganization available to the working man. A Chapter 13 plan can be thought of as a means whereby a person can consolidate his debts, and pay back his creditors in installment payments which do not bear interest. During the time his plan is in effect and being carried out, he can avail himself of the protections of the bankruptcy court.

A Chapter 13 plan is extremely valuable when a person has priority tax debts which the IRS is collecting or about to collect through wage levies or seizures of property. You may recall I stated earlier that priority income tax debts, indeed any priority debt,[10] cannot be discharged in bankruptcy. A person with priority tax debts can, however, dispose of those debts through a Chapter 13 plan. Here is how it works.

Let us imagine that you have *non-priority* tax debts in the amount of $50,000. This would include taxes for years in which you have filed a timely return, the assessment is at least 240 days old *and* the tax is for a year which pre-dates the bankruptcy filing by at least three years. Let us suppose that you have $10,000 in *priority* tax debts. This would include debts which are *not* at least three years old, or for which a return was *not* timely filed,[11] or for which an assessment is *not* at least 240 days old.

Filing a petition in Chapter 7 would discharge the non-priority debts, but would not discharge the priority debts. So while you could expect to clear the slate of $50,000 worth of lingering tax bills, $10,000 in priority, nondischargeable debts would remain. Once the order of discharge was issued by the bankruptcy court, the IRS would again poise itself to levy wages and bank accounts in order to satisfy the remaining debt. This would leave you with just a pittance to live on each month while the IRS takes the majority of your wages.

---

[10] Bankruptcy Code §507(a).
[11] If the return was filed late, the debt on that return will be priority unless the return was filed at least two years prior to the filing of a petition in bankruptcy.

Under a wage earner's plan, you would propose a plan by which the IRS would be paid the priority taxes in full over a period of time. You would be permitted to submit a form which disclosed your gross earnings and net earnings after all payroll deductions are subtracted. From there, you would submit a budget which disclosed all of your necessary monthly living expenses for such things as food, shelter, clothing, medical care, insurance, transportation, recreation, etc. Many of these items the IRS fails to take into account when it determines a payment plan for you.

The difference between your monthly net income and the monthly budget is called "disposable income." The disposable income is the amount which is used to fund your plan. Under the Bankruptcy Code,[12] installment payments under the plan cannot extend beyond five years. Ideally, installment payments should not go beyond three years unless outstanding priority debts and limited disposable income make a three year pay-back plan impossible.

To illustrate this idea, let us suppose you have a gross monthly income of $1,500[13] and payroll deductions of $350. Your net income is therefore $1,150. Let us further suppose that your monthly budget totals $800. This would include rent, auto payments, gasoline, insurance, medical bills, food, clothing, utilities, telephone, and other fixed or regularly recurring expenses which are "reasonably necessary to be expended for the maintenance or support of the debtor or a dependent of the debtor, and if the debtor is engaged in business, for the payment of expenditures necessary for the continuation, preservation, and operation of such business."[14]

The difference between $1,150 (your net income) and $800 (your monthly budget) is $350. This is the amount of your disposable income, or the amount of money available each month in which to fund a plan of repayment to the priority creditors.

You will recall that priority tax debts in our example were $10,000. The non-priority, dischargeable debts were $50,000. To be acceptable, a plan of repayment must make full provision to completely pay all debts entitled to "priority under §507."[15] In addition, courts have said that a Chapter 13 plan most provide for

---

[12] Bankruptcy Code §1322(c).
[13] If married, the debtor in Chapter 13 may include the income of his spouse to fund the plan, even though the spouse may not be a debtor. This acts to increase the availability of disposable income to fund a plan.
[14] Bankruptcy Code §1325(b)(2) (A) & (B).
[15] Bankruptcy Code §1322 (a)(2).

the payment of *some* (but not all) of the non-priority or unsecured debts. Payment of as little as just a few percent of those debts can be acceptable. And, because the payments under Chapter 13 are handled by the Chapter 13 Trustee, provision for payment of the trustee must also be made. The fee charged by the Chapter 13 Trustee varies from district to district, but is generally in the vicinity of 10 percent of the money handled under the plan.

From this, we can determine just how much we are to pay to the trustee in order to complete the plan. Here are the amounts: Priority debts, $10,000; non-priority debts, 10 percent (for example) of $50,000 or $5,000; and trustee's fee, 10 percent of amount handled under the plan. Since $15,000 is to be paid under the plan, the trustee's fee will be $1,500. Hence, your total payout would be $17,500. With $350 available each month to fund the plan, we can easily determine that the total payment of $17,500 can be accomplished in 50 months.

The payment would be made each and every month to the trustee handling the case. The payments would be applied by the trustee to the creditors in the order of priority. After the plan is completed, the court is required to "grant the debtor a discharge of all debts provided for by the plan. . ."[16] The *only* debt which will not be discharged by a successfully completed Chapter 13 plan is one for alimony or child support.

Under our example plan, the debtor would be discharged of $45,000 in non-priority taxes after having paid all the priority taxes and just 10 percent of the non-priority taxes. Perhaps more importantly, the unpaid balance *does not* bear interest. Even if you could get the IRS to agree to such an installment arrangement administratively, it would be impossible to persuade them to waive interest on the unpaid balance. Hence, the savings to you in interest alone could easily *equal* the amount of non-priority taxes discharged.

Earlier in this Chapter, when discussing who could discharge taxes, I made the statement that if no return is filed or if fraud is associated with a tax return or tax liability, such a tax could not be discharged. This is true *only* with respect to Chapter 7 cases. It is *not* true with respect to Chapter 13 cases. Only *priority* taxes cannot be discharged under Chapter 13 and must be paid in full in deferred monthly payments. A tax is priority only if it:

---

[16] Bankruptcy Code §1328(a).

a. is less than three years old (computed from the date the return should have been filed to the date of filing the petition in bankruptcy);

b. has been assessed for fewer than 240 days prior to filing in bankruptcy; and

c. may be assessed after the petition in bankruptcy has been filed.

Even if no return was filed or was filed late, or the IRS has claimed that fraud is involved with the tax debt, that does not prevent the tax from becoming discharged under a properly proposed and fully executed Chapter 13 plan.

The beauty of a successful Chapter 13 case can best be explained with the example of Pat, a Minneapolis factory worker. Pat did not file tax returns for several years. The IRS mailed Pat a notice of deficiency for 1979 and 1980, with which he did nothing. After the 90 days expired, the tax was assessed and shortly thereafter, the IRS began levying Pat's wages, leaving him with just $150 each month.

In the meantime, the IRS mailed a second notice of deficiency to Pat, this one covering the years 1981, 1982 and 1983. Again, Pat did not petition the Tax Court and the tax was quickly assessed. After receiving a notice and demand for payment of the second assessment, Pat contacted the Revenue Officer assigned to the case. "I would like to get a payment arrangement," Pat said. "I cannot live on $150 per month."

Snidely, the Revenue Officer popped, "I already have the best payment arrangement there is—all our money!" Unwilling to work with Pat, the Revenue Officer made it clear that Pat had better seek other remedies if he wanted any relief.

Shortly after the conversation, Pat filed a Chapter 13 petition. The automatic stay provisions of the Code immediately lifted the wage levy and Pat had his wages to himself once again. He then submitted the necessary forms and proposed a plan of repayment to the IRS. The plan proposed that of the $9,983 owed for the non-priority taxes, only about 7 percent or $729 would be paid over the period of the plan! Of course, all of the priority taxes would be paid under the plan over five years.

The plan was submitted to the trustee and after some procedural bantering, was accepted and approved by the court. Pat was taking home $1,578 per month before taxes. With the wage levy in effect, he was not receiving enough on which to live. Pat's budget reflected that he had $400 per month available to fund his plan, so his future payments were based upon that figure. With the approval of his plan by the trustee and the court, Pat will be, upon completion of his plan, successful in discharging $9,254 in federal income taxes. More importantly, he will do so without suffering another day under the stranglehold of an IRS wage levy.

The Magic of Federal Bankruptcy Laws—

Believe it or not, *mere* discharge of federal income tax debts is not the only benefit that the bankruptcy laws have to offer. I am not even sure that discharge is the *best* attraction within the Bankruptcy Code. Other provisions of the Bankruptcy Code can act to completely turn the tables on the IRS. Used properly, even if a person cannot bankrupty a tax liability because of the fact that the debt may be either secured or priority, the provisions I am about to discuss can end virtually any tax collection nightmare.

1. **The Automatic Stay.** Bankruptcy Code §362 is called the "automatic stay." I have mentioned it a few times in this chapter already. Under this provision of the law, when a petition under *any* Chapter of Bankruptcy is filed, the automatic stay kicks into effect. What this means, quite simply, is that no creditor may initiate or continue any action whatsoever to "recover a claim against the debtor that arose before the commencement of the (bankruptcy) case."[17]

With respect to the IRS, what this means is that wage levies must stop, now! When a petition in bankruptcy is filed most bankruptcy clerks will provide a document entitled, "Notice of Commencementof a Case." The form is quite simple in nature and merely notifies anybody to whom the document is given that a petition in bankruptcy has been filed. After commencing a bankruptcy case, it is a good idea to provide a copy of this notice to the IRS Revenue Officer in charge of the case, as well as to your employer. This will lead to an immediate release of the levy.

Another remarkable aspect of the stay is that it prevents the IRS from taking any "act to obtain possession of property of the estate or of property from the estate or to exercise control over property of the estate."[18] What this means is, not only can the IRS no longer seize wages, it cannot seize any other property, real or personal. Perhaps most significantly, even if it has already seized

---

[17] Bankruptcy Code §362(a)(1).
[18] Bankruptcy Code §362(a)(3).

property, *it cannot sell* that property. And to go even one better, at the request of the citizen, the IRS must *return* the property which it has seized but not sold.

In 1983, the Supreme Court ruled in the case of **United States v. Whiting Pools, Inc.,**[19] that property seized by the IRS is nevertheless "owned" by the citizen until it is actually sold. Because the stay prevents the IRS from selling property after the case has been commenced, the citizen has the right under Code §542(a) to *demand* that property be returned.

In one case with which I was involved, the IRS had seized a man's house and had it on the selling block! The IRS had an Anoka, Minnesota home under seizure and was prepared to sell it by sealed bid to pay 1978, 1979 and 1980 back income taxes. The assessment was in excess of $65,000. The house, with a market value of about $85,000, was about to be sold for the whopping sum of $2,004.53. How such an incredibly low sale price could be justified is anybody's guess, but there it was—in black and white!

The problem began, like so many do, with missed communication and misunderstanding. Don, a small businessman, had received a notice of deficiency from the IRS asserting a large tax bill for each of the three years mentioned. Don is a plumber, not a lawyer or accountant, so he had no idea what to do with the notice. Unfortunately, those to whom Don went for help were probably also plumbers, and the advice he had received was quite off the mark, to say the least.

Don had managed to get a perfunctory petition filed with the Tax Court, but after the initial paperwork was generated, he quickly became trapped in the undercurrent of court rules and procedures. He had no idea what he was *supposed* to do, what he *was* doing, or what the IRS was doing. Before too long, the court lost patience and dismissed Don's case for failure to follow the court's rules. The result was a tax assessment well in excess of $20,000. That amount would *triple* before any relief would come.

After years had passed during which Don had ignored (due to inability to pay) notices and demands for payment from every level of th IRS, a Revenue Officer was assigned to the case. By this time, I was trying to help Don pull the chestnuts out of the fire. The IRS had mailed a second notice of deficiency, this one covering 1981 and 1982. He began stumbling through Tax Court alone once

---

[19] 462 U.S. 198 (1983).

more, but before the matter had gotten out of hand, I got into the act and steered the ship in the correct procedural direction. By the time the second case was completed, the claim was reduced from over $8,500 to just $1,537.

Remaining, however, was the collection problem created by the first foul-up. I made contact with the Revenue Officer and explained that the Tax Court assessment was grossly overstated. I pointed out that since Don's case had been dismissed for failure to follow the rules, he never did get a hearing on the merits of his tax liability. I further explained that income tax returns would show the correct liability to be in the neighborhood of $1,500 per year; vastly below that determined by the Tax Court.

The Revenue Officer put the monkey on my back. He stated that no steps would be taken to sell Don's home, now under seizure, until he got his past returns filed. Once the returns were filed, we could explore the possibility of an audit reconsideration. This would allow the overstated assessment to be eliminated and replaced with the correct, substantially lower amounts shown on the returns.

We worked feverishly to prepare the returns and have them submitted to the Revenue Officer. After months of sifting through antique records, the task had been completed. The returns were submitted, and Don was riding high—until the bottom fell out.

After we had fulfilled our part of the bargain in every particular, the Revenue Officer welched on his end. "We are going to have to go through with the sale of the house," he sadly reported. "It would be unfair to others who have had property seized if we were to release this home," he said.

How it was *unfair* to live up to his agreement I have not yet figured out, but there we sat.

A heated discussion with the Revenue Officer ensued. I was livid and let him know it. "Clearly," I charged, "you can see that the assessed liability exceeds the *correct* liability by tens of thousands of dollars. The *fair* thing to do is to abate the assessment!"

"Well," he hedged, "I just don't think I can do that. After all, Don brought these problems on himself, and he is just going to have to pay the fiddler."

"Pay the fiddler," I cried! "Are you interested in revenge, or are you going to follow the law?!"

Defensive now, the officer replied, "I have the assessment and I'm going to collect it. The house will be sold."

"Suit yourself," I touted. "But if you don't want to cooperate with me, we will just bankrupt that liability and you will get nothing!"

Just like most "experts," this expert responded by saying, "You can't bankrupt taxes."

"Not only will we bankrupt these taxes," I stressed, "but you will also be forced to release the house. And if you try to go ahead with the sale after we file the petition, we will apply to the court for an order holding *you* in contempt!"

Unsure now, he stated, "I don't want anything to do with contempt, but I have every right to sell the house. It is under seizure."

"It may be under seizure," I bellowed, "but it *isn't yours until you sell, and you haven't* sold it yet! Not only that, you *can't* sell it before we file bankruptcy! You just do not have enough time."

The officer calmly responded by saying, "That's not the law. As long as the property is seized, it is ours."

"How many bankruptcy cases have you worked?" I demanded to know.

"Hundreds," he said confidently, "and I don't think what you're saying is right."

"Well then you're gonna get an education," I pronounced.

The petition in Chapter 13 was filed in early April. While the Revenue Officer continued to rattle his saber, he was set straight by those apparently more in the know than he. The sale, set for April 15, did not go through. Nor will it. The **Whiting Pools** case will see to that!

In another case, Collins had his van seized by the IRS while he was at work. The van was seized on the 14th of March and Collins filed a Chapter 13 petition four days later. After filing the petition, Collins followed up with a motion for turnover under Bankruptcy Code §542(a). He cited **Whiting Pools** as the authority for his suggestion that the court should order the IRS to release the van.

After a hearing in the Houston Federal Bankruptcy Court, the IRS was ordered to release the van to Collins. Though the IRS clearly wanted to sell the van for a fraction of what it was worth, the automatic stay in §362 and the turnover provisions of §542(a) prevented it. Like Don, Collins got his property back from the IRS.

2. *Exempt Property.* The idea of filing a petition in bankruptcy is unsettling to many people. For the most part, I have seen the attitude prevail that bankruptcy is a way of "cheating" creditors, or worse, that one "loses everything" in bankruptcy. Neither impression is true.

With respect to "cheating" creditors, the ability to discharge lingering debts is a *right* created by the United States Constitution.[20] The first bankruptcy law in the United Staes was passed in 1800. It was patterned after the English law which dated to the time of Henry VIII, though the United States' legislation broadened both the rights of creditors and debtors in bankruptcy. Whereas in England, bankruptcy statutes functioned primarily to the benefit of creditors, drawing upon the insight of the great William Blackstone,[21] our American founders greatly expanded bankruptcy to benefit debtors as well as creditors. In his *Commentaries*, Book II, *The Rights*, Chapter 31, Blackstone observes:

> "But at present the laws of bankruptcy are considered as laws calculated for the *benefit* of trade, and founded on the principle of humanity as well as justice; and to that end they confer some privileges, not only on the creditors, but *also on the bankrupt or debtor himself*. On the creditors; by compelling the bankrupt to give up all his effects to their use, without any fraudulent concealment; on the debtor; by exempting him from the rigor of the general law, whereby his person might be confined, at the discretion of his creditor, though in reality he has nothing to satisfy the debt. . ." (Emphasis added) *Commentaries*, Book II, page 427.

Hence, we see that bankruptcy was established as a means of "humanely" resolving the question of creditor/debtor relations, principally as an alternative to "confinement," or jail-for-debt. Beginning with the act of 1841, rehabilitation of the debtor has become an object of increasing concern to Congress. With that legislation, the idea of a *voluntary* petition filed by the debtor himself was introduced into our society. The object was to provide

---

[20] See Article 1, Sec. 8, Clause 4.

[21] Blackstone was the 18th Century's most prominent legal scholar. As an English jurist, Blackstone occupied a seat on the bench of the Court of Common Pleas, 1770-1779 at Michaelmas. Blackstone was revered for his insight into the rights and liberties of Englishmen. In his *Commentaries on the Laws of England*, Book 1, Chapter 1, he recorded a ringing diatribe on these rights. Unlike most jurists, Blackstone practiced what he preached and this was reflected in the decisions which issued from his court. More than any other jurist, Blackstone's influence over the thinking of our forefathers was visibly profound. Blackstone's inexorable posture in support of individual liberties was replete throughout the rulings of our early American judges, and is dangerously absent from the writing of contemporary jurists. Blackstone's four volume series, *Commentaries on the Laws of England*, were first published in 1769. He died in Westminster, England in February of 1780. His Commentaries are still revered as legal classics.

[22] *The Constitution of the United States of America*, Analysis and Interpretation, pages 300-301, 1972, U.S. Government Printing Office, Stock No. 5271-00308, prepared by the Congressional Research Staff.

the debtor with a means of resolving his unmanageable condition of debt. It was observed that the interests of society in general are not served by citizens burdened with stagnating debt.[22] Bankruptcy is man's answer to the divine principle of forgiveness.

With respect to the idea of "losing everything," there are two issues which must be considered. First, if one does not seek the protection of the bankruptcy court, you can be assured that the IRS will see to it that you do "lose everything." The true hardship occurs when the IRS sells, say, $100,000 worth of your property for the grand total of perhaps $15,000. When the $15,000 is then applied to a $150,000 tax liability, where does that leave you? It leaves you in the position of having no assets whatsoever and yet are still faced with a huge tax bill which you have no way to pay! And the IRS harassment will only continue.

Secondly, both Congress and the various State Legislatures have passed "exemption" statutes which permit a debtor in bankruptcy to retain certain assets. The exemptions vary widely from state to state, but generally permit a debtor to retain his personal belongings such as clothing, furniture, an automobile (up to a certain value), tools and equipment necessary to earn a living (up to a certain value), and, perhaps, a homestead. Therefore, one is not "wiped out" and left as poor as a church mouse when the bankruptcy is complete.

The value and description of the property which is exempt under state law will vary, as I mentioned, from state to state. Some state statutes are liberal in the amounts of exemptions which they offer. Minnesota, for example, provides that an automobile worth up to $2,000 and other personal property, worth a total of $4,500 is exempt. On the other hand, Florida exempts only $1,000 *total* in all assets of any description. Still, you can be sure that a person will generally fair much better at the hands of the bankruptcy court than he will at the hands of the unbridled IRS Collection officers.

3. *The End of the Tax Lien.* The effect of a discharge on a federal tax lien has been much debated. Due to the uncertain nature of the interrelationship between the Bankruptcy Code and the Tax Code, much confusion has been generated over this topic. I believe however, that my understanding of the two can shed

---

[22] The Constitution of the United States of America, Analysis and Interpretation, pages 300-301, 1972, U.S. Government Printing Office, Stock No. 5271-00308, prepared by the Congressional Research Staff.

some light upon how this issue is resolved.

Section 522(c) of the Bankruptcy Code provides that any property which is exempt either under state or federal law "is not liable during or after the case for any debt" which the citizen had incurred prior to filing bankruptcy. An exception to that general rule is the source of much of the confusion. The exception provides that the rule *does not apply* to a debt that is secured by a *"tax lien,* notice of which is properly filed."[23]

This is read by the IRS to mean that no property is exempt from the IRS' power of seizure and sale, bankruptcy or no bankruptcy. Such a narrow reading ignores two important facts. First, the stay which was discussed earlier remains in effect until a discharge occurs in the case. This is universally recognized as a bar to the IRS' power of seizure and sale. Secondly, *tax law,* not just bankruptcy law, places express limits upon the IRS' ability to seize a citizen's property.

Section 6334 of the Internal Revenue Service Code establishes those limits. With the passage of the Taxpayers' Bill of Rights Act,[24] Congress has *increased* some of those limits. Exemption levels for both personal effects and furniture, as well as books and tools of the trade, business or profession, have been increased from $1,500 respectively, to $10,000 respectively.[25] So even though the Bankruptcy Code may provide that the IRS' lien may remain in effect as to property which it classifies as exempt, the IRS would nevertheless be *prevented* from acting upon that lien to the extent that such property falls under the exemption within the Tax Code I just described. For more details, see Chapter Six, Part 2(B).

Even beyond that, it is *well settled* that the tax lien remains in effect *only* as to property which the debtor owned *at the time* he filed bankruptcy. It is settled and recognized that the lien *does not* attach to property which a debtor acquires after the bankruptcy has been filed. This property, referred to as "after-acquired property," is free of the constraints of the tax lien.[26] One court, in direct response to the government's contention that the lien survived to encumber "after-acquired property," described the situation this way:

". . .in our opinion, . . . the dominant purpose of the change (in

---

[23] Bankruptcy Code §522(c)(2)(B).
[24] S. 1774, passed in October of 1988.
[25] Taxpayers' Bill of Rights Act, §13(c), amending Code §6634(a)(2) and (3).
[26] **In re Braund,** 289 F. Supp. 604 (9th Cir. 1970).

bankruptcy law) was to relieve a debtor of the burden of these older taxes after bankruptcy. The government's interpretation would permit it to enforce (to the extent of assets acquired by the discharged debtor) collection of all its taxes, regardless of their age, if a lien had been filed. This would to so substantial a degree frustrate the real purpose of the amendment that Congress surely must not have intended the result." **United States v. Sanabra**, 424 F.2d 1121 (7th Cir. 1970).

So while the lien is valid as to property which the debtor owned at the time the bankruptcy is commenced, *it is not valid* as to any property which is acquired *after* the bankruptcy is commenced. That property includes wages paid after the petition is filed. Hence, for all practical purposes, the filing of a bankruptcy petition kills the tax lien from that day *forward*. This allows the debtor to purchase property after commencement of the bankruptcy case which will not be subject to any tax lien that may have been filed prior to the commencement of the case. This benefit must surely be perceptible to the reader.

4. *Redetermination of a Tax Liability.* As we have already examined throughout this book, the IRS regularly makes determinations of tax liabilities which are grossly overstated. Due to the complexity of the procedural aspects of the tax laws, a person without the benefit of experienced counsel will be at the mercy of the IRS when it comes to arbitrary tax-increase determinations. Under settled *tax* law, there are only two ways in which a person may contest a determination of the IRS. The first is to petition the Tax Court within 90 days of receiving a Notice of Deficiency. The second is to pay the tax, then file a claim for refund, followed by a suit for refund.

I have seen countless persons fall prey to the IRS because they either did not understand how to petition the Tax Court or did not understnad that they had the right to petition the Tax Court. Once the time for petitioning the Tax Court has expired, the option of paying the tax and commencing refund litigation is often out of the question due the amount of the tax involved. An exceedingly high assessment cannot be paid, and as a result, no review option is available.

While this is a prevailing mode of thought, I have learned that it too is *meritless*. Among the numerous benefits of a bankruptcy case, Bankruptcy Code §505 stands out as perhaps the most beneficial. Section 505(a) gives the bankruptcy court the authority to "determine the amount or legality of any tax, any fine or penalty relating to a tax, or any addition to tax, whether or not previously assessed, (and) whether or not paid."

The advantages of §505 spring from the page in a flurry of renewed hope. Under this provision of the law, when a person has been denied the ability to contest an IRS determination for any reason, he will be provided that opportunity once a case in bankruptcy is commenced. Even if the underlying tax is determined by the court to be nondischargeable because it is a priority debt, the assessment may nevertheless be modified by the court to reflect the correct amount of tax due as opposed to the inflated amount claimed to be due by the IRS.

In one case, the benefits of §505 saved thousands of dollars for a citizen in bankruptcy. The IRS had assessed taxes blindly against Don for several years. By the time a petition in bankruptcy had been filed, the IRS was demanding just over $69,000. But Don could not have owed more than $10,000. This could be proven if only he could get a hearing. But Don missed the boat with his notice of deficiency and could not afford to pay the tax in order to begin a refund proceeding. That left §505 and bankruptcy as the only hope.

By the time the dust had settled in Don's bankruptcy, the $69,000 tax assessment had been reduced to $8,557.40. Don then began making payments in the amount of $237.40 each month to a Chapter 13 trustee in order to pay off the amount of the newly-corrected assessment. Don stood to lose his home on account of a tax liability which was over eight times greater than what he owed. Section 505 prevented that disaster from occuring.

5. *The Adversary Proceeding.* Bill had been assessed income taxes in the excess of $1.5 million. Just exactly how one person could be accused of owing so much in back taxes is a book unto itself, but nevertheless, Bill was stuck. With barely $20,000 per year in income and that kind of liability collecting interest each day, there is no question that Bill needed help with the problem. He turned to his lawyer and Chapter 7 for relief from the debt.

A bankruptcy petition was filed by Bill's attorney. After a discharge had been issued by the court, the IRS notified Bill that it would begin seizing his pay in satisfaction of the debt. Bill and his lawyer were at a loss. Both had believed that the discharge would keep the IRS at bay, but the IRS had different ideas. With the IRS on the doorstep, a wage levy in hand, Bill turned to me.

Without delay, an adversary proceeding under the authority of Part VII of the Bankruptcy Rules was commenced. An adversary proceeding is nothing more than a civil lawsuit presented within the context of the bankruptcy court. The adversary proceeding can be used in a number of circumstances, and is used commonly by the debtor to raise the question of whether certain debts have been discharged in bankruptcy. In this case, Bill sued the IRS claiming its debt was now invalid as a result of the Chapter 7 he had filed.

The first step Bill took after filing the adversary proceeding was to apply to the court for an order preventing the IRS from carrying out its threatened collection action before the court could resolve the suit. An order of this type is referred to as a "preliminary injunction." Shortly after filing the application, the court granted Bill's request for a preliminary injunction. The court ordered the IRS to keep its hands off Bill's paycheck. In the meantime, the case would progress, with our goal that of obtaining an order from the court confirming that Bill's taxes were fully discharged.

Before the adversary proceeding was filed, I had a conversation with the local court clerk. I explained that Bill had gone through a Chapter 7 and despite the discharge, a "certain creditor" was making collection threats. We intended with our adversary proceeding, I explained, to stop that action.

The clerk chuckled as I explained Bill's plight. "Did I say something funny," I asked, somewhat miffed that she would laugh at such a dismal situation.

"Not at all," she quickly responded. "It just occurred to me that this creditor you mentioned has to be the IRS."

"How did you know?" I asked, puzzled.

"They are the only ones who don't seem to have any respect for the court," she said.

Since this early conversation occurred, I have come to learn that the IRS is of the opinion that taxes cannot be discharged in bankruptcy. Witness Publication 908. As a result, it stands to reason that they would not respect a discharge from the bankruptcy court. Consequently, one must be prepared to go on the offensive with regard to the IRS. This is done in one of two ways.

First, a letter outlining the law and facts of the case may be written to the IRS Special Procedures Section. SPS is the division of the IRS which handles bankruptcy problems. The letter would seek an admission that the taxes in question have been discharged and demand an abatement of the liability in question. As an alternative, should the IRS refuse to abate the assessment, an adversary proceeding could be filed. The suit would seek an order from the bankruptcy court *declaring* that the taxes have been discharged and ordering the IRS to abate the assessment. The choice of forum is made by the IRS. It can either abate the tax willingly or face the court through the adversary proceeding.

Planning for Bankruptcy—

With the knowledge that taxes may be discharged in bankruptcy, we have opened an entire new area of tax planning; planning for bankruptcy. Planning for bankruptcy must be as deliberate and careful a process as that used by the rich in planning their financial affairs. One man I knew filed a petition in bankruptcy with the help of an attorney. Neither knew that his federal tax liabilities, the reason he was driven to insolvency, were dischargeable. The petition was filed prematurely by just *four days*. This negligence resulted in nearly $40,000 in taxes escaping the Chapter 7 discharge.

The planning process begins with identifying several important dates. The dates on which certain events have occurred determine whether the liability is a priority debt or a non-priority debt. I have already pointed out the significance of this distinction. Let us review the events which shape the direction of a tax bankruptcy.

First, you must be certain that the tax liabilities are at least three years old. This period is computed beginning with the date the return *should have been filed.* Using the example of the year 1985, the three-year period would begin on April 15, 1986. Thus, tax year 1985 would be three years old on or after April 15, 1988.

Secondly, the tax assessment must be in effect for at least 240 days. The assessment occurs on the date the return is filed, or, 90 days after a notice of deficiency is mailed but not appealed to the Tax Court, or, the date in which the Tax Court renders a decision against you, whichever event is the most recent. The assessment date is critical and must be pinpointed. If you filed an offer in compromise *before* the 240-day period expired, the period is extended. It will be lengthened by the amount of time which the offer was pending before the IRS, plus 30 days. If the offer was filed *after* the 240-day period expired, the offer will have no effect on this time computation.

Thirdly, the return must have been filed in a timely manner. If it were filed late, *two years* must lapse between the time the return was filed, and the time the petition in bankruptcy is filed.

Only when *all three* of these time constraints are met will a tax be considered non-priority and fuly dischargeable. Tax liabilities which do not meet each criterion are *priority* debts and will not be discharged in a Chapter 7 bankruptcy. They can, however, be disposed of with a Chapter 13 plan as we have already discussed.

An important step one should take when considering bankruptcy is to request a copy of his "Individual Master File," or IMF. The IMF is the computer-maintained statement of account which we have discussed in this book at various times. An IMF is maintained for each individual, and is filed according to his social security number. A request directed to the IRS Service Center with which you file your tax returns will secure a copy of your IMF. Be sure to specify the tax years in question, and provide your social security number. Because of IRS disclosure laws, you will also have to verify in writing that you are seeking your own personal IMF record. Without this verification, the IRS will not disclose the material.

You should also request a copy of the code translator used to read the IMF. Without it you will be lost, as each transaction recorded in the IMF is coded with a number. For example, the entry "150 041586 $2,198.34" indicates that a return was filed on April 15, 1986, and that the amount of $2,918.34 was assessed on that same date. Subsequent assessments made pursuant to an audit or Tax Court decision will be reflected with a separate code.

The IMF is critical. Without it, you cannot pinpoint the date on which any assessment was made. Even though you may know the date on which the Tax Court rendered its judgment against you, the resultant tax liability may not have been assessed until days, weeks, or even months later. As you already know, if your bankruptcy petition is filed just *one day* premature, you risk the possibility that some taxes may not be discharged.

By isolating the dates of each event, you will be able to determine when to file your petition in a Chapter 7 or Chapter 13 proceeding. Remember, if no return was filed for the year in question, or if fraud were involved with the tax in question, a Chapter 7 will not discharge the debt. Chapter 13 however, will, provided the remaining rules are met. Also, if your tax assessments are priority debts due to their age and you are suffering under enforced collection action now, Chapter 13 may be the only sensible alternative.

If you elect to delay the filing of a bankruptcy petition in order to fall within one or more of the rules we have discussed, you must be prepared to deal with IRS collection efforts which may come your way. ACS will send notices and demands for payment. It will send a final 30-day notice. And it may file liens and levies. Chapter Six details the steps which may be taken to neutralize these collection efforts while you wait.

EXHIBIT 7-2 (page 1)

5700 Special Procedures

page 5700–364
(12–5–86)

Exhibit 5700–113

Dischargeability of Taxes in Bankruptcy

(Reference: IRM 57(13)4.42:(1))

This chart should be used to determine whether a specific tax liability has been discharged in the proceeding.

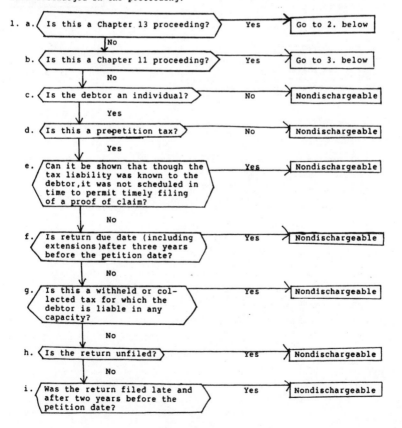

EXHIBIT 7-2 (page 2)

Exhibit 5700-113 Cont. (1)

Dischargeability of Taxes in Bankruptcy

(Reference: IRM 57(13)4.42:(1))

No

j. Was this a fraudulent return?   Yes   Nondischargeable

No

k. Did the debtor in any manner willfully attempt to evade or defeat the tax?   Yes   Nondischargeable

No

l. Is this income tax?   No   Dischargeable

Yes

m. Was the tax assessed within 240 days before the petition date?   Yes   Nondischargeable

No

n. Was the tax assessed within 240 days, plus the time an offer in compromise with respect to the tax was pending plus thirty days, before the petition date?   Yes   Nondischargeable

No

o. Was the tax not assessed but assessable at the time of the bankruptcy petition (e.g. a notice of deficiency had been issued or the taxpayer executed a waiver extending the statutory period for assessment)?   Yes   Nondischargeable

No

Dischargeable

2. a. Was the tax "provided for" by the debtors Chapter 13 plan? *   No   Nondischargeable

Yes

b. Work through the steps of item 1. of the flow chart. Is the result "dischargeable"?   Yes   Dischargeable

No

c. Did the debtor receive a hardship discharge under Section 1328(b)?   Yes   Nondischargeable

No

Dischargeable

EXHIBIT 7-2 (page 3)

Exhibit 5700–113 Cont. (2)

Dischargeability of Taxes in Bankruptcy

(Reference: IRM 57(13)4.42:(1))

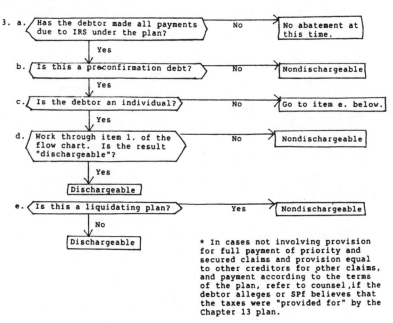

3. a. Has the debtor made all payments due to IRS under the plan? — No → No abatement at this time.

Yes

b. Is this a preconfirmation debt? — No → Nondischargeable

Yes

c. Is the debtor an individual? — No → Go to item e. below.

Yes

d. Work through item 1. of the flow chart. Is the result "dischargeable"? — No → Nondischargeable

Yes

Dischargeable

e. Is this a liquidating plan? — Yes → Nondischargeable

No

Dischargeable

* In cases not involving provision for full payment of priority and secured claims and provision equal to other creditors for other claims, and payment according to the terms of the plan, refer to counsel, if the debtor alleges or SPf believes that the taxes were "provided for" by the Chapter 13 plan.

Conclusion—

The IRS' failure to tell the truth about federal income taxes and bankruptcy is deplorable. While the IRS has recalled its Publication 908, it remains to be seen whether the real story will be told in the revised edition. If the agency does wish to tell the truth, I have a suggestion. Perhaps its revised Publication 908 could include a copy of the bankruptcy flow chart which appears as Exhibit 5700-113 in IRS Manual Part 5700. The chart, relatively easy to follow as IRS charts go, clearly shows that taxes are dischargeable in bankruptcy. I have included the three page chart in this Chapter as Exhibit 7-2.

Since this information does appear in the IRS manual, there is no legitimate reason why it should continue to be hidden from the public. Anything less than the straight story on bankruptcy is a crime! Regardless of what the IRS elects to do with Publication 908, you have learned the truth. Tell a friend!

Table of Abbreviations

"C.B." — Refers to Cumulative Bulletin.

"Cir." — Refers to the stated circuit court of appeals, i.e., 8th Cir.

"Code" — Unless otherwise indicated, refers to the Internal Revenue Code of 1986, as amended.

"F.2d" — Refers to the Federal Reporter, Second Series, published by West Publishing Co., St. Paul, MN.

"F.Supp." — Refers to the Federal Supplement, published by West Publishing Co., St. Paul, MN.

"IRM" — Refers to the Internal Revenue Manual.

"MT" — Refers to an IR Manual Transmittal.

"Rev. Proc." — Refers to a Revenue Procedure.

"Rev. Reg." — Refers to a Revenue Regulation.

"S.Ct." — Refers to The Supreme Court Reporter, published by West Publishing Co., St. Paul, MN.

"T.C" — Refers to a Tax Court Regular Decision.

"T.C. Memo" — Refers to a Tax Court Memorandum Decision.

"U.S." — Refers to the United States Supreme Court Reports, published by the U.S. Government Printing Office.

"U.S.C." — Refers to the United States Code, at the stated title and section, i.e., 26 USC §6334.

About the Author

Daniel J. Pilla has dedicated himself to the presentation of taxpayers' rights and their freedoms. As a Tax Litigation Consultant, he has recognized that there is a common ground on which both the taxpayer and tax collector can tread. He has also recognized that for the taxpayer to share this common ground, it will be necessary for the taxpayer to assert his rights to do so.

He will tell you, however, that before any rights can be asserted, one must have a working knowledge of what those rights are. Without this knowledge, history shows that the rights of the taxpayer will be trampled by those set to the task of tax collection. Without the assertion of these rights there is no way to prevent it.

Just as Dan Pilla has dedicated himself to teaching Americans what these rights entail, he challenges each of us to learn and assert these rights whenever possible. He challenges each individual to protect the liberties afforded them by the Constitution. For only through the protection of individual liberties can we all work together to keep this country strong in the hands of God.